Human Rights Interventions

Series Editors
Chiseche Mibenge
Stanford University
Stanford, CA, USA

Irene Hadiprayitno
Leiden University
Leiden, Zuid-Holland
The Netherlands

The traditional human rights frame creates a paradigm by which the duty bearer's (state) and rights holder's (civil society organizations) interests collide over the limits of enjoyment and enforcement. The series departs from the paradigm by centering peripheral yet powerful actors that agitate for intervention and influence in the (re)shaping of rights discourse in the midst of grave insecurities. The series privileges a call and response between theoretical inquiry and empirical investigation as contributors critically assess human rights interventions mediated by spatial, temporal, geopolitical and other dimensions. An interdisciplinary dialogue is key as the editors encourage multiple approaches such as law and society, political economy, historiography, legal ethnography, feminist security studies, and multi-media.

More information about this series at
http://www.palgrave.com/gp/series/15595

Gabriel Blouin-Genest
Marie-Christine Doran • Sylvie Paquerot
Editors

Human Rights as Battlefields

Changing Practices and Contestations

palgrave
macmillan

Editors
Gabriel Blouin-Genest
Department of Political Science
Virginia Tech
Blacksburg, VA, USA

Marie-Christine Doran
School of Political Studies
University of Ottawa
Ottawa, ON, Canada

Sylvie Paquerot
School of Political Studies
University of Ottawa
Ottawa, ON, Canada

Human Rights Interventions
ISBN 978-3-030-06294-1 ISBN 978-3-319-91770-2 (eBook)
https://doi.org/10.1007/978-3-319-91770-2

Cover design: Tjaša Krivec

This Palgrave Macmillan imprint is published by the registered company Springer Nature Switzerland AG
The registered company address is: Gewerbestrasse 11, 6330 Cham, Switzerland

The photograph on the front cover was taken by Marie-Christine Doran during her recent fieldwork in the Norte Grande *of Chile. This wall is a testament to the indigenous and human rights struggles in Chile. It is but one of many that are covered with meaningful words for anyone who is aware of the violence perpetrated upon human rights defenders in Latin America and around the world. Written in Spanish, this declaration to all defenders of human rights from below reads:*

"Do not be afraid
Do not be silent
Or you will die"

In solidarity, we stand with you,
The editors and authors of this book

Acknowledgments

The editors and authors of the book would like to deeply thank Dr. Anca Pusca, Senior Editor of International Relations and Security Studies at Palgrave Macmillan, for her wonderful help, insights, and advice throughout the whole preparation of this book. We would also like to thank Katelyn Zingg, Editorial Assistant at Palgrave Macmillan, for her constant and friendly help in guiding us through all the steps of the preparation of the manuscript.

Thank you to all the extraordinary people, on all continents, who make human rights happen every day and believe in human dignity and equality: we have so much to learn from you all and this book is a modest tribute to your courage and determination. Thank you for so generously sharing your inspiring views during fieldwork research, despite some very challenging and dangerous conditions, especially in the case of indigenous right defenders affected by the criminalization of dissent. Thank you to the Social Sciences and Humanities Research Council of Canada for its great support in many of these fieldwork researches. The support of the University of Ottawa and Virginia Tech is also greatly appreciated, in particular the departments of political science from these two universities.

Special thanks also to the *Casa de Memoria José Domingo Cañas* (JDC) and Marta Cisterna for giving us the permission to use pictures of the mural paintings and installations of the *Casa de Memoria JDC*, in Santiago de Chile. Even though we weren't able to use these deeply moving pictures for the cover of the book in the end for technical reasons, we want to acknowledge the extraordinary work of the *Casa* in making the public, and especially children, aware of the importance of fighting past and present human rights violations on a day-to-day basis.

And last but not least, thank you to our wonderful undergraduate and graduate students for their enthusiasm in studying the constant reinvention and many expressions of human rights from below, as well as to our loved ones for their support and all the great discussions about a better world.

Gabriel Blouin-Genest, Marie-Christine Doran and Sylvie Paquerot

Contents

Notes on Contributors

Olabanji Akinola is a PhD (ABD) candidate in the collaborative PhD program in Political Science and International Development Studies at the University of Guelph, Ontario, Canada. Akinola holds a Master of Arts (MA) in International Studies with specialization in Political Science from the Graduate Institute of International and Development Studies, Geneva, Switzerland, and another MA in Political Science and International Development Studies from the University of Guelph, Ontario, Canada. His research interests revolve around politics, human rights, governance, and socioeconomic development in Africa, and he has published book chapters, journal articles, book reviews, and policy briefs on these topics.

Judith Bessant is a professor at RMIT University, Melbourne, Australia, and an adjunct professor at the School of Justice, QUT, Australia. She publishes widely and has also worked as an advisor for governments and non-governmental organizations. In 2017 she was awarded an 'Order of Australia' (AM) for her significant service to education as a social scientist, an advocate, and an academic. Recent and forthcoming publications include *The Precarious Generation: A Political Economy of Young People* (with Farthing and Watts, 2017), *Young People Re-Generating Politics in Times of Crises*, and *The Great Transformation, History for a Techno-Human Future* (2018).

Gabriel Blouin-Genest is an assistant professor at the Department of Political Science, Virginia Tech. Blouin-Genest teaches courses in global governance and public policy. His research interests include health politics and policies, health security and pandemics, global health institutions and practices, human rights, water and food politics as well as the complexity theory. His work has been published in *Health: An Interdisciplinary Journal for the Social Study of Health, Illness and Medicine*; *The Journal of Human Rights and the Environment*; *Health Policy and Technology*; *SociologieS*; and *Cultures & Conflicts*. Blouin-Genest is also the co-author of *L'eau en commun* (PUQ, 2012) and of several chapters published (or in the process of being published) by Peter Lang, UBC Press, and Athéna Press.

Charles Bosvieux-Onyekwelu is a sociologist, specialized in socio-history, the sociology of law, and the sociology of elites. His PhD thesis was on the socio-history of public service under the French Third Republic at the Université de Paris-Saclay (France). He is a research and teaching fellow at the Université de Lorraine and also teaches a course on law and gender at Sciences Po. He has held teaching positions at the Université Paris 1 Panthéon-Sorbonne, the Université du Maine, and the Université Paris Ouest Nanterre La Défense, where he taught human rights, sociology of law, and political theory.

Ñusta Carranza Ko is Assistant Professor of Political Science in the Department of History, Political Science, and Geography at Ohio Northern University. She received her PhD in Political Science from Purdue University and holds a MA in Politics from New York University, MA in International Relations from the University of Windsor, and a BA in Political Science from McGill University. Her research interests include cross-regional research on transitional justice processes in Latin America and East Asia, including policies of memorialization in Peru and South Korea and questions of indigenous peoples' rights in Peru.

Fabio Cristiano is a lecturer at the Department of Political Science, Lund University (Sweden), and a visiting research fellow at the Kenyon Institute—Council for British Research in the Levant in East Jerusalem. His research interests lie at the intersection of international relations (IR), cyberwarfare, and critical theory. He is finalizing his thesis on Palestinian cyberwar and hacking, engaging with the concept of jihad to explore how sovereignty and subjectivity are reproduced in relation to virtuality. He has published on cyberwar, war simulations, Palestine, and gaming/augmented reality. Other areas of interest are cyber-diplomacy and internet as human rights. He convenes various courses on IR theory, war theory, Israel/Palestine, development studies, and digital pedagogy in Lund.

Surma Das is a sessional lecturer at the Political Science Department at the University of Alberta in Edmonton. Her research and teaching interests are in the areas of women's rights, human rights, right to health, and development in South Asia. Her dissertation, funded through an International Development Research Center (Canada) (IDRC) Doctoral Award, examined the discursive power of framing women's right to maternal health as a human right to prompt political action for preventable maternal deaths in developing countries. She was recognized for academic excellence and thought leadership by the standing section on Population, Reproductive and Sexual Health of the American Public Health Association in 2016. In 2015, she received honorable mention for the Kari Polanyi Levitt Prize for Best Graduate Student Annual Essay Contest held by the Canadian Association for the Student of International Development.

Marie-Christine Doran is an associate professor at the School of Political Studies, University of Ottawa, and a researcher in different international networks on post-conflict and human rights, including the International Panel on Exiting Violence (www.ipev.org). She is director of a research team on violence, criminalization of right's defense and democracy in Latin America, funded by the Social Sciences and Humanities Research Council of Canada. She has been a fellow at the Center for the Study of World Religions at Harvard University, where she taught on fundamentalism and violence, as well as human rights and religion, and a visiting professor in France and Latin America. Her published work focuses on political violence, post-conflict, criminalization of social movements, struggles for justice, memory, and human rights from below within democratic renewal, on which she has recently published a book at Karthala, featuring the case of Chile: *Le Réveil démocratique du Chili: une histoire politique de l'exigence de justice*. She is working on a new book *Criminalizing Democracy: The Hidden Face of Violence in Latin America* to be published by Routledge in 2019, and has published many peer-reviewed articles and book chapters on related subjects. She is also a consultant for the Ministry of Global Affairs, Government of Canada.

Mikey Erb holds an MA in Political Science from Virginia Tech. While he has studied international relations theory, political theory, and women and gender studies, he specializes in analyzing the power structures surrounding queer and gender issues. He has taught as a graduate teaching assistant at Virginia Tech in the subject area of selected world issues as well as race, gender, and ethnicity. He works for the Government Accountability Office (GAO).

Ozan Kamiloglu is a PhD candidate at the School of Law, Birkbeck College, University of London where he has also been Lecturer. His current research is on human rights and the ethical turn, in which he focuses on the period after the fall of Soviets and tries to analyze how human rights discourses change with the unipolar world order. Some of his publications include "Violence Is the Other", *London Journal in Critical Thought: Fanaticism, Politics and the Subject of Justice*, Interview with Alberto Toscano, *Birkbeck Law Review*; *Bruno Latour, Law and International Justice*—An Interview With Dr. Kirsten Campbell, *Birkbeck Law Review;* Interview with Étienne Balibar, *PostExpress.*

Sylvie Paquerot is an associate professor at the School of Political Studies and an associate researcher at HRREC—Human Rights Research and Education Centre—University of Ottawa; CEDIM—Center for Studies on International Law and Globalization—UQAM; Paquerot's research focuses on environmental issues from the perspective of international human rights law. Her work also seeks to better understand the links between democracy and human rights in the contemporary political context and the changing nature of the right to self-determination. Her recently published works include "Socio-Economic Rights and the Environment: A Path to Political Responsibility?", in Porter and Jackman (eds) *Reconceiving Human Rights Practice for the New Social Rights Paradigm*, Irwin Law Books (2014) and "The Integration of the Right to Water in International Law: Circumventing and Bypassing State Sovereignty", in Terje Tvedt, Owen McIntyre and Tadesse Kassa Woldetsadik (eds), A HISTORY OF WATER LAW, SERIES III: *Sovereignty and the Development of International Water Law*, IB Tauris & Co Ltd, Volume 2, Series 3 (2015). She is a board member of France-Libertés Foundation.

Rob Watts is Professor of Social Policy at RMIT University, Melbourne. He has published books including *The Foundations of the National Welfare State* (1987), *States of Violence and the Civilising Process: On Criminology and State Crime* (2016), and *Public Universities, Managerialism and the Value of Higher Education* (2017). His co-authored books include *Sociology Australia* (3rd edition) (with Bessant, J., 2007), *Talking Policy: Australian Social Policy* (with Bessant, J., Dalton, T. & Smyth, P., 2007), and *The Precarious Generation: A Political Economy of Young People* (with Bessant J. and Farthing, R.).

CHAPTER 1

Introduction: Becoming Human Rights Subjects Through New Practices

Gabriel Blouin-Genest, Marie-Christine Doran, and Sylvie Paquerot

Since the official formation of the United Nations (UN) in 1945 and the proclamation of the Universal Declaration of Human Rights (UDHR) three years later, human rights have undergone a never-before-seen internationalization—a form of globalization of its own. Having become, according to Bertrand Badie (1999), "humanity's first common goods," human rights are now found almost everywhere and invoked at all levels of society—from micro practices to global treaties—by completely different types of actors. This internationalization of human rights fuels the paradox of today's politics of human rights: they are claimed by Northern and Southern countries alike, and by governments as much as by private stakeholders and NGOs. Sometimes, actors contest the legitimacy of human rights; in other circumstances, the same actors are quick to call on

G. Blouin-Genest
Department of Political Science, Virginia Tech, Blacksburg, VA, USA
e-mail: gblouin@vt.edu

M.-C. Doran (✉) • S. Paquerot
School of Political Studies, University of Ottawa, Ottawa, ON, Canada
e-mail: Marie-Christine.Doran@uottawa.ca; spaquero@uottawa.ca

G. Blouin-Genest et al. (eds.), *Human Rights as Battlefields*, Human Rights Interventions,
https://doi.org/10.1007/978-3-319-91770-2_1

these same rights to reinforce their own activities, policies or laws. Human rights are also used to justify the actions and practices of actors on all sides of the political spectrum.

This paradox fuels the reflections investigated here, where human rights—understood as fundamental commitments made by states—represent a reference point for political action and "commonality" regardless of the obvious limits that are exposed on a daily basis to their concrete implementation. Human rights discourses and practices are, in some sense, used as a legitimization tool that helps the oppressed participate vocally in violent societies no matter their accomplishment. This book explores the struggles and new meanings emerging from the use of human rights as a political tool in the context of this conflicting commonality.

As with any shared rules and norms governing what human beings have "in common" (Blouin-Genest and Paquerot 2016), human rights are neither neutral nor objective: they are political, contested and conflictual. They involve what we call political "battlefields" (idem), which refers to political spaces that undergo constant changes and in which political conflict—and the struggles for meaning (Laclau and Mouffe 1985)—is expressed by translation and transformation processes. We argue that these processes contribute to the modification of the scope and understanding of human rights, as will be explained in depth in Chap. 2 of this volume where the theoretical and conceptual framework are developed.

Yet, even in cases where stakeholders and social actors have clearly re-appropriated rights discourse, any innovations or breakthroughs are often seen as having been allowed by international laws (Lavaud and Lestage 2006), as though actors were detached from and "objects" of human rights, instead of subjects. This perspective is particularly true when the cases at stake involve oppressed or subaltern actors, which is demonstrated in several chapters in this volume: the intersectional nexus of oppression involving women, children and Indigenous Peoples is revealed through the struggles of "human rights from below" (see the Chaps. 8 by Das, 9 by Carranza Ko and 10 by Doran). It is particularly important to document the dynamics of the re-appropriation, and even the reformulation, of human rights practices by social actors who are directly involved in conflicts and contestations that have been framed by the human rights context, rather than from the exclusive perspective of states and international institutions. That being said, the very important transformation dynamics at play within the institutional context are also revealed through these processes of translation. The role of institutions in the conceptual translation of human rights is very clearly documented in several chapters of this volume, including those by Bosvieux-Onyekwelu (Chap. 3), Paquerot (Chap. 4), Kamiloglu (Chap. 5) and Blouin-Genest & Erb (Chap. 11).

Notwithstanding their current inscription in international laws, documents and practices, human rights are consistently and dynamically used by actors as political tools to justify their actions, regardless of the dominant meaning of those rights and the "struggles for meaning" that stem from these re-appropriations (Doran 2016). Far from being fixed and imposed, human rights are flexible objects that adapt well to contexts, situations and uses, and thus their meanings or understandings can be modified without necessarily being anchored to new international law documents or practices. We suggest that these malleable meanings allow us to shed new light on the political processes that are at the heart of movements and actions that contest and change human rights through new and often unconventional practices. These practices may even challenge spaces conquered by political forces or legal mechanisms that are presented as being on the side of the oppressed, as some of the chapters in this book reveal particularly in Chap. 6 by Bessant and Watts, as well as in Chap. 12 by Cristiano).

Interestingly, it is the internationalization and flexibility of human rights that have made them contentious political objects: human rights are at the same time everywhere and nowhere, easily claimed and used to support contested practice, only to be repudiated the moment they no longer fit the main narrative of the actor(s) in question. They structure political conflicts, as rights are both the causes of and solutions for such encounters. Some have criticized this situation, arguing that human rights lost their effective power because they are constantly being translated and modified, without ever truly being implemented. Indeed, as indicated by Slaughter (2009), human rights have become "banalized."

The normalization, generalization and overall banalization of human rights is not, however, a limitation on the human rights research agenda, as we demonstrate in this volume. On the contrary, such a recognition of how human rights are being harnessed by multiple structures and actors represents a unique opportunity to understand what human rights have created, rather than focusing only on their legal interpretation, as framed by international documents, treaties and practices. In short, it opens human rights research to the study of new practices that are changing and redefining the meaning, understanding and use of human rights.

In this context, this edited volume seeks to understand the roles and functions of human rights, both in today's international society as well as in diverse national contexts, what is *created* by them instead of what they *consist of*, and how they are defined per se through international law. This approach requires us to look at how new and contemporary human rights practices emerge from social/political struggles and conflicts, and position themselves as standards, rules or values that are used as political tools to defend specific issues, ideas or projects. Understood as such, human rights appear to emerge from below (De Sousa Santos and Rodríguez-Garavito 2005), that is, from local and micro actors, issues or contestation, rather than being exclusively imposed from above, and most notably, by international law documents or practices.

It is this political and conflictual dimension of human rights practices that this book explores, thus adding a layer of complexity to the existing literature and research on human rights. As such, the key questions organizing this edited volume are:

- *What role do human rights play today, beyond their origin and inscription in international law?*
- *What political function can be attributed to the debates surrounding these rights, and the conflicts in which they are situated?*
- *To what extent are human rights active agents of social and political change, particularly when consideration is given beyond their technical implementation and recognition?*

Through recognizing that human rights become a type of "argument for authority" (Arendt and Mattei 1972) as well as a legitimization tool, the research problems that guide this edited volume challenge the idea that they are an obligatory point of passage in the development of new laws, despite their ineffective enforcement. Indeed, new human rights practices, especially conflictual ones, are an inherent part of their own redefinition of role and scope. As demonstrated by the different chapters in this volume, we are particularly interested in the political functions of human rights, the paradoxes that accompany their use as political tools, their (in)effective materialization and implementation, the debates, conflicts and struggles that frame human rights practices, and how human rights are contested, claimed and recognized beyond their liberal and western origin, which, therefore, shapes alternative conceptualizations.

The objective of this edited volume is thus threefold:

1. Generate a conceptual framework to understand human rights and their changing/evolving political dimensions;
2. Document key case studies/contexts in which human rights are expressed in terms of political battlefields, and;
3. Examine the ambivalence and limitations of such theoretical/conceptual apparatus.

The different case studies explored in this edited volume target the reality that contemporary human rights (notably through the UDHR but also in other institutional spaces such as the Interamerican Human Rights System ICHR) have become a highly recognized legal/legitimate landmark that influence many jurisdictions, actors and practices, while at the same time fall short of being minimally realized. As recalled by Doise (2003), this situation underlines the paradox of a "coexistence of a very strong adherence to fundamental principles and an equally strong awareness that they never completely apply to social reality" (p. 1). Yet, we believe that the factors that explain this paradox have to be illustrated and analyzed in specific, concrete cases where the power relations surrounding human rights as highly invested signifiers (Laclau and Mouffe 1985) can be seen at work. The present volume takes on this challenge. Because social reality is ever-changing and affected by meanings in flux, which opens up a space for subjectification and liberty (Doran 2016), the field of human rights has to be examined constantly. Following this introduction, these issues will be tackled throughout the chapters of this book, as detailed below, as well as in Chap. 2 "Human Rights as Battlefields: Power Relations, Translations and Transformations. A theoretical Framework" by Blouin-Genest, Doran and Paquerot.

The first section of this volume, *The changing nature of human rights and their political boundaries: new definitions, longstanding debates* presents Chap. 3 by Charles Bosvieux-Onyekwelu, Chap. 4 by Sylvie Paquerot and Chap. 5 by Ozan Kamiloglu.

The second section, *Overcoming the frontiers of discrimination and structural violence: intersectional struggles of human rights from below and transformations of Political space*, features Chap. 6 by Judith Bessants and Rob Watts, Chap. 7 by Olabanji Akinola, Chap. 8 by Nusta Carranzo Ko and Chap. 9 by Surma Das.

The third section, *Social contestation and the broadening of human rights' meanings* presents Chap. 10 by Marie-Christine Doran, Chap. 11 by Gabriel Blouin-Genest and Mikey Erb and Chap. 12 by Fabio Cristiano.

The final insights of the conclusion in Chap. 13 by Blouin-Genest, Doran and Paquerot tackles the overall meanings of human rights as a battlefield in order to deepen and enlarge democratic space and practice, while challenging the limits of liberal representative democracies, within the field of human rights, as well as outside of it.

A Vivid Picture of Human Rights Struggles and Their Political Effects Today: Overview of the Chapters

The contributions assembled in this volume present us with a rich array of case studies from almost all the continents and a variety of contexts, including the practices of very diverse actors and institutions. These solidly documented studies are articulated in a general effort to analyze and assert the more theoretical dimensions that these cases may contribute to our general understanding of what we could call—inspired by Bourdieu's notion of *champ* (field)—the *field of Human Rights* as observed today. To a certain extent, these contributions converge to elucidate the new power relations and political spaces that have been created through the endurance of struggles for meaning that stem from the appropriation and transformation of human rights by diverse actors. Even though the various cases analyzed in this volume illustrate important specific considerations, their global effects converge in challenging, and sometimes overcoming, political boundaries (Doran 2016) set around the currently dominant meanings of human rights. Through specific patterns in the appropriation, translation and transformation of human rights, the following chapters help us to identify these effects and to understand new political spaces that have been opened—or have yet to be opened—in the field of human rights.

In a number of cases, we can identify a convergence that reveals deeply entrenched patterns of often intersectional oppression. In these cases, struggles for human rights are always the necessary starting point to reveal the multifaceted aspects of these oppressions, as well as the mechanisms of legitimization that maintain them. These struggles cross through the materiality of discourses, as revealed in Bosvieux-Onyekwelu's important contribution in Chap. 3 about the gender presumptions of the initial French conceptions of human rights. His chapter tackles the centrality of gender at the heart of the foundational definitions of human rights and helps to shed light on crucial issues regarding the preassigned place of women in liberal, western societies, from whence human rights were developed. The issue of power and its contestation revealed in "The gender of human rights" furthermore highlight concerns related to the #MeToo movement, which takes on a whole new dimension as we can relate those concerns to very well accepted conceptions of gender that overdetermined the possibilities of current definitions of human rights heritage.

In the same vein, Nusta Carranzo Ko and Surma Das both bring vivid and inspiring case studies of human rights struggles of women in Peru and India who have known the most dispossession and discrimination in their countries. The studies reveal their amazing path to empowerment and their continuing struggle to redress past and present violence. In Chap. 8, "Forcibly sterilized: Peru's indigenous women and the battle for rights," Carranza Ko explains with remarkable depth how the dominant paradigm of reconciliation in Peru excluded the terrible case of massive sterilization that was forced on Indigenous women during Fujimori's authoritarian regime. Only the extraordinary persistence and determination of Indigenous women's human rights struggles in Peru have been able to elucidate the intersectional nature of these tremendous violations, which were so entrenched in structural racism and the legacy of the recent authoritarian regime that many people in Peru thought of forced sterilization as a beneficial action for poor and underprivileged people. Their success in overthrowing this despicable discourse of legitimization of structural racism, led to the additional success of Indigenous women in Peru who have shown the extent to which Peru's dual society remains far from justice and equality for Indigenous people, even though they represent roughly 25% of the population.

In Chap. 9, "Politicization of rights-based development and marginalization of human rights from below: the case of maternal health rights in India" by Surma Das, we are presented with a rich analysis of the consequences for what at first would appear to be progress toward the reduction of preventable maternal deaths in India, where the number of such deaths is the second-highest in the world. The author challenges the generally well-known human-rights framework for development—the rights-based approach—which has succeeded in highlighting the political dimensions of such deaths and framing them as "maternal" human rights issues. However, this apparent victory triggered new power relations that affected previous human rights advocacy efforts in India, which were focused on "reproductive" health and rights prior to international involvement. The insightful analysis of Das thus clearly shows that the well-intentioned focus on maternal health, largely encouraged by international advocacy networks and institutions, may be detrimental to the much holistic approach of women's reproductive rights from within India's domestic tradition of human rights advocacy.

Another main line of argument in this book occurs through the many contributions that converge to show that identifying power relations at work is only possible by carefully looking at the precise definitions and applications of human rights in specific contexts. Through this type of analysis, we are able to explain the slow progress of human rights defense in the world today, as well as some regressive tendencies. As Sylvie Paquerot's engaging contribution on the world's most precious resource—water—demonstrates so clearly in Chap. 4, "The right to water: the political function of human rights as an expression of the contradictions in globalization," the apparent victory of having water recognized internationally as a main issue of global economic governance conceals a major flaw that has always been part of the ambivalent nature of the dominant liberal definition of human rights. As Paquerot argues in her analysis of the last 20 years' advocacy on the right to water, the possibility of acknowledging access to water as a right in international institutions does not prevent the growing tendency to concurrently privatize water. Thus, years of efforts from human rights and water advocacy networks whose aim was to define water as a common good and secure it from privatization and commodification have been neglected by what would otherwise appear to be a great achievement in the international recognition of the importance of water by the United Nations General Assembly and the Human Rights Council in 2010. Even though the struggles over the meaning of human rights, and in this particular case, the right to water, may still reverse this definition, Paquerot's discerning analysis is key to understanding the dominant liberal, individualist paradigm that is at work when human rights are translated in the international system.

A similarly enlightening analysis is conducted by Ozan Kamiloglu in Chap. 5, "Politics of neutrality, human rights and armed struggles: The Turkey example." Kamiloglu tackles the delicate issue of power that is based on the hegemonic definitions and redefinitions of human rights by major transnational advocacy actors such as Amnesty International. In this truly engaging analysis, the author asserts that the proposed definition of armed opposition groups as oppressors in contexts where armed resistance is seen by many as the only means to overthrow authoritarian regimes or political forces, as it is in Turkey. In this case, these definitions may trigger new processes of ostracization, and the repression of the Kurd movement and the armed resistance group PKK (Kurdistan Workers Party). This chapter thus shows that predominant conceptualizations (or myths) behind the field of human rights, such as neutrality and universality, can also be the sites of new processes of discrimination and must, therefore, be examined carefully from within the context in which they will be applied. This contribution thus brings us to the idea of universality as the main feature of human rights defense.

In a rich case study of Nigeria that converges within this line of argument, Olabanji Akinola courageously and convincingly illustrates in Chap. 7, "Who is a child? the politics of human rights, the Convention on the Right of the Child (CRC), and child marriage in Nigeria," that the slow progress of human rights for children since the implementation of the CRC in African countries is not due as much to political, social or even cultural obstacles in each African country, as it is largely a result of the way in which human rights for children have been defined in both international institutions and national legislative bodies. The enlightening analysis of the Nigerian case clearly reveals that the very definition of human rights and their translation by legislative systems hold primary importance in providing—or retrieving—access to the most fundamental human rights for the most vulnerable human beings in Africa and around the world, our children.

In Chap. 6, "Child prisoners, human rights and human rights activism: beyond 'emergency' and 'exceptionality'—an Australian case study," the remarkable contribution of Judith Bessant and Rob Watts provides a political analysis of both the implementation of human rights and the debate about power relations within the field. They convincingly trace the process by which political and legal systems may converge despite their temporary opposition in human rights cases. By means of their analysis of the process by which spaces of exceptionality are used by the legal system to challenge unfair and discriminatory political decisions toward poor and Indigenous child prisoners in Australia, the authors contend that the founding principle of popular sovereignty is excluded from both the legal and political systems when their disputes are resolved in spaces of exceptionality.

The third and final main line of argument emerging from the contributions to this book can be seen in the assessments of the possible transformations—and even counter-hegemonic articulations—that may occur due to new human rights meanings.[1] Emerging from very diverse perspective—from Indigenous redefinitions of key concepts from international and national legislatures on natural resources, to the genealogy of the human right to health, or even the use of internet as a human right—three contributions to this book shed light on the political effects of human rights from below that go beyond the appropriation, or even the translation, of international legislative tools for human rights.

In Chap. 10, "Indigenous struggles for the redefinition of human rights in natural resources conflicts: beyond the strategic use of international legislation," Marie-Christine Doran's contribution, based on field work, examines the precise sites of *struggles for meaning* between national and international legislation around human rights, Indigenous rights and natural resources, and their transformation through political imaginaries that are articulated in the discourse and practice of indigenous rights defenders in Chile. Doran's extensive material demonstrates that this rich indigenous collective action repertoire in Chile goes far beyond the strategic use of international legislation. In fact, the evidence in this chapter points to a transformation of hegemonic meanings—even those developed in international conventions for the protection of Indigenous rights—which lead to a truly innovative—and sometimes even poetic—dimension of new indigenous meanings for human rights. This contribution sheds light on the recurrent use of violence that is allowed due to the permanence of the legislation of the authoritarian regime that affects Indigenous people from North to South despite the celebrated stability of Chile's democratic institutions. In doing so, Doran clearly demonstrates how indigenous definitions of rights, justice and democracy challenge this ongoing oppression through the continual creation of positive contributions to democracy and rights perspectives, even under the most adverse conditions. Ultimately, as the Chilean case illustrates, it is the right to full political representation, deliberation and participation that is contained within Indigenous conceptions of human rights.

In Chap. 11, "Improving HIV/AIDS drugs access: a genealogy of the human right to health from below," Gabriel Blouin-Genest and Mikey Erb tackle one of the most illustrative examples of the transformative effects of human rights from below: the right to health. Through a solid, evidence-based analysis, this chapter underlines how the language and practice of human rights have been used to produce, translate, modify and/or contest the reality of the human right to health. To do so, Blouin-Genest and Erb use HIV/AIDS, and in particular the question of access to essential drugs and medicines, as their main case study. They show that the human right to health, rather than being imposed from above by international actors, emerged from below, especially through the work of civil society, community groups and activists involved human rights "battlefields."

Finally, Chap. 12 by Fabio Cristiano, "Internet access as human right: a dystopian critique from the occupied Palestinian territory," presents us with a cutting-edge contribution, that was analyzed in a very challenging context wherein the collection of data was itself high-risk. In this truly enlightening study, Cristiano shows that internet access is a tool for population control that is used by all the political authorities from both sides whose aim is to control political liberties for the Palestinian population. The claim for internet as a human right remains first and foremost at the heart of the claim for liberty that fuels the desire for transformation in the Palestinian society. The virtual cry for internet as a human right has allowed the Palestinians in the occupied territories to focus on resistance to both the oppression of the Israeli state and to the general repercussions for liberties that followed the Arab spring uprisings in the region. Ultimately, the resistance to all forms of political control that are embodied by the claim for internet as a human right is both a tool of the social re-construction of Palestine as an imagined territory, and a fundamental reminder that humans may dream of liberty even if they have never seen a concrete example of it.

Ultimately, all the cases analyzed in this book demonstrate that beyond all the possible appropriations, translations or re-articulations of human rights lies their truly fascinating nature: their profound and solidly asserted universality stems from the very possibility of finding in human rights the basis for the continued contestation of their own sedimented meanings. This profound critical standpoint arises from the polysemic, yet always renewed, utopian idea of liberty. This extraordinary idea at the core of contemporary human rights will always prevail in shedding light on oppression and in opening new space for imagining emancipation. As the immortal verse by Paul Eluard says "*Sur les armes des guerriers, Sur la couronne des rois, J'écris ton nom: Liberté...*/On the weapons of warriors, on the crowns of kings, I write your name: Liberty."

Note

1. Please refer to Chap. 2 "Human Rights as Battlefields: Power Relations, Translations and Transformations. A theoretical Framework" for a detailed explanation of these concepts and their usefulness from an analytical point of view.

References

Arendt, Hannah, and François Mattei. 1972. *La crise de la Culture*. Paris: Gallimard.

Badie, Bertrand. 1999. *Un monde sans souveraineté: les États entre ruse et responsabilité*. Paris: Fayard.

Blouin-Genest, Gabriel, and Sylvie Paquerot. 2016. Environmental Human Rights as a Battlefield: A Grammar of Political Confrontation. *Journal of Human Rights and the Environment* 7 (1): 132–154.

De Sousa Santos, Boaventura, and César A. Rodríguez-Garavito, eds. 2005. *Law and Globalization from Below: Towards a Cosmopolitan Legality*. Cambridge: Cambridge University Press.

Doise, Willem. 2003. *Human Rights as Social Representations*. London/New York: Routledge.

Doran, Marie-Christine. 2016. *Le réveil démocratique du Chili: une histoire politique de l'exigence de justice: de la transition à l'Assemblée constituante (1990–2016)*. Paris: Karthala.

Laclau, Ernesto, and Chantal Mouffe. 1985. *Hegemony and Socialist Strategy: Towards a Radical Democratic Politics*. 1st ed. London: Verso.

Lavaud, Jean-Pierre, and Françoise Lestage. 2006. Les redéfinitions de l'indianité. *Esprit* 1: 42–64.

Slaughter, Joseph. 2009. *Human Rights, Inc.: The World Novel, Narrative Form, and International Law*. New York: Fordham University Press.

PART I

The Changing Nature of Human Rights and Their Political Boundaries: New Definitions, Longstanding Debates

CHAPTER 2

Human Rights as Battlefields: Power Relations, Translations and Transformations—A Theoretical Framework

Gabriel Blouin-Genest, Marie-Christine Doran, and Sylvie Paquerot

Introduction: Are Human Rights Taken for Granted?

What are human rights exactly? How are they used—and sometimes abused—in contemporary politics? How can we understand them beyond their traditional—and contested—meaning as "rights inherent to all human beings."[1] What does this meaning entail? If all human beings are stakeholders of the same rights, large scale racism, gender violence, or poverty remind us of their nonexistence for most of us.

G. Blouin-Genest (✉)
Department of Political Science, Virginia Tech, Blacksburg, VA, USA
e-mail: gblouin@vt.edu

M.-C. Doran • S. Paquerot
School of Political Studies, University of Ottawa, Ottawa, ON, Canada
e-mail: Marie-Christine.Doran@uottawa.ca; spaquero@uottawa.ca

G. Blouin-Genest et al. (eds.), *Human Rights as Battlefields*,
Human Rights Interventions,
https://doi.org/10.1007/978-3-319-91770-2_2

Human rights are largely un-problematized and unchallenged social objects and practices. Interestingly, and even though their general understanding seems to be minimally shared, at least when it comes to their "dominant understanding" (Donnelly 2013, pp. 24–25) found in the Universal Declaration of Human Rights (UDHR 1948), the question of the adequacy between this common sense meaning and possible conflicting/contradictory practices is still up-to-date. In fact, beyond the vague understanding of human rights as standards, rules or legally sanctioned values emerging from international law, practices or documents, the reality of human rights practices, especially when they come from actors involved in day-to-day contestation and implementation, largely appears to be under-documented and analyzed in academic literature. In particular, the theoretical and conceptual framework needed to assert the importance of non-state and community actors in the day-to-day construction and reinforcement of human rights appears to be missing, despite multiple examples of international organizations and NGOs documenting these crucial actions from non-state and community actors.

Authors such as Boaventura de Sousa Santos or Arturo Escobar, among others (Doran 2010, 2017), have documented the extreme vitality of human rights emerging "from below," which remains, however, largely under-analyzed in the human rights literature. This current understatement of human rights from below stems from what many scholars have observed: human rights are often taken for granted as a de facto component of liberal democracy (e.g. Gauchet (2002) or Badie (2002)). Understood as such, human rights are left emptied of their potential for contestation. This "neutralization" structures a well ordered civil society, thus excluding human rights from the political realm.

As Chantal Mouffe suggested, political liberalism's dominant version of liberty rejects conflict and antagonism from the horizon of rights and thus leads to the "end of politics," rejecting challenges and debates from the political space (Mouffe 1994, pp. 7–25). Raymonde Monnier, in her analysis of the 1789 French Declaration of the Rights of Man and of the Citizen, and the subsequent use of the word "democracy" (Monnier 1999), reminds us that the liberal and Western origin of human rights is very clear about one main idea: liberty cannot be truly accomplished without equality of rights, which represents popular sovereignty in democracy. As such, equality of rights—and human rights—will be the locus of constant struggles, either for their implementation or as a defense against, for example, the usurpation of power by a state or other group disconnected from popular sovereignty and democracy.[2]

Yet, some scholars have analyzed the progressive disappearance of this conflictual nature of human rights as exemplifying their use as tools for Western domination (Mutua 2002), as being compatible with neoliberalism (Gustafson 2002) or even as being manipulated by dictatorships (Haughney 2012). This perspective comes in part from the "globalization" of human rights as an ideology accompanying the free market (Tosel 1995) and the multiple uses of human rights rhetoric as legitimizing strategies for state actors. Routinized use of human rights rhetoric contributes to the de-politicization of democracy itself by suggesting that an institutional space for human rights exists when, in fact, the more challenging arena of contestations and conflicts opened up by human rights practices is negated.[3] Frequent in many Latin American or African countries (such as the RDC), this problematic situation was recognized by the United Nations Committee on Human Rights Office and the Inter-American Commission on Human Rights, which decided in 2017 to create a Joint Action Mechanism to Contribute to Protection of Human Rights Defenders in the Americas[4] in countries that adhere to and promote human rights but nonetheless persecute human rights activists. The killing of hundreds of human rights defenders in countries that recognize and implement human rights frameworks underlines the paradox of contemporary human rights practices.

This paradox, in turn, leads us to ask the following questions: What is created by human rights? What are their current uses today, outside of their practical setting in international law, documents and practices, or their philosophical origin? The theoretical and conceptual framework outlined in this chapter supports that human rights, before being a legally recognized instrument inscribed in international law, are first and foremost a contested object shaped by struggles, debates and contestation from actors involved in concrete actions, mobilization and activism. In short, this chapter develops the conceptual/theoretical framework needed to understand how human rights, rather than being created from above, have in fact arisen from particular settings and through actions, practices, documents and narratives emerging from communities and groups involved in the issues and rights at stake.

The main argument supported here is that human rights should be understood as a space for *struggles for meaning* (Laclau and Mouffe 1985; Laclau 2000) or "battlefields," understood as "[t]he social and political space through which different human rights actors become organized and mobilized in order to claim a specific understanding/practice of these rights through the logic of emancipation from their original context or objectives." (Blouin-Genest and Paquerot 2016, p. 140). The conceptual and theoretical framework behind this understanding of human rights as "battlefields" emphasizes the place/space merging—and framing—the comprehension of human rights as materializing from struggles and contestations in which actors are involved firsthand. This understanding calls for a re-politicization of human rights that shows how they can challenge both the political and social orders and how they are used to broaden society's democratic space.

In order to do so, we first look at the conflicting history of human rights and their dominant understandings, followed by an exploration of their emergence from below. We conclude with a conceptual analysis of their uses in/for contentious politics.

Human Rights: The Conflicting (Hi)Story of Political Landmarks

Human rights are sometimes understood as fixed objects, reproduced in international law documents, practices and organizations. They appear as conceptual objects created once and for all in the specific post WWII context. Human rights are rarely analyzed for their fluidity and malleability, and especially not in terms of how community groups and activists are key to the definitional and conceptual process of what human rights are outside of their setting in international law. The objective of this chapter is to start a re-problematization of the dominant understanding of human rights. This re-problematization is also a call for a re-politicization of human rights.

Since the creation of the United Nations (UN) in 1945, human rights went through several evolutions, contestations and paradigmatic shifts: "[t]he concept of rights is expanding rapidly, propelled by increased knowledge and experience, changing societal challenges and conditions, and realization of the inherent limits in the earlier rights concepts and practices." (Mann 2006, p. 1940). These changes are analyzed quite differently depending on the perspective adopted and/or the place from which they are analyzed. From being a necessary tool for the emancipation of different "oppressed" or "victimized" groups to being used as moralistic instruments for neocolonialism and liberalism, human rights have been characterized by conflicting positions and interpretations. Human rights have been an active "battlefield" for multiple—and various types of—actors (Blouin-Genest and Paquerot 2016; Doran 2016).

Human rights have been used by different actors to both be recognized themselves as legitimate *and* have a cause or issue captured by the authority and the moral value that comes with the concept/idea of human rights, shaping what Hafner-Burton Tsutsui called the "paradox of empty promises" (Hafner-Burton and Tsutsui 2005), according to which these expectations are never met. We should not be surprised, then, to find human rights being invoked at almost every political level and by so many contradicting actors. Their legitimacy and validity are at the same time contested, invoked, challenged or captured: some actors invoke human rights in specific contexts and contest them in others; they are often used as political tools against enemies, while in other cases serving the purpose of protection against aggression. This paradoxical situation conceals the need for the re-politicization of human rights, which entails a shift to understand them as political objects shaped by struggles and contestation.

The conflicting and contradictory uses of human rights are well summarized by Doise,

> [w]hen it comes to human rights, the twentieth century has seen the best as well as the worst: there have been efforts that have never been tried before to create the institutional basis for the respect of these rights, but also mass relentlessness to violate them systematically. (Doise 2003, p. 1)

China, Chiquita, Coca-Cola and North Korea are all actors that at some point invoked human rights in order to defend *their* actions or protect themselves *from* external interventions. These actors are also consistently the target of human rights groups and activists, as well as the UN, mainly because of constant human rights violations perpetrated under their authority (and despite being party to multiple international human rights conventions and treaties).

Thus, conflicts, contestations and oppositions are what characterize contemporary human right practices and understanding. Rather than having a fixed understanding imposed from above, coming from international law documents, practices and regulations, human rights are subject to constant redefinition, contestation and reframing by actors. Some of them, as suggested above, are powerful entities using human rights as a strategic tool while at the same time violating them or actively supporting their violations; yet, other actors are directly involved in human rights practices that oppose and contest the power of these "illegitimate" human rights strategists. This specific process of resistance arising from human rights "from below" is tackled in this book and fuels the idea that human rights still have a solid subversive power despite their rhetorical and strategic use by transnational companies and dictatorships.

As pointed out by Ife, "[h]uman rights from below would reject any notion of either needs or rights as being determined, a priori, from above whether as universal human rights or as common human needs. [...] Human rights from below rather see both needs and rights as constructions. They are defined by human beings in social, political and cultural contexts" (Ife 2009). Human rights are thus objects of constant re-appropriation.

Drawing on the example of global water governance, Borrero Navia reminds us that human rights remain "always in practice in an environment of forces in conflict, a prolonged process of social and political struggle [which] precedes their recognition" (Borrero Navia 1994, p. 15). We can add that even when recognized, conflicts and struggles persist in shaping the role human rights and how they frame and shape dominant understandings. In fact, as we argue in this book, conflicts and oppositions are what characterize contemporary human rights practices.

The conflicting and complex history of human rights shows how deeply interconnected with conflicts, struggles and contestations human rights are. Interestingly, and despite their conflicting nature, human rights are nonetheless deeply rooted in the history of "modernity"[5] and modern political liberalism. Democracy, secularization and free will seem to be inseparable from the contemporary idea of human rights. In this perspective, human rights refer to the principles of freedom and equality and to the fundamental right of every human being to self-determination, the right to decide for oneself.

Human rights are nonetheless deeply contested and rearticulated on a consistent basis, even in their Western/liberal practices. Although the roots of human rights can be found in multiple civilizations and cultures (Leuprecht 2011, p. 112), their translation/materialization into international law, documents and practices largely originates from the paradigm of Western modernity and liberalism, at the heart of which political freedom appears as its core element. Interestingly, and despite their Western and liberal origin, there are very few international law concepts that seem to be shared, at least in their common sense understanding, as much as human rights. They have even attained a form of "banalization" (Slaughter 2009) at the international level. This form does not mean that they are not criticized or opposed, but that they are used as a common ground for discussion through conflicts and oppositions. This role is why we argue that human rights can be considered as "battlefields."

Contemporary human rights (through the UDHR in particular) have thus become a highly recognized legal and political landmark, influencing many jurisdictions, practices, treaties and activist mobilizations while at the same time falling short of being minimally realized, implemented and respected. The largely shared common understanding of human rights is only equaled by their overwhelmingly common violations. As such, there is a paradoxical "coexistence of a very strong adherence to fundamental principles and an equally strong awareness that they never completely apply to social reality." (Doise 2003, p. 1).

What is probably the most striking element about human rights is that, even though they are invoked/contested by conflicting actors, constantly violated and not even close to being minimally implemented at the global scale, they nonetheless come with a surprising aura of incontestability and legitimacy. Human rights represent today a sort of "argument for authority" (Arendt and Mattei 1972) a "political landmark" despite their clearly ineffective enforcement and realization. This "banalization" of human rights (Slaughter 2009) leads to the question of their translation from a fixed meaning in international law documents to their actual use by actors, and especially community-based actors and activists involved in mobilization.

The Translation of Human Rights from Below

A recognition that what is taken as a given, in this case the dominant understandings of what human right are, needs to be problematized is key to our endeavor here. We thus position our theoretical/conceptual framework within what Paul Rabinow, among others, has identified as the necessary deconstruction and investigation of "social practices [that] have hence become effective forces in the social world" (Rabinow 1996, p. x). This position allows us to show how the constitution of dominant—and unchallenged—understandings regarding human rights, how they are perceived and taken for granted, is in fact specifically peculiar and has its own historical context, and its own social conditions and political foundations

(Rabinow 1996, p. 241). When it comes to human rights, this peculiarity allows us to show that their dominant meanings or common sense understandings emerge for somewhere, and thus, must be problematized and challenged as contextual political objects.

Understood as "[…] a particular way of analyzing an event or a situation: not as a given but as a question" (Collier and Lakoff 2008, p. 11), problematization[6] seeks to challenge dominant and well-recognized understanding of reality (in our case, of human rights). Our theoretical framework is thus in great part inspired by the Actor Network Theory (ANT), as we show that shared knowledge about human rights emerges through interactions and multidimensional relationships between actors—especially community-based actors and activists—rather than being imposed from above, through the symbolic power of international law and practices. Thus, we argue that human rights should be understood as relational entities rather than fixed objects. This relational understanding, again, reminds us of how ANT could be useful in the re-problematization of human rights. As argued by Law, "[…] entities take their form and acquire their attributes as a result of their relations with other entities" (Law 1999, p. 3). They are relational, rather than being fixed or imposed: "[…] what appears to be topologically natural, given in the order of the world, is in fact produced in networks" (Law 1999, p. 8). Conflicts, oppositions and dissensus characterize these networks,[7] they represent these interactions, and thus create meanings, and frame practices, even if they are conflicting ones.

Meaning and understanding thus emerge from "[…] the summing up of interactions through various kinds of devices, inscriptions, forms and formulae, into a very local, very practical, very tiny locus" (Latour 1999, pp. 16–7). Relations, movements, oppositions, struggles and exchanges structure uniformity and coherence of social objects (idem). They emerge through networks. These networks represent the battlefields for the emergence of meanings regarding human rights. As documented in the different chapters in this volume, they also involve micro actors and practices, rather than simply processes coming from above, from imposed practices and understandings (i.e. international law practices, documents and organizations related to human rights).

These understandings and meanings are produced from various practices rendering the documentation of human rights practices from various loci, empirical materials and perspectives (of which this book is an example, in the end) more than urgent. This urgent need, again, echoes ANT, as it "privileges neither natural (realism) nor cultural (social constructivism) accounts of scientific production, asserting instead that science is a process of heterogeneous engineering in which the social, technical, conceptual, and textual are puzzled together (or juxtaposed) and transformed (or translated)." (Ritzer 2005, p. 1). This understanding of ANT equally applies, we argue here, to human rights. We thus find the development of meanings of contemporary human rights in various material, discursive and textual practices, which justifies our use of different types of empirical material to document emerging human rights practices in this book.

Accordingly, by positioning human rights analysis within such networks, we characterize human rights as spaces/places for dispute over power, as the locus of claims and productive confrontations, thus situating human rights in line with an analysis where the nature of power itself changes. Struggles, conflicts and oppositions are key to this process:

> [w]ithin all sociotechnical networks, relational effects result from disputes between actors, such as attempts at the advancement of a particular program, which necessarily results in social asymmetry. Therefore, ANT can also be considered a theory of the mechanics of power: the stabilization and reproduction of some interactions at the behest of others, the construction and maintenance of network centers and peripheries, and the establishment of hegemony. Rather than power as possession, power is persuasion, 'measured' via the number of entities networked. Power is generated in a relational and distributed manner as a consequence of ordering struggles. (Ritzer 2005, p. 2)

Throughout these struggles, contentious issues and oppositions, what we call battlefields, objects are translated, they evolve and change: "[t]ranslation (transport with deformation), as distinguishable from diffusion (transfer without distortion), is both a process and effect" (Ritzer 2005, p. 2). Human rights emerge from these translations where conflicts, opposition and dissensus are key to the production of human rights. More importantly for us, they emerge from below. What has to be questioned and documented, then, is how human rights emerge from below, through struggles and conflicts, rather than being imposed from above, by transnational actors or practices.

Human rights, in light of such a framework, appear to have the purpose of supporting the oppositions that enable the emergence of political debates beyond the sanitized view of peaceful relationships in society.

They emerge from actors and practices that are not de facto delineated by pre-existing paradigms or structures. They broaden, we argue, a society's democratic space by challenging the social and political order. The concept of a political "field"[8] is central to this understanding of human rights as the place/space where meaning emerges through struggles, conflicts and oppositions.

Understood as such, human rights have a form of independence from their liberal and Western origin. They should not, then, be conflated with their—conflicting and paradoxical—use and instrumentalization by different actors. They need to be understood as a place for interaction between actors within different networks, a place/space where power struggles, societal relations and interactions are translated, creating meanings and understandings that can thus be invoked, contested or resisted. They can then become "battlefields."

Battlefields, 'Struggles for Meaning' and the Counter-Hegemonic Potential of Human Rights from Below

In addition to the possibilities opened up by ANT, the theoretical perspective of discursive hegemonic relations developed by Ernesto Laclau and Chantal Mouffe enables us "to understand that society and politics are deeply constituted by 'struggles over meaning'" (Doran 2016, p. 44). This perspective sheds light on the fact that there are "deep power relations at play in the process of constitution and subversion of meaning and that we might seize them and analyze them to see effective social and political change" (Doran 2016, p. 45). In this view, the social space can be seen as a system of meaning or intelligibility based on a certain number of discursive formations and universes, some of which are hegemonic and distribute social status, roles and legitimacy to certain actors, thus establishing "frontiers" and barriers, which form a relatively stable discursive horizon, including many converging discursive formations (Foucault 1969), presented as objective. However, as the social is always affected and reopened by the constant and contingent flux of meanings that discursively constituted subjects form, deform and reform, there may occur situations where, using Laclau and Mouffe's terminology, 'antagonisms' directly contest the hegemonic definition of 'nodal points'[9] that are crucial for hegemonic discursive formations. These antagonisms represent other meanings for the same words/concepts that contest the hegemonic meaning. They may be transformed and translated into discursive chains that will make many voices converge and achieve counter-hegemonic meaning, thus contesting and sometimes transforming the shared meaning of a particular signifier. There may be many specific important 'sites of antagonism' in a given social space and when they become contested by many articulations of meaning or discourses:

> Any discourse is constituted as an attempt to dominate the field of discursivity, to arrest the flow of differences, to construct a centre. We will call the privileged discursive points of this partial fixation, nodal points. (Lacan has insisted on these partial fixations through his concept of *points de capiton*, that is, of privileged signifiers that fix the meaning of a signifying chain. [...]) (Laclau and Mouffe 1985, p. 112)

Key for us here is that new meanings stem from a direct contestation of and confrontation with old ones. These new meanings may also be reversed, in turn, because the flux of meaning is always at play in the 'constitutive exteriority' of which the social is made (Doran 2016, pp. 41–69). This perspective thus calls upon a scenario of struggles for meaning that may be observed in order to "empirically show the emergence of struggles for meaning having measurable political effects" (Doran 2016, p. 53). Deeply rooted in this perspective is the idea that politics—or the political—is a conflictual space (or *moment* in Husserlian terms) where meanings and significations are challenged or dislocated by contesting antagonisms, and then become rearticulated in new ways: "'Politics' is an ontological category: there is politics because there is subversion and dislocation of the social. This means that *any* subject is, by definition, political" (Laclau 1990, p. 61).

This process of challenging established meanings and rearticulating counter-hegemonic ones is observable, we argue in this volume, from the perspective of human rights from below, which appear as particularly meaningful and fruitful contested objects. The contributors to this volume document and analyze multiple practices of human rights from below that challenge dominant or deviant uses of human rights. Some of the case studies clearly highlight struggles and confrontations, while others show more advanced processes of subversion and the emergence of new counter-hegemonic meanings. Throughout the different case studies explored, we witness discursive interactions apprehended by ANT and the counter-hegemonic potential identified by Laclau and Mouffe's theory of power at the heart of discursive relations.

The possibilities opened up by this double framework show that the liberal, or purely harmonious, theory of human rights that is dominant in human rights literature is not enough to account for this great variety of cases and their trickle-down effects on human rights struggles, contestations and practices.

Human Rights and Contentious Politics: The Effective Potential to Transform Democracy

As underlined by Blouin-Genest and Paquerot (2016), "[h]uman rights [...] establish themselves not only as a formal limit imposed upon power, but as a space for claims and contestation against this same power, simultaneously structuring the vocabulary of, and means for, actions organized in their own name—that is, in the name of human rights." (p. 137). Human rights are a place/space for "claims and contestations" (p. 138).

Understood as a space/place for political claims, contestation and resistance without a necessary or permanent effectivity, human rights reveal their political nature. Consensus and compromise give way to confrontation and opposition as organizational factors of what is shared, even if this sharing comes from conflicts and oppositions. It is thus the productive power of human rights on social organization that is recognized and acknowledged in this volume.

Confrontations, oppositions and conflicts create opportunities for new political meanings and produce new social structures. Going against the compromise-oriented focus of traditional liberalism, where conflicts and oppositions are seen here as elements of division and disorganization, this book rather underlines the importance of "contentious politics" (Tilly and Tarrow 2015), of how conflicts, opposition and dissensus should be understood as productive political and social factors.

Conflicts, oppositions and dissensus are the shared language of the "common" (Dardot and Laval 2015), which is profoundly embedded with contemporary human rights practices: "contentious politics involves interaction in which actors make claims bearing on someone else interests, [...] in which governments are involved as targets, initiators of claims, or third parties. Contentious politics thus brings together three features of social life: contention, collective action and politics" (Tilly 2008, p. 5).

Confrontation is not to be avoided. Rather, when embraced for its productive factor, it enables common ground and common language for social/political interaction. Understood as such, human rights embody what we share at the global scale, even though deeply contested and largely unrealized.

This framing of human rights means going against the search for consensus typically assumed in democratic settings:

> [it] present[s] a new way to think about democracy that is different from the traditional liberal conception of democracy as a negotiation among interests [...]. [W]hile we desire an end to conflict, if we want people to be free we must always allow for the possibility that conflict may appear and to provide an arena where differences can be confronted. (Mouffe and Castle 1998)

In this perspective, human rights entail a direct relation to liberal democracy's most basic features: political representation and participation. Kriegel (1986, p. 291) contends that the actual Universal Declaration of Rights relies on an "intangible basis" because the right to political participation is not guaranteed whatsoever, leading to a superficial application of rights because stakeholders may not contest political decisions on the basis of their rights.

It is precisely the possibility of challenging political order through dissensus, oppositions and contestations—to enlarge the participatory and democratic setting—that is opened up by the theoretical and conceptual framework of human rights from below that is developed in this volume.

Notes

1. http://www.ohchr.org/EN/Issues/Pages/WhatareHumanRights.aspx, accessed on January 10, 2018.
2. The tyranny of *La Terreur* perfectly illustrates this usurpation of power when Robespierre and his followers decided to eliminate the popular component of the French Revolution. Despite this treason, the fundamental intuition of the 1789 Declaration of the Rights of Man and of the Citizen, that rights will have to be constantly defended from the standpoint of popular sovereignty and democracy, remains entirely true today.
3. In many countries with a strong legal and human rights framework, such as Colombia for example, belonging to a human rights organization was seen during the armed conflict that ended in 2016 as the equivalent of supporting the leftist guerillas, which often translated into death warrants for human

rights defenders (IPEV report, Chapter 9, 2018, http://www.ipev-fmsh.org/).
4. See http://www.ohchr.org/EN/NewsEvents/Pages/DisplayNews.aspx?NewsID=22282&LangID=E.
5. See Bauman (1990) for a critical analysis of modernity.
6. Collier and Lakoff themselves refer to the Foucauldian concept of problematization, as being the "discursive or non-discursive practices that bring something into the game of truth and falsehood and constitutes it as an object of thought" (Foucault 1994, p. 1489).
7. We are aware of the many conceptual problems associated with the use of the term "network". As Bruno Latour points out, this term must be understood for its specific ANT meaning, as being the process through which information undergoes a series of transformations involving several actors, thus modifying and interpreting the information, and not for its common sense of "[…] transport without deformation, an instantaneous, unmediated access to every piece of information" (Latour 1999, p. 15).
8. For Bourdieu, "the political field is a place, where, within the competition between those involved, political results, problems, programs, analyses, concepts, and events are created and between which ordinary citizens […] must choose" (Bourdieu 1981, pp. 2–4).
9. Nodal points are important and visible sites of power relations where the subversion and transformation of previous hegemonic meaning can be seen at play (Laclau and Mouffe 1985).

References

Arendt, Hannah, and François Mattei. 1972. *La crise de la culture*. Paris: Gallimard.

Badie, Bertrand. 2002. *La diplomatie des droits de l'homme. Entre éthique et volonté de puissance*. Paris: Fayard.

Bauman, Zygmunt. 1990. Modernity and Ambivalence. *Theory, Culture & Society* 7 (2–3): 143–169.

Blouin-Genest, Gabriel, and Sylvie Paquerot. 2016. Environmental Human Rights as a Battlefield: A Grammar of Political Confrontation. *Journal of Human Rights and the Environment* 7 (1): 132–154.

Borrero Navia, J.V. 1994. *Environmental and Water Law in the South: Latin America, Asia, Africa – Second International Water Tribunal-1992*. Utrecht: International Books.

Bourdieu, Pierre. 1981. La représentation politique [Éléments pour une théorie du champ politique]. *Actes de la recherche en sciences sociales* 36 (1): 3–24.

Collier, Stephen J., and Andrew Lakoff. 2008. The Problem of Securing Health. In *Biosecurity Interventions: Global Health and Security in Question*, 7–32. New York: Columbia University Press.

Dardot, Pierre, and Christian Laval. 2015. *Commun: essai sur la révolution au XXIe siècle*. Paris: La Découverte.

Doise, Willem. 2003. *Human Rights as Social Representations*. London/New York: Routledge.

Donnelly, Jack. 2013. *Universal Human Rights in Theory and Practice*. Ithaca: Cornell University Press.

Doran, Marie-Christine. 2010. Les effets politiques des luttes contre l'impunité au Chili: de la revitalisation de l'action collective à la démocratisation. *Revue internationale de Politique comparée* 17 (2): 103–126.

———. 2016. *Le réveil démocratique du Chili: une histoire politique de l'exigence de justice: de la transition à l'Assemblée constituante (1990–2016)*. Paris: Karthala.

———. 2017. The Hidden Face of Violence in Latin America: Assessing the Criminalization of Protest in Comparative Perspective. *Latin American Perspectives* 44 (5): 183–206.

Foucault, Michel. 1969. *L'archéologie du savoir*. Paris: Gallimard.

———. 1994. Le Souci de Ia Vérité. *Dits et Écrits 1954–1988: IV 1980–1988*.

Gauchet, Marcel. 2002. *La démocratie contre elle-même*. Paris: Gallimard.

Gustafson, Bret. 2002. The Paradoxes of Liberal Indigenism: Indigenous Movements, State Processes, and Intercultural Reform in Bolivia. In *The Politics of Ethnicity: Indigenous Peoples in Latin American States*, ed. D. Maybury-Lewis, 267–306. Cambridge: Harvard University Press.

Hafner-Burton, Emilie M., and Kiyoteru Tsutsui. 2005. Human Rights in a Globalizing World: The Paradox of Empty Promises. *American Journal of Sociology* 110 (5): 1373–1411.

Haughney, Diane. 2012. Defending Territory, Demanding Participation: Mapuche Struggles in Chile. *Latin American Perspectives* 39 (4): 201–217.

Ife, Jim. 2009. *Human Rights from Below: Achieving Rights Through Community Development*. Cambridge: Cambridge University Press.

Kriegel, Blandine. 1986. *Les chemins de l'État*. Paris: Calmann-Lévy.

Laclau, Ernesto. 1990. *New Reflections on the Revolution Our Time*. London: Verso.

Laclau, Ernesto. 2000. *La guerre des identités, Grammaire de l'émancipation*. Paris: La Découverte/M.A.U.S.S.

Laclau, Ernesto, and Chantal Mouffe. 1985. *Hegemony and Socialist Strategy, Towards a Radical Democratic Politics*. London: Verso.

Latour, Bruno. 1999. On Recalling ANT. *The Sociological Review* 47 (S1): 15–25.

Law, John. 1999. After ANT: Complexity, Naming and Topology. *The Sociological Review* 47 (1_suppl): 1–14.

Leuprecht, Peter. 2011. *Reason, Justice and Dignity: A Journey to Some Unexplored Sources of Human Rights*. Boston/Leiden: Martinus Nijhoff Publishers.

Mann, J.M. 2006. Health and Human Rights: If Not Now, When? *American Journal of Public Health* 96 (1): 1940–1943.

Monnier, Raymonde. 1999. Démocratie et Révolution française. *Mots* 59 (1): 47–68.
Mouffe, Chantal. 1994. *Le politique et ses enjeux : pour une démocratie plurielle*. Paris: La Découverte/MAUSS.
Mouffe, Chantal, and Dave Castle. 1998. Hearts, Minds and Radical Democracy. *Red Pepper* 1, online. https://www.redpepper.org.uk/hearts-minds-and-radical-democracy/
Mutua, Makau. 2002. *Human Rights. A Political and Cultural Critique*. Philadelphia: University of Pennsylvania Press.
Rabinow, Paul. 1996. *Essays on the Anthropology of Reason*. Princeton: Princeton University Press.
Ritzer, George, ed. 2005. *Encyclopedia of Social Theory*. London: Sage.
Slaughter, Joseph. 2009. *Human Rights, Inc.: The World Novel, Narrative Form, and International Law*. New York: Fordham University Press.
Tilly, Charles. 2008. *Contentious Performances*. New York: Cambridge University Press.
Tilly, Charles, and Sidney G. Tarrow. 2015. *Contentious Politics*. London: Oxford University Press.
Tosel, André. 1995. *Démocratie et libéralismes*. Paris: Editions Kimé.
UDRH. 1948. Universal Declaration of Human Rights. *UN General Assembly*.

CHAPTER 3

The Gender of Human Rights: The French Debate Over "les droits de l'Homme"

Charles Bosvieux-Onyekwelu

Bending French Human Rights Law into Gender-Friendly Language (Introductory/Theoretical Section)

Despite becoming a "landmark" (Doise 2013) and a new "lingua franca" (Moyn 2010) on a global scale over the last 50 years, human rights are repeatedly contested from the perspectives of race, gender, and political philosophy (Lacroix and Pranchère 2016) from various geographical regions (Baretto 2013; Chakrabarty 2000; Otto 1997). This chapter intends to study the French debate over the spelling and writing of the phrase corresponding to "human rights" in English. According to the *Académie Française*, a French institution bestowed with the mission of guarding the French language, "*Droits de l'Homme*" [Man's rights] is the proper expression, as the institution defends that the masculine gender is the generic gender. It would therefore have the capacity of describing people of both sexes or genders, while the feminine genre could not. In this sense, the

C. Bosvieux-Onyekwelu (✉)
École des hautes études en sciences sociales (EHESS), Centre Maurice Halbwachs (CNRS-EHESS-ENS), Paris, France
e-mail: charles.bosvieux-onyekwelu@normalesup.org

G. Blouin-Genest et al. (eds.), *Human Rights as Battlefields*, Human Rights Interventions,
https://doi.org/10.1007/978-3-319-91770-2_3

expression "*les droits de l'Homme*" seems logical, as "*Homme*" [man] is supposed to represent the whole humanity.[1] On the opposite end, an assembly of activists, politicians, and academics called "*Droits humains pour tou-te-s*" [Human Rights for All] argues that the use of the term "*Homme*" perpetuates the "neutral masculine" norm. Hélène Bidard, a member of the organization and local councilor in Paris in charge of gender equality, thus maintains that "it would not spring to anyone's mind to utter 'women's rights' and think that, by doing so, they speak on behalf of the whole humanity" (Bidard 2015).

This debate has persisted for about 20 years, France being the only Western country that translated "human rights" as "*droits de l'Homme*" [Man's rights], a choice that has been more and more questioned. Recently, the issue has been on the news when 314 teachers of all levels of the French educational system decided to sign a petition entitled "*Nous n'enseignerons plus que 'le masculin l'emporte sur le feminin'*" [We will not teach anymore that the "the masculine prevails over the feminine"]. This petition is the latest event of a month-long debate on the issue of what is called in France "*écriture inclusive*" [inclusive writing],[2] a form of writing that debunks a founding grammar rule of the French language: the neutrality of masculine nouns. Indeed, the French language divides its words into two categories, masculine and feminine, but the rule of the "neutral masculine" commands that one uses the masculine plural (e.g. "*les avocats*" [the lawyers]) even if there are men and women among the lawyers in question, and even if there are more women than men. Conversely, advocates of inclusive writing state that one should spell it "*les avocat-e-s*" or "*les avocat·e·s*", the "e" bearing the mark of the feminine. The battle between the defendants of "*droits de l'Homme*" [Man's rights] and the proponents of the alternative wording "*droits humains*" [human rights] therefore takes place in the same kind of controversy, and forms part of an overarching debate over the politics of language.

Women's rights, which were officially stated in the 1945 United Nations Charter and in the 1948 Universal Declaration of Human Rights (UDHR), became more of a pressing issue at the World Conference on Human Rights held in Vienna in 1993. Two years later, in her remarks during the United Nations Fourth World Conference on Women in Beijing (September 8, 1995), Hillary Clinton proclaimed a mantra that would help popularize the phrase: "If there is one message that echoes forth from this conference, it is that human rights are women's rights. And women's rights are human rights" (Sunder 2003, p. 1407). The celebration of the

50th anniversary of the UDHR (1998) also contributed to bring this question to the political agenda of international organizations and NGOs. In contrast, a plea from French politician Ségolène Royal in defense of "*les droits humains*" [human rights] during an official visit to China as part of her presidential campaign in 2007 raised a few eyebrows and even amused some political pundits. Considering the vast rhetorical and historical background, this chapter aims to take human rights and their expression in language seriously. By characterizing human rights as a territory of conflict (Blouin-Genest and Paquerot 2016a) rather than peaceful and extended international "lingo", it questions the idea of human rights as "a grammar of the 'in-common'" (Blouin-Genest and Paquerot 2016b) and attempts to relate it to efforts to build inclusive forms of language.

The question this chapter tackles implies law, language, and grammar. It situates human rights in a Bourdieu-esque political and legal field, in which those involved compete for a specific yet rare form of symbolic good: the universal. In a critical approach to law, it takes it as an instrument of domination in the hands of insiders "experienced in the use of forms and formulas as weapons", whereas laymen "are condemned to submit to 'the power of form', that is, to the symbolic violence perpetrated by those who, thanks to their knowledge of formalization and proper judicial manners, are able to put the law on their side" (Bourdieu 1987b, 850). To understand the exclusion of women from democratic politics, the power of form Bourdieu mentions is then construed as closely connected to the way law is conveyed in words, following the idea that "the question of how the sexes are represented in language is not only of linguistic interest but constitutes a transdisciplinary field of research where linguistic aspects intersect with psychological and sociological issues" (Stahlberg et al. 2007, p. 163). Taking my cue from John Austin, I try to explore the problem of the wording of women's rights in the light of the distinction between "performative utterances" and "constative utterances" (Austin 1962, p. 6): saying "*droits de l'Homme*" [Man's rights] instead of "*droits humains*" [human rights] (and persisting in doing so) is, I contend, a form of "speech act" (ibid., p. 146), identical to what we mean when saying "I bet" or "I promise". In other words, the utilization of an expression such as "*droits de l'Homme*" participates in making women invisible in law and thus fails to encompass a large part of the population that does not identify as masculine.

Drawing on this theoretical and disciplinary angle, this piece asks to what extent a gendered or gender blind vision of human rights reflects inequalities between men and women in society: what role does law, in particular (French) universalistic Republican law, play in the reproduction or transformation of these inequalities? More specifically, how should the question of cultural influences between the English-speaking and French-speaking worlds be considered, for example, in the light of differences between judicial systems, linguistic or grammatical issues? I then follow the thought of Carol Smart when she states: "Instead of asking 'How law can transcend gender?', the more fruitful question has become, 'How does gender work in law and how does law work to produce gender?'" (Smart 1992, p. 6). Indeed, when we talk about human rights, it is natural to visualize men. For example, treaties about the protection against torture or war crimes tend to be written with a male approach, for instance thinking about the rights of male prisoners in times of war and forgetting the impact of rape or hunger on women and girl children (Charlesworth 1999, pp. 381–88).

This chapter is primarily based on material I have been marshaling for both my teaching and my research.[3] This material is diverse and mixes political theory and literature with legal history and sociology of law. It focuses on the French version of this debate, and compares it with other French-speaking countries such as Canada (Quebec) and Switzerland.[4] Gender thus serves as a tool for surpassing these disciplinary divisions (including that between Private and Public Law). In a diachronic approach to the problem, the content of French linguistics will be used to recall the struggle of grammarians in the seventeenth century to legitimate the equivalence between the masculine and the neutral in order to enhance a "masculine sociodicy"[5] (Bourdieu 2001, p. 40), as perceivable in the history of the expression "*droits de l'Homme*" [Man's rights]. Later on, the active position of the *Académie française* to make French speakers see the phrase "*droits de l'Homme*" as gender-neutral (called "*épicène*" in French) clashes with the growing alertness of feminist circles toward intellectual bullying, a confrontation I document in the second stage of this chapter.

A Diachronic Approach to the Problem

It is usual for legal controversies to be conveyed in technical terms, given that law is both a practice and an academic discipline. In the case of the correct spelling of "human rights" in French, the technicality of the debate arises from the grammatical aspect of the question, that is, the superiority of the masculine as denoting neuter. As highlighted by Eliane Viennot's work (Viennot 2006), this superiority is contingent, and rests upon the activism of a social group the feminist scholar calls "*la clergie*" (a mix between lawyers, theologians and grammarians). Accordingly, the dispute over the phrase "*droits de l'Homme*" [Man's rights] is far-reaching in history and ingrained in a national language. It appeals to philology and needs to be traced back to the sixteenth and seventeenth centuries to help understand how women (as individuals and as a collective entity) have been crossed out of the history of human rights.

The Lingo Down to an "h"

In order to comprehend why some, in the spelling of "*droits de l'Homme*" [Man's rights], focus on the "h" of "*Homme*" [Man], it is necessary to dwell upon the grammatical aspect of the problem. French has a binary grammatical system that applies to all linguistic material (nouns, pronouns, adjectives, participles, etc.) available in the language. In English, on the contrary, there is no gender in articles, but there can be one in nouns (actor/actress, prince/princess, waiter/waitress) and pronouns (he/she). Additionally, French does not have a third gender equivalent to neuter, as opposed to Latin. Some words can be both masculine and feminine ("*amour*" [love], "*œuvre*" [work]), and real gender-neutral words (such as "*enfant* [child]", "*tu* [you]") can be found in this language. Canadian author Louise-Laurence Larivière remarks (Larivière 2007, p. 47) that the same word being used for the generic ("*l'Homme*" as a human being) and the specific ("*l'homme*" as man) is caused by the evolution of the language. In Latin, there were indeed two substantives to refer to these distinct realities: "*homo*" and "*vir*" (the same in Ancient Greek: "*anthropos*" and "*andras*"). Apart from a few words derived from it ("*viril* [manly]", "*virilité* [manhood]"), the French did not retain the Latin "*vir*" to refer to the male human being. The most important point, however, is that in English too the same kind of masculinist preaching occurred, as remembered by grammarian John Kirkby (pp. 1705–1754): "The masc. Person answers to the general Name, which comprehends both Male and Female; as Any Person, who knows what he says" (Kirkby 1746, rule 21). In this line of thought, the substantive "mankind" is used to refer to all human beings.

In France, Viennot's different works on women and power have enhanced the idea that masculine sociodicy through language was not necessarily an eternal truth. To outline the fact that this prevalent use only dates back to the seventeenth century, she evokes "a long effort to masculinise our language" (Viennot 2014, p. 10). Before that, it was the feminine that was seen as neutral, as opposed to today. This started to change in 1647, when the notorious grammarian Vaugelas maintained that "because it is nobler, the masculine form must prevail over the feminine every time they are taken together" (Vaugelas 1647, p. 264). This famous statement epitomizes the linguistic component of the subordination of women. Indeed, the logic of the "ancient language" was "to mark sex difference instead of feminine" (Viennot 2014, p. 51), in order to avoid ambiguity. When scholars like Vaugelas—one of the first members of the *Académie française*—came to linguistic power, their efforts impacted nouns—feminine substantives expressing creative activities such as "*autrice*" [author], "*compositrice*" [composer], "*peintresse*" [painter] were banned—as well as the agreement of verbs and adjectives. Later on, the masculine being the "noble gender" was imposed when French became the national language through access to schooling (1830s for boys, 1880s for girls). From this state of affairs, Viennot finds two lessons to learn:

> The first one is the violence imposed on the French language by those who undertook to amend it for it to illustrate "the greater nobility of masculine gender". None of their interventions in this matter was self-evident; they were all accomplished in spite of the language, its traditions and its logic. The second one is the energy they had to consume, for what was quite a modest outcome in the end, until institutions took over from their desires: primary and secondary school, higher education, bureaucracy, banks and so on. (Viennot 2014, p. 103)

The French academic concludes that language is just one more field where the war of knowledge took place, namely not free knowledge (the one that intimately enriches a person) but knowledge as an instrument of power, the only one that, according to Viennot, "*la clergie*" understood.

From an Exclusionary Practice to an Oblivious History

In 1789, when the first *Déclaration* was inscribed into positive law, the balance of power between sexes considerably evolved in favor of men: it became conventional for women to take their husband's last name (and even first name) when married. Thanks to a thorough analysis of the archives from that time, Anne Verjus stresses that the man of the French Revolution is neither a representative of his sex nor a simple owner or a bare individual, but an incarnation of the *pater familias* in the Latin sense (Verjus 2010). Furthermore, it is worthy to note that, in several passages of her slapstick version of the 1789 *Déclaration*, Olympe de Gouges refers only to women. In the preamble, for example, she writes: "Considering that the ignorance, neglect or contempt of women's rights is the sole cause of public misfortune and of the corruption of governments" (de Gouges 1791, p. 102). In other sections, however, both men and women are considered, like in article II: "The goal of any political association is the conservation of the natural and imprescriptible rights of man and woman" (*id.*). In comparison, Mary Wollstonecraft's book (*A Vindication of the Rights of Woman*) is not as centered on women, and, unsurprisingly for the time, uses the substantive "mankind". Although, under the French Revolution and even in 1848, people still called themselves "*citoyen*" and "*citoyenne*" [citizen] (even if women were then excluded from citizenship), 1789 elicited a model of citizenship whereby, for someone to be recognized as a rational being, it was mandatory to possess two features considered as implementing the principle of equality issued from the Revolution: "manliness and being a 'good Frenchman'" (Sénac 2017, p. 12).

It is beyond reasonable doubt that in the *Déclaration des droits de l'Homme et du citoyen* [Declaration of the rights of Man and of the citizen], the term "*Homme*" [Man] was not chosen for its alleged generic value (despite the capital letter), but specifically to refer exclusively to people of masculine gender, as explained by Amnesty International: "For those who wrote the *Déclaration*, the word 'homme' encompassed one gender only. They never intended that it included the feminine gender. They never considered granting women the rights they bestowed on men" (Amnesty International 1998, p. 4). Interestingly, this choice of the term "*Homme*" [Man] came after a debate at the National Assembly about whether or not women were equal to men. Even though they had a significant role during the French Revolution, the Assembly decided that, because of a lack of intelligence, women had to be excluded from the *Déclaration*. This formal text, a source of pride for many French people and still influential nowadays, was therefore the first legal step to marginalize women and materialize their domination by men. More importantly, the reduction of the woman to her body and to a procreating function became an excuse to put her away from any public role in society. Such a gendered vision of politics[6] relates to the wider setting of an archaeology of the public sphere. Even if, in the prime of the Third Republic (1880s),

French political leaders strove to untighten the stranglehold of family patriarchy, most of them were not willing to grant citizenship to women, as they wanted nothing but to "create a moral environment in the home that would help to make citizens out of men and teach civil virtue to male children" (Nord 1997, p. 63). This trend is sharper in the republican context, where ideal citizenship values, in comparison with the liberal model, "the public sphere, a place for emancipation" versus "the private sphere, the place of need" (Bereni and Revillard 2009, p. 31). It is then clearly set out that there are domestic restraints that jeopardize women's public commitment, undermining their ability to voice a different version of the "*droits de l'Homme*" [Man's rights].

The main debate in France, however, is over the 1948 Declaration, one of the most influential documents in terms of the protection of human rights. When it was drafted in English, a controversy emerged because the drafters wanted to call it the "Universal Declaration of Man Rights". Eleanor Roosevelt, one of the few female redactors, protested and later succeeded in convincing her co-drafters to replace "Man Rights" by "Human Rights", even though the former is used several times in certain articles of the Declaration. France is the only French-speaking country that translated it with "*droits de l'Homme*" [Man's rights]: the Quebec authorities, for example, opted for the more neutral phrasing "*droits de la personne humaine*" [rights of the human person]. It is nevertheless of paramount importance to precise that in 1948, things did change, in contrast to 1789. The first article starts with "*tous les êtres humains naissent libres et égaux en dignité et en droits*" [All human beings are born free and equal in dignity and rights], therefore replacing "*Homme*" [Man] by "*êtres humains*" [human beings]. Moreover, in 1789, the word "*Homme*" was used 13 times and "personne" did not come up, whereas in 1948, the term "*Homme*" appears only 8 times, as opposed to "*personne*", which is written 20 times. There was therefore an attempt to decrease the discrimination of the 1789 *Déclaration*, although the authors did not manage it entirely, since the title, the most visible element of the Declaration, was not changed, throwing a certain paradox into relief as well as an embarrassment in terms of vocabulary.

France is unquestionably not the only Western country to have carried out a direct or indirect misogynous legislation. The Russian thinker Moses Ostrogorski, who wrote major texts on modern democracy and universal suffrage, states in the introduction to his comparative legal study that "everywhere, history encounters women in a completely subordinate position. In the sense that it rules the relationships between the members of society, law gives its blessing to such a constraint on the woman" (Ostrogorski 1892, p. VII). The phrasing of human rights in French is not only about the words when opponents of gender equality use it, as in the following examples. In 1929, the Canadian Supreme Court resorted to an article of the 1867 Constitution and to the pseudo-ambiguity of the word "*personne*" to assert that women could not be appointed to the Senate (Lamothe 2007, p. 129). In Switzerland, the lawyer Léonard Jenni took action to the Federal Court on behalf of Hilda Lehman in 1923. He claimed that while the terms "*citoyen* [citizen]" and "*Suisse* [Swiss]" were written under a masculine form, they were to be interpreted, in the federal Constitution and in the acts of Parliament, as equally applicable to women. The jurisdiction turned him away, and maintained its ruling in 1956 and in 1965. Canadian linguist Jacqueline Lamothe explains that the female inhabitants of Zurich obtained their right to vote at a local level only in November 1970, after seven "*votations* [referendums]" and an intense process of judicial review. These complaints made them "extremely sensitive to denomination, as it can serve to include or exclude, depending on the spirit of the times" (ibid., p. 131). In the case of human rights, the history of ideas thus teaches that "women have a history all right", but that this is a history "both of what was and of what was not allowed to be" (MacKinnon 1987, p. 39).

Contemporary Feminist Activism: A French Institutional Response to the Mobilizations on the Field

The contemporary continuation of the feud over the "*droits de l'Homme*" [Man's rights] leads us to the central institution of linguistic power in France, the *Académie française*. Composed (in theory) of 40 "*immortel-le-s* [immortals]", this house is in charge of all matters (spelling, vocabulary, usages, translations) pertaining to the French language. Concisely, it is responsible for the equivalent of both Received Pronunciation (RP) and BBC English or the Queen's English in the UK. Over the last 20 years, feminist activism has entered the heartland of the *Académie*'s work, with mobilization for the feminization of words and titles as well as for "*parité linguistique* [linguistic parity]" in French. Be it for a more gender-neutral, gender-inclusive or non-discriminatory language, people involved in this symbolic fight found themselves at odds with the *Académie française* and its spin-off, the *Commission générale de terminologie et de néologie* [General Commission for Terminology and Neology] (now "*Commission d'enrichissement de la langue française*" [Commission for the Enrichment of the French Language]). This agency was founded in 1996 with a mandate to update and control the vocabulary of public structures. The conservatism of the *Académie française*, which differentiates France from other French-speaking areas like Quebec or Switzerland, has been underlined and criticized by a number of activists, most of them being academics. It can be furthered stressed by relating it to the grass roots feminist mobilizations that occurred outside France, in a manner that directly challenges the universalism of both French republicanism and human rights international law.

Hardly a Gender-Friendly House: The Académie Française and the Vindication of Orthodox French

On June 14, 1984, the *Académie française* issued a statement in which the members of the institution reminded the public that "in French like in other Indo-European languages, there is no relationship of equivalence between *grammatical gender* and *natural gender*" (quoted by Baider et al. 2007, p. 8). In this recommendation against the feminization of titles and functions, the "*immortel-le-s*" consider that giving up on the masculine generic would be "detrimental to the spirit of the language". For them, the usage of the masculine generic means that "in the case in question, the opposition between sexes is not relevant" and that "they can be mistaken for each other". The thrust of the *Académie*'s argument is based on what linguists call hypernymy: for example, "citrus" is the hypernym of "lemon", "orange", "mandarine", "clementine", and so on; "dog" is the hypernym of "poodle", "dalmatian", "teckel", and so on. Yannick Chevalier, Hugues Constantin de Chanay and Laure Gardelle posit a distinction between a type A (the examples of citrus or dog) and a type B of hypernymy (sometimes called "self-hypernymy" or "self-domination") where the hypernym is identical with one of its hyponyms, which is the case when people assume that "*Homme*" [Man] includes "*les femmes*" [women]. Chevalier et al. wrote that "the statute of masculine as a hypernym is more a discursive practice than a linguistic fact" (Chevalier et al. 2017, p. 25). The line of argument followed by the *Académie française* is further annihilated (pp. 21–22), but the crucial point for my demonstration is that even within the academic field, the *Académie*'s perspective remains controversial.

As mentioned above, the members of the *Académie* invoke "the spirit of the language", a phrase that indicates that the problem of this semantic row lies in France's pride in its Enlightenment and of its Revolution. The 1789 *Déclaration*, being almost sacred, would explain why, from the *Académie*'s point of view, the French population would still be very much attached to the phrase "*droits de l'Homme*" [Man's rights]. As Agnès Callamard (Callamard 1998, p. 28), a French expert on human rights, argued, when talking about "*droits de l'Homme*", the French have the glorious battles of the revolutionaries in mind. Hence why the expression "*les droits de l'Homme*", which encompasses all human beings, including women, must not be changed simply for the sake of what the "*Académicien-ne-s*" see as "political correctness" of "frivolous feminist claims". What is this position worth, though, when it is obvious that even the national and official organization for human rights in France, the "*Commission nationale consultative des droits de l'homme* [*sic*]" [National Consultative Commission for Human Rights], does not even spell its own name with a capital "h"?[7] Even the UN website uses "*droits de l'homme*", and, what is more, people cannot hear the difference orally. Furthermore, the *Académie*'s argumentation that the phrase "*droits humains*" [human rights] would sound "*anglo-saxon* [sic]"[8] is vapid as the Spanish and the Italians have no trouble translating "human rights" into "*derechos humanos*" and "*diritti humani*". Viennot is, therefore, right when she proclaims that "there are good reasons to suppose that we are dealing with an ancient dream: the one of Eve's being born from Adam's rib" (Viennot 2014, p. 93). By maintaining that the capital "H" is the be-all and end-all of the problem, the *Académie* holds out for a biblical vision of the French language, the purpose of which no longer being to express the difference of sexes (as was the case up to the seventeenth century), but the primacy of the masculine.

Although guides to foster more gender-friendly writing of French in Quebec, Switzerland and Belgium have existed since the 1970s, France had to wait until 1999 for the publication of *Femme, j'écris ton nom* (Becquer et al. 1999). This official landmark was part of a more general policy initiated by the "*gauche plurielle*"[9] of the French Government and their adoption of the Constitutional Act on "*parité*" [parity] (1998). Nevertheless, in spite of the Prime Minister's circular in relation to the feminization of trades, functions, ranks, and titles (March 6, 1998), the report submitted in 1999 by the *Commission générale de terminologie et de néologie* follows the same line as the 1984 Declaration of the *Académie*: it states that "precisely, the legal subject has no sex".[10] According to French sociologist (specialized in gender issues) Michel Bozon, there is a connection between the conservatism of the *Commission générale de terminologie et de néologie* (in charge of proposing new words and phrases to the *Académie française*) and the *Académie* itself. For him, both are predominantly white and male (5 women out of 36 current members at the *Coupole*[11]), and a few "*immortel-le-s*" are even automatic members of the *Commission* (Bozon 2006, p. 147). The attitude of both institutions vis-à-vis the use of "gender" in French also betrays their "ideological attachment to masculine gender as a vehicle of universality" (*id.*). The recommendation of the *Commission* regarding how to translate "gender" (July 22, 2005) is indeed critical toward this concept: it states that even in English, it deviates from the original (grammatical) meaning of the word. Such a reaction from this public structure is barely surprising given that even in 1999, when the French Government was progressive and when some semblance of "*parité*" [parity] was on its way, the *Commission* insisted on the generic value of the masculine. This linguistic conservatism spread to certain media and political circles. In 2006, for instance, when Royal chose to talk about "*droits humains*" [human rights] in Beijing, the journalist Isabelle Mandraud seemed to find it particularly peculiar. In her article, she always wrote "*droits humains*" in italics and with quotation marks. Even though this phrase is the exact translation of the 1948 UDHR, she analyzed it as a mistake on the part of Royal, rather than something deliberate, saying that the politician wanted to decrease the impact of the phrase "*droits de l'Homme*" [Man's rights] for diplomatic reasons. Treating the expression as if it was different from the French translation, she asserted: "Madame Royal chose to utilise the vocable 'droits humains', an Anglo-Saxon term [*sic*] devoid of gender connotation, broader than the term '*droits de l'homme*', yet not as centered on individual liberties" (Mandraud 2006, p. 3).

This linguistic conservatism seems to be completely unlike the experience of academics with an expertise in gender studies. Pierrette Vachon-L'Heureux notes "a great difference between official policies that assert the existence of a masculine that is said to be generic, and feminist scholars who see this construction as a new avatar of masculine domination" (Vachon-L'Heureux 2007, p. 74). For them, linguistic parity includes a wide range of writing practices, which are designed to fight gendered representations that are more or less conveyed by the dominant role of French grammar as masculine. Feminization is then as much about a political commitment as an obligation of scientific relevance in the description and the analysis of the social world. As former Prime Minister Lionel Jospin (who was on the forefront of this debate) once said, "our language evolves: it is obviously not untied from the stakes of our time. '*Parité*' has its place in language" (quoted by Becquer et al. 1999, p. 6). Therefore, the point is to convince a majority of people that generic formulations are discriminatory and collectively denounce their so-called neutrality. As a matter of hope for those who believe in an inclusive language, Catherine Coutelle was finally able, in March 2016, to amend the French law on the duty of alertness of parent companies and ordering institutions. This left-wing MP and President of a delegation (at the French Parliament) for the protection of women's rights fought for a year to amend the first article of the law, managing to replace "*de l'homme*" by "*humains*".

The possible examples from outside France come from two federal states where French speakers are in minority: Switzerland (with Romandy) and Canada (with Quebec). In the former, the fourth article of the federal Constitution was amended on June 14, 1981, and now expresses: "Men and women have equal rights." Since this revision, at both the county and national level, official texts endeavor to be written in gender-neutral forms and to follow the *Écrire les genres* (Moreau 2002) guide. Edited by a feminist writer who had been commissioned by the "*Bureau fédéral de l'égalité* [Federal Bureau for Equality]", this guide includes ten rules of writing that set an example. Rule ten is an encouragement to:

> Use the expression "*droits de la personne humaine* [rights of the human person]" instead of "*droits de l'Homme*" [Man's rights], unless you are referring to the French historical document. If it is to refer to the 1789 *Déclaration des Droits de l'Homme et du Citoyen* [Declaration of the rights of Man and of the citizen] or to any other francophone historical document entitled "*Droits de l'Homme*", the official title should be used. However, when referring to United Nations documents in different languages and being translated and interpreted, "*personne*", "*personne humaine*", "*êtres humains*" [human beings] should be used.

In Quebec, the arrival of feminine forms of titles, occupations, and functions with the momentum of North-American feminism in the 1970s forced experts and authorities (namely the *Office québécois de la langue française* [Quebec Agency for French language]) to reflect on how to accommodate their patrimonial vocabulary. In the *Charte des droits et libertés de la personne du Québec* (1975), the preamble only uses "*être humain*" [human being] et "*personne humaine*" [human person], but never "*l'homme*" [man]. There are two documents from the *Office québécois de la langue française*: one in 1986 about the use of feminine forms and one in 1991 about the feminization of texts. Together with the comprehensive guide, commercialized by the official publisher "Les publications du Québec", *Avoir bon genre à l'écrit* (Guénette and Vachon-L'Heureux 2007), they form the most directly available resources for French speakers who aim toward a gender-friendly use of their language. Interestingly, and in comparison with France, Canada is a country that is obliged to deeply consider US English, due to its physical border and history. Nevertheless, its authorities do not see the phrase "*droits humains*" [human rights] as a form of linguistic imperialism.[12] This is not to simply say that the grass is always greener, but to note the characteristics of a territory—North America—a pioneer in the field of gender studies.

Women's Mobilizations on a Global Scale: A Threat to the Universality of Human Rights International Law?

The peculiarity of the French debate can be better pinpointed by looking behind a national perspective and focusing on international human rights law. Indeed, there is a similarity between the former and French public law. In both cases, the strength of a universalist ideology is defied by mobilizations emerging from below and out of the scope of institutions, which indirectly emphasize a key point made by Verjus. In a critique of Pierre Rosanvallon's history of universal suffrage in France (Rosanvallon 1992), the former states that it is a wrong perspective to assume that it had been necessary for women to become individuals to include them in citizenship, without taking into account the fact that it is the definition of representation itself that needed to be modified to get to that point where voters do not represent the nation anymore, but only themselves. In other words, explains Verjus, "there is not solely 'individualization' or republicanization of populations that are 'incompatible' with the republican ideal, but also adaptation of 'ideas' to the necessity of inclusion" (Verjus 2017, p. 245). The same rationale can be found with regard to international human rights law, which tends to overlook the fact that there are also rights that are specifically *women's rights*, for example, female genital mutilation or child marriage, a blind spot for supporters of the term "*droits de l'Homme*" [Man's rights]. In that respect, Hilary Charlesworth affirmed: "We know, for example, of the distinctive burdens placed on women through food and medical shortages caused by conflict. When food is scarce, more women than men suffer from malnutrition, often because of cultural norms that require men and boys to eat before women and girls" (Charlesworth 1999, p. 388). This idea of women's rights being singled out is difficult to handle: one may hypothesize that there are not specific rights, but, instead, specific situations of abuses of universal rights, which necessitate specific obligations for states. In internal laws, the question of recognition of femicide would be another bone of contention. Yet what Joan Scott observed in her study of French feminism and the rights of Man can be remembered: "In order to protest women's exclusion, they had to act on behalf of women and so invoked the very difference they sought to deny" (Scott 1996, p. X).

Some more analysis can be injected by probing the findings of Madhavi Sunder's thrilling study on the conciliation of women's rights with religion. The example she mainly concentrates on is taken from Morocco, but it directly echoes the French dispute over the veil.[13] Sunder explains:

> Human rights law continues to define religion in the twenty-first century as a sovereign, extralegal jurisdiction in which inequality is not only accepted, but expected. Law views religion as natural, irrational, incontestable, and imposed—in contrast to the public sphere, the only viable space for freedom and reason. Simply put, religion is the "other" of international law. (Sunder 2003, p. 1402)

This state of affairs is not in line with what Sunder calls "the New Enlightenment", which refers to the fact that "today, individuals seek reason, equality, and liberty not just in the public sphere, but also in the private spheres of religion, culture, and family" (ibid., p. 1403). In that regard, law does not compare with new intellectual specialties such as cultural studies and subaltern studies, which fostered such evolution.

The story Sunder recounts is about Moroccan women mobilizing in 2004 to amend the family Code (*moudawana*) of the kingdom in a more egalitarian way, and spreading the word to the organization called *Musawah* ("equality" in Arabic), a global movement for equality and justice in Muslim family law that gathers 250 feminist campaigners coming from 47 different Muslim countries. In this narrative, what is striking is the political intelligence of the strategy set up by women: at a meeting in Berlin in May 1995, representatives from 16 Muslim countries meeting to discuss strategies for improving women's human rights in their regions concluded that "the production of material using indigenous concepts and ideas to support international rights documents" was a project of "highest priority" (ibid., p. 1446). In the case of Morocco, women got their point across and achieved their goal by first invoking Islamic principles, then the equality clause contained in the Moroccan Constitution, then the Convention on the Elimination of All Forms of Discrimination Against Women (CEDAW) and, lastly, other international law writings. This reversal in the hierarchy of norms offers a case in point: it can indeed be considered as a form of translation of the grammar of human rights. As Sunder perceptively remarks, "while a confrontation narrative informed by subaltern studies reads Muslim women as remaking international law, and not simply receiving it, the traditional legal narrative of law in transition elides this" (ibid., p. 1415).

Conclusion

The controversy discussed in this chapter is somehow more top-down than bottom-up. It opposes activists—not only women—who think the language of human rights should be more inclusive, to masculinist gatekeepers who frown upon what they consider to be a preposterous attempt to introduce a more progressive use of French. Rationally speaking, the case of those averse to the generalization of "*droits humains*" [human rights] is seen to be flimsy; some of their arguments are spurious. Bourdieu once said: "I tend to think that, in social sciences, the language of rules is the asylum of ignorance" (Bourdieu 1987a, p. 187). This statement fits with the argument expressed in this chapter, targeting both lawyers and grammarians. Following the guide *Écrire les genres*, the vocable "*droits de l'Homme*" [Man's rights] should remain a historical reference, even if it questions the existential identity of some organizations born with it (e.g. the French *Ligue des droits de l'Homme*, whose current leaders do not want to change their name to "*Ligue des droits humains*"). It seems that French institutions are not heading toward a more gender-neutral writing of human rights either, as current Prime Minister recently issued (November 22, 2017) a circular in which he urged all the members of government to ban inclusive writing from official texts.

More broadly, the effort to demasculinize the way we speak is, this chapter argues, a practice of *empowerment*. That is tantamount to saying that switching to "*droits humains*" [human rights] is not just a verbal dispute. Like in Bourdieu's theory, a violence that is symbolic does not mean it is not real. A lot of examples in history (think about the controversy over the interpretation of "occupied territories" in UN resolution 242 on the withdrawal of Israeli troops after Six-Day War) could testify that fighting with words is also fighting with the meaning of things. In plain language, if we give away the words, we give it all away. Put another way, there can be a performative goal in our habits of speaking and our practice of writing. Only words? Not quite. A lot of what we say is actually only words, which does not mean it does not hurt, like hate speech, as investigated by Laura Beth Nielsen: "Such speech is harm in and of itself, because of the way it makes women feel and act when in public as well as the role it plays in creating and reinforcing systems of gender hierarchy in the public sphere" (Nielsen 2002, p. 279). Words are not inconsequential. Words represent a problem and a solution. If human rights are a battlefield, I see no reason why we should not use words as allies.

Notes

1. Sam Moyn's effort (Moyn 2010) to differentiate the "Rights of Man" from "Human Rights" (the former being linked to the construction of a closed space within nation-states, as opposed to the latter, which expanded in the late 1970s and is essentially grounded on a global and non-adversarial vision of politics) is compelling, but fails to give justice to the linguistic problem this chapter analyzes.
2. This autumn, the publisher Hatier issued a history textbook for primary school pupils, which was entirely in inclusive writing, a decision that caused quite an uproar among opponents of such an evolution of the French language. See https://www.editions-hatier.fr/article/magellan-et-galilee-questionner-le-monde-ce2-ed-2017-livre-eleve [accessed on January 30, 2018].
3. In 2015 and 2016, I taught Human Rights to law students at the Université du Maine and then at the Université Paris Nanterre. This year, I led a course seminar in the Euro-American program of Sciences Po entitled "Social, Political, Legal Obstacles to Gender Equality". Researchwise, I organized with Véronique Mottier a workshop on "Law and Gender: Political Agendas?" last summer at the congress of the *Association française de science politique*. Lastly, I use the fieldwork of ongoing post-doctoral

research, funded by the *École des hautes études en sciences sociales* (EHESS), on legal firms *pro bono* work (oriented toward cause lawyering and human rights).

4. As mentioned above, this debate is both about France and about the French language. Hence why the sources used in this chapter are mostly in French. Unless specified otherwise, all the translations into English are from me. It is also noteworthy to precise and admit that my perspective is Western-centered, and that I have no knowledge about the usage of the "*parité linguistique*" [linguistic parity] in French-speaking African countries.
5. Initially coined by Max Weber in his work on the sociology of world religions, the term of sociodicy has then been reused by Bourdieu. It refers to the theoretical justification, by the ruling class, of its own privileges (see Bourdieu 2001, p. 19).
6. By "gendered vision of politics", I mean, following the lead of Joan Landes, that "the collapse of the old patriarchal order gave way to an increasingly gendered conception of the public sphere" (Landes 1988, p. 2).
7. http://www.cncdh.fr/fr/linstitution [accessed on June 30, 2017].
8. See Elisabeth Badinter's reaction when contacted by the organization "*Droits humains pour tou-te-s*" [Human Rights for All] in order to join their manifesto: "*Sorry, but I do not like the Anglo-Saxon* [sic] *phrase 'droits humains', which does not mean anything in French.*" Retrieved from http://droitshumains.unblog.fr/2015/05/08/elisabeth-badinter-fait-fausse-route/comment-page-1/#comment-24 [accessed on June 30, 2017].
9. The "*gauche plurielle*" is the left-wing coalition that came to power after the 1997 general elections. It comprised the Socialist Party, the French Communist Party, the Green Party, and the Radicals.
10. http://www.ladocumentationfrancaise.fr/rapports-publics/994000415/index.shtml [accessed on June 30, 2017].
11. The Coupole is the building where the *Académie* is located.
12. However, in Quebec, there had been, and still is, a debate between "*droits de la personne*" [rights of the person] and "*droits humains*" [human rights]. Many French-speaking academics consider that it is something as a balance of disadvantages: "*personne*" has the disadvantage that it can include moral persons and "*droits humains*" has the disadvantage to be an Anglicism (I am grateful to Sylvie Paquerot for drawing my attention on this aspect of the problem).
13. For more on this issue see Guénif-Souilamas and Macé 2004, Hennette-Vauchez and Valentin 2014, and Scott 2007.

References

Amnesty International. 1998. *Pour un langage non sexiste des droits humains*. Retrieved from https://www.amnesty.org/download/Documents/156000/org330021998fr.pdf.

Austin, John. 1962. *How to Do Things with Words*. Oxford: Oxford University Press.

Baider, Fabienne, Edwige Khaznadar, and Thérèse Moreau. 2007. Les enjeux de la parité linguistique. *Nouvelles questions féministes* 26: 4–12.

Baretto, Jose-Manuel, ed. 2013. *Human Rights from a Third World Perspective: Critique, History and International Law*. Newcastle: Cambridge Scholars.

Becquer, Annie, Bernard Cerquiglini, and Nicole Cholewka. 1999. *Femme, j'écris ton nom : guide d'aide à la féminisation des noms de métiers, titres, grades et fonctions*. Paris: La Documentation française.

Bereni, Laure, and Anne Revillard. 2009. La dichotomie public-privé à l'épreuve des critiques féministes : de la théorie à l'action publique. In *Genre et action publique : la frontière public-privé en questions*, ed. Pierre Muller and Réjane Sénac, 27–55. Paris: L'Harmattan.

Bidard, Hélène. 2015. *Il ne viendrait à l'idée de personne de parler des droits de la femme en pensant parler de l'humanité toute entière*, December 10. Retrieved from http://droitshumains.unblog.fr/2015/12/10/helene-bidard-il-ne-viendrait-a-lidee-de personne-de-parler-des-droits-de-la-femme-en-pensant-parler-de-lhumanite-toute entiere/comment-page-1/.

Blouin-Genest, Gabriel, and Sylvie Paquerot. 2016a. Environmental Human Rights as a Battlefield: A Grammar of Political Confrontation. *Journal of Human Rights and the Environment* 7 (1): 132–154.

———. 2016b. Les droits humains comme grammaire de 'l'en-commun'. *SociologieS*. Retrieved from http://sociologies.revues.org/5654.

Bourdieu, Pierre. 1987a. *Choses dites*. Paris: Éditions de Minuit.

———. 1987b. The Force of Law: Toward a Sociology of the Juridical Field. *Hastings Law Journal* 38: 814–853.

———. 2001. *Masculine Domination*. Cambridge: Polity Press.

Bozon, Michel. 2006. Censure linguistique du genre : une résistance politique ? *Travail, genre et sociétés* 16: 143–147.

Callamard, Agnès. 1998. 'Droits de l'homme' ou 'droits humains' ? Le sexisme à fleur de mots. *Le Monde diplomatique*, p. 28, March.

Chakrabarty, Dipesh. 2000. *Provincializing Europe: Postcolonial Thought and Historical Difference*. Princeton: Princeton University Press.

Charlesworth, Hilary. 1999. Feminist Methods in International Law. *American Journal of International Law* 93 (2): 379–394.

Chevalier, Yannick, Hughes Constantin de Chanay, and Laure Gardelle. 2017. Bases linguistiques de l'émancipation : système anglais, système français. *Mots, les langages du politique* 113: 9–36.

De Gouges, Olympe. 1986 [1791]. Déclaration des droits de la femme et de la citoyenne. In *Œuvres*, 101–112. Paris: Mercure de France.

Doise, Willem. 2013. *Human Rights as Social Representations*. London: Routledge Editor.

Guénette, Louise, and Pierrette Vachon-L'Heureux. 2007. *Avoir bon genre à l'écrit: guide de rédaction épicène*. Québec: Les publications du Québec.

Guénif-Souilamas, Nacira, and Éric Macé. 2004. *Les féministes et le garçon arabe*. La Tour d'Aigues: Éditions de l'Aube.

Hennette-Vauchez, Stéphanie, and Vincent Valentin. 2014. *L'affaire Baby Loup ou la nouvelle laïcité*. Paris: LGDJ.

Kirkby, John. 1746. *A New English Grammar*. Menston: Scolar Press Facsimile.

Lacroix, Justine, and Jean-Yves Pranchère. 2016. *Le procès des droits de l'homme : généalogie du scepticisme démocratique*. Paris: Éditions du Seuil.

Lamothe, Jacqueline. 2007. Désexisation ou parité des textes institutionnels ? *Nouvelles questions féministes* 26: 126–132.

Landes, Joan. 1988. *Women and the Public Sphere in the Age of the French Revolution*. Ithaca: Cornell University Press.

Larivière, Louise-Laurence. 2007. Dis-moi comment tu te nommes et je te dirai qui tu es. *Nouvelles questions féministes* 26: 47–56.

MacKinnon, Catharine. 1987. Difference and Dominance: On Sex Discrimination. In *Feminism Unmodified: Discourses on Life and Law*, 32–45. Cambridge: Harvard University Press.

Mandraud, Isabelle. 2006. À Pékin, Mme Royal cherche à concilier mondialisation et 'droits humains'. *Le Monde*, p. 8, January 8.

Moreau, Thérèse. 2002. *Écrire les genres : guide romand d'aide à la rédaction administrative et législative épicène*. Genève: État de Genève.

Moyn, Sam. 2010. *The Last Utopia: Human Rights in History*. Cambridge: Harvard University Press.

Nielsen, Laura Beth. 2002. Subtle, Pervasive, Harmful: Racist and Sexist Remarks in Public as Hate Speech. *Journal of Social Issues* 58 (2): 165–180.

Nord, Philip. 1997. Les origines de la Troisième République en France (1860–1885). *Actes de la recherche en sciences sociales* 116 (1): 53–68.

Ostrogorski, Moses. 1892. *La femme au point de vue du droit public : étude d'histoire et de législation comparée*. Paris: Rousseau.

Otto, Dianne. 1997. Rethinking the Universality of Human Rights Law. *Columbia Human Rights Law Review* 29: 1–46.

Rosanvallon, Pierre. 1992. *Histoire du suffrage universel en France*. Paris: Gallimard.

Scott, Joan. 1996. *Only Paradoxes to Offer: French Feminists and the Rights of Man*. Cambridge: Harvard University Press.

———. 2007. *The Politics of the Veil*. Princeton: Princeton University Press.

Sénac, Réjane. 2017. *Les non-frères au pays de l'égalité*. Paris: Presses de Sciences Po.

Smart, Carol. 1992. The Woman of Legal Discourse. *Social and Legal Studies* 1: 29–44.

Stahlberg, Dagmar, Friederike Braun, Lisa Irmen, and Sabine Sczesny. 2007. Representation of the Sexes in Language. In *Social Communication: A Volume in the Series Frontiers of Social Psychology*, ed. Klaus Fiedler, 163–187. New York: Psychology Press.

Sunder, Madhavi. 2003. Piercing the Veil. *Yale Law Journal* 112 (6): 1401–1472.

Vachon-L'Heureux, Pierrette. 2007. Au Québec, la rédaction épicène devient une proposition officielle. *Nouvelles questions féministes* 26: 70–80.

Vaugelas, Claude-Favre. 1647. *Remarques sur la langue française utiles à ceux qui veulent bien parler et bien écrire*. Paris: Didot.

Verjus, Anne. 2010. *Le bon mari : une histoire politique des hommes et des femmes à l'époque révolutionnaire*. Paris: Fayard.

———. 2017. Historiciser les catégories d'analyse : le cas du genre à l'époque de la Révolution. In *Vers une histoire sociale des idées politiques*, ed. Chloé Gaboriaux and Arnault Skornicki, 239–250. Villeneuve d'Ascq: Presses universitaires du Septentrion.

Viennot, Éliane. 2006. L'irrésistible ascension des clercs. In *La France, les femmes et le pouvoir : l'invention de la loi salique (Ve-XVIe siècle)*, 206–294. Paris: Perrin.

———. 2014. *Non, le masculin ne l'emporte pas sur le féminin ! Petite histoire des résistances de la langue française*. Donnemarie-Dontilly: Éditions iXe.

Wollstonecraft, Mary. 1891 [1792]. *A Vindication of the Rights of Woman with Strictures on Political and Moral Subjects*. London: T. F. Unwin.

CHAPTER 4

The Right to Water: The Political Function of Human Rights as an Expression of the Contradictions in Globalization

Sylvie Paquerot

As a vital natural resource, water has always drawn the attention of public authorities, more often than not, as a question of power. Deeply related to the control of territories and essential to life, the distribution and conditions of access to this vital resource have been at the core of how social relations are organized. Internationally, however, water was taken into account only as a source of conflict between states until the second half of the twentieth century.

But water, by its very nature, is hardly reducible to such a setting. Because water does not respect borders, sovereignty has had to be managed in a number of cases, and thus considered in light of regulations that take into account the physical reality of water: (1) not to cause significant damage and (2) reasonable and fair use. The main concern in this domain of international law has been—and largely remains—to find peaceful solutions to conflicts that may arise between two or more sovereign states regarding a "shared resource." International law was created by sovereign

S. Paquerot (✉)
School of Political Studies, University of Ottawa, Ottawa, ON, Canada
e-mail: spaquero@uottawa.ca

G. Blouin-Genest et al. (eds.), *Human Rights as Battlefields*, Human Rights Interventions,
https://doi.org/10.1007/978-3-319-91770-2_4

states to govern those states. More specifically, the main function of the law has been to regulate state interrelationships in order to avoid conflict: "[…] it was only in the 20th century that the concept of 'water resource' appeared"[1] (Margat 2000, p. 124).

In the 1970s, the international community began to expand the number of situations in which water was taken into account. In 1972, the first expansion took place in the context of environmental issues in Stockholm (UN 1972). This shift in perspective was followed by a targeted international conference on water to respond to requests made at the conferences on food (UN 1974) and on human settlements (UN 1976): the 1977 Mar del Plata Conference convened by the General Assembly of the United Nations (UN 1975). Indeed, the International Drinking Water Supply and Sanitation Decade known as the first International Decade for Water, 1981–1990 (UN 1980), was declared following this conference.

A first significant shift in perspective can then be traced to the Mar del Plata International Conference on Water in 1977, where, for the first time, water was identified not only as a shared resource but also, and primarily, as a condition of development and as a human right. At the Mar del Plata Conference, 116 States (UN 1977, p. 94) asserted that "all people, regardless of their stage of development and their social and economic conditions, have the right to have access to drinking water in quantities and of a quality equal to their basic needs" (UN 1977, Res. II a) and "that it is universally recognized that the possibility of having access to this element is essential to human life and the complete development of human being as an individual and as a member of society" (UN 1977, Res. II b).

The emergence of the right to water at this time served to shift priorities at the international level. Until that point, the issue of freshwater had only been addressed in the context of interstate relations around transboundary resources. However, the shift brought a focus to the uses of water and the needs of citizens, especially from the point of view of development. It is the responsibility of States to meet the needs of their population, including through international cooperation. This perspective was put forward at the conference:

> While most of international law covers relations between states, human rights law and some aspects of international environmental law go beyond interstate relations to focus on the rights and duties of states within their borders. This trend is likely to grow, because most environmental and resource law concerns not just states but also humans within states. (Dellapenna and Gupta 2008, p. 448)

The awareness of the cross-cutting nature of water issues seems to have been acquired in international fora in that period based on three changes: (1) States themselves began to approach the issue according to different priorities—beyond interstate relations in the consideration of transboundary resources; (2) the number of international organizations interested in the issue of water increased significantly and covered very diverse aspects of the problem; and (3) civil society, having had little input into the debates surrounding interstate relations, had new space for engagement due to environmental and human considerations.

The decision to decree an International Decade on this issue (1981–1990) was made in order to prioritize the objective of giving access to drinking water to all human beings. The decree was followed by multiple direct and indirect interventions, directives, and declarations on the subject from several UN international organizations and the General Assembly itself. In addition, the importance of international public funding in the management of water resources, along with the number of UN agencies and programs operating in this area (WWAP 2003), indicated a clear recognition of the requirement for cooperation (Sohnle 2002, pp. 88–89). However, until the 1990s, the 1977 statement that access to water should be regarded as a human right did not include a conflictual or political dimension, since it had been framed in terms of (relatively) uncontroversial universal norms (Petiteville 2016). Therefore, our focus will be on the shift in perspective that took place following the first International Water Decade, rather than this first acknowledgement of water as a human right.

Specifically, this chapter will focus on the various actors and their roles in the evolution of the definition of the issue of access to water, beginning with the end of the first Decade on Water in 1990 until the formal recognition of access to water as a human right at the UN Human Rights Council and at the General Assembly in 2010. We will demonstrate how and why the emergence of new actors concerned with access to water on the international scene—their strategies, alliances, and clashes—has resulted in the imposition of certain guiding principles on international action in the realm of water, through the mobilization of legitimacy arguments. We argue that the "politicization" of freshwater issues has been driven by how those issues are treated economically, how they have been coopted by international financial institutions (IFIs) and how they have been "privatized" through new forms of global governance. This shift in ideology and the use of human rights discourse has forced institutional actors, including both international institutions and states, to take the demands of civil society into account as an essential factor for legitimacy. However, following the analytical framework of actor network theory presented in Chap. 2, we will see how the sense, scope, and content of the right to water—which has finally been recognized in the institutional system following a process of sociological translation from a liberal perspective—does not respond to the original claims for that right.

Staging the Economic "Nature" of Water

The implementation of fundamental rights is first and foremost the responsibility of each state for the population within its territory; however, the conquest of the water market—seen as the grabbing, pollution, depletion, or squandering of this resource—goes far beyond national borders. Whether it is the privatization of distribution or sanitation infrastructure, the construction of large dams, massive pollution by mining or oil companies, intensive irrigation, or any other of a variety of water-involved projects, these issues involve transnational stakeholders and are at the heart of the globalization of the economy. The competition for resources is global and explains the advent of the question of the human right of access to water. For almost two decades, these seemingly dichotomous approaches to water (economic and rights-based) at the international level have given rise to a vast political confrontation (Paquerot 2006) that takes place outside the framework of liberal negotiation, through which states have so far addressed most major environmental issues (Conca 2006).

The Configuration of Actors at the End of the International Decade for Water

The various opinions and assessments following the first International Decade for Water were mixed. Interpretations diverge on whether the Decade was a partial success or a failure in providing access to drinking water to all human beings. There were practically as many people deprived of water and sanitation at the end of the decade as at the beginning; however, this result may have been due to the growth of the world population, among other factors. Some experts highlight that the outcome would have been disastrous without the efforts that were made (Nguyen and Dausset 1999). That being said, the General Assembly, noting that the goal of providing clean water and sanitation to the entire world had not been achieved, called for increased efforts to achieve this goal by the end of the century.

Two international water-related events marked the end of the Decade, during which we see the emergence of the terms of the ideological confrontation that would occupy the international scene for the next two decades: the Montreal Conference and the New Delhi Conference. The Montreal Conference was an international meeting of non-governmental organizations (NGOs), convened under the leadership of OXFAM-International, wherein the Montreal Charter was adopted (Charte de Montréal 1990). This Charter was submitted as a reference document for the Global Consultation on Drinking Water and Sanitation, to be held in New Delhi under the leadership of the United Nations Development Program (UNDP). The Montreal Conference was the first time that at least some non-state actors for water-related issues organized to participate in an international forum on a common rather than a dispersed basis. The Charter of Montreal opens with the affirmation of access to water as a human right and its inseparability from other human rights. Affirming that access to water and sanitation is primarily a political issue (Charte de Montréal 1990, Principle 1), it calls for "a reform of dominant economic development patterns that waste and pollute the planet's limited resources" (Charte de Montréal 1990, Principle 1).

We can roughly compile the actors present on the international scene in the field of water at that time. Among states, three trends are perceptible. First, for many countries in the South, challenges around access to water are framed in terms of development and infrastructure. The New Delhi Conference, which officially closed the International Decade for Water, was characterized by this perspective as the goal of "a minimum for all, rather than a maximum for a few" (Mayrand 1999, p. 15) was affirmed. We see the two other trends manifest in developed countries: on the one hand, a propensity to handle the issue through development aid and, on the other hand, a growing concern for the environmental effects of the misuse of water, in the wake of the ideological shift to sustainable development. It should also be noted that at this time, states were generally not defining access to water as a human rights issue.

Among international organizations, each intervenes according to its "field of competence" and the two institutions most present were therefore the UNDP and the World Bank (WB), as they are both dedicated to international development. The orientation of the Decade gave a prominent role to these two organizations, but several others continued to work on water issues according to their sectoral competencies.[2]

Finally, with regard to non-state actors, this period was characterized by a large presence of charitable and development NGOs, as well as an increased presence of environmental NGOs who were concerned with pollution and the proliferation of large dams. Also present were the so-called professional NGOs, such as associations of engineers or hydrologists, which contributed both to the development of knowledge and to development projects prior to and during the Decade, often in close collaboration with the UNESCO's World Hydrological Program.

The Terms of the Controversy

These two conferences are significant: since the early 1990s, the orientations of the IFIs in the field of water have been more clearly defined and have become increasingly dominant. As a result, in the first half of the 1990s, we witnessed the first major privatization of distribution and sanitation services in the South—in particular in Manila and Buenos Aires—as well as the publication of the World Bank's policy in the field of water (WB 1994). This increasingly market-oriented solution to water problems induced a gradual integration and "politicization" of NGO involvement.

In 1992, shortly before the Rio Earth Summit, the second session of the International Water Tribunal in Amsterdam[3] focused on water management issues in Asia, Africa, and Latin America, and incorporated the people's right to these resources beyond the specific problem of pollution that had been its previous concern. The International Water Tribunal built upon a Declaration that was prepared by a group of legal experts from different parts of the world[4] (Declaration of Amsterdam 1992) and based on existing international principles. The Tribunal applied these principles to all water resources and not only to transboundary resources, which indicated a desire to remove the water issue from the narrow framework of interstate relations (Amsterdam 1992, p. 8). The Amsterdam declaration includes, inter alia: the principle of intergenerational equity; the right to water in sufficient quantity and quality as a human right; and the consideration that water cannot be appropriated because it is a common good that should be under the stewardship of humanity. The principles defended by NGOs are broadly in line with those that would be put forward in Rio de Janeiro.

The International Conference on Water and the Environment (WMO 1992), held in Dublin shortly before the Rio Summit, sets out, inter alia, the following principles: "Freshwater, a fragile and non-renewable resource, is essential for life, development and the environment" (WMO 1992, Principle 1); and "water, used for multiple purposes, has economic value and should therefore be recognized *as an economic good*" (WMO 1992, Principle 4) (emphasis added). By virtue of this principle "it is essential to recognize the fundamental human right to safe water and adequate hygiene at an affordable price" (WMO 1992, Principle 4). Thus, in Dublin, the notion of "economic good" as applicable to water resources appeared and it would eventually be included in almost all the UN documents in this area.[5]

There is no explicit mention of water in the final declaration of the Rio Summit; however, Action 21 in Chapter 18 contains a number of more specific principles for water resources. Furthermore, the recognition of the right to access water in the terms of the Mar del Plata Conference is reiterated (UN Action 21, 1992), the vital character of water resources having been laid down in the introduction of the chapter, which states:

> Water is necessary for all aspects of life. The overarching goal is to ensure that the world's population has adequate supplies of good quality water at all times while maintaining the hydrological, biological and chemical functions of ecosystems, adapting human activities to the limiting capacity of nature and fighting the vectors of water-related diseases. (UN Action 21, para. 18.2)

There is also the recognition of water as an economic good, as proposed by the Dublin Conference, but in terms that allow this vital resource to, at least partially, remain outside economic and market regulations. Thus, it is said that:

> Integrated water resources management is based on the idea that water is an integral part of the ecosystem and is a natural resource and a social and economic good whose quantity and quality determine the allocation. [...] In the development and use of water resources, priority must be given to meeting basic needs and protecting ecosystems. However, beyond these requirements, users should pay a fair price. (UN Action 21, para. 18.8)

Based on the outcomes of these various international conferences in the early 1990s, we can see that (1) the trend toward economic solutions is strong; (2) NGOs begin to regroup (Montreal Conference, Water Tribunal) and consider the issues around water from an integrated perspective; and (3) international "public" institutions and states, while integrating the economic dimension, retain the Mar del Plata perspective of water as a development issue.

The World Water Council: New Governance and Privatization of the Water Agenda

In 1994, the World Bank launched its general policy in the field of water in which it specifies the conditions for economically rational water management. Two years later, in 1996, a new organization was constituted, the World Water Council (WWC), which is difficult to situate in the traditional categories of actors of the international arena: neither state, nor international institution, nor NGO, this Council combines the qualities of all types of international actors. Here we see a typical example of new forms of "horizontal" governance that brings together all the "stakeholders" who share the same perception of the problem. Indeed, if NGOs gathered at the Montreal Conference to share a common vision of the problem—access to water as a human right and political responsibility—then actors who shared the other vision—an economically rational water resource management—now had their own shared space for dialogue.

Though it was not an international public body, the WWC included multiple UN agencies and several governments in its membership, and it was largely funded by the World Bank and various multinational corporations in the field of water (Sohnle[6] 2002, p. 444). As such, the WWC initiated the First World Water Forum in 1997 with a ministerial conference; a practice that has recurred every three years thereafter. The evolution of international principles was largely influenced by these "private" international meeting events while the status and interventions of the WWC remain more than ambiguous.[7] The WWC has around 350 members in 50 countries and is referred to as the "leader of the World Water Movement" on its website.

If we understand "international civil society" as referring to all groups of people who come together based on specific shared interests in order to advocate for those interests in the international, public sphere, and if, by extension, we consider "international political society" to be predominantly of states and international "public" institutions, then the WWC has more in common with private spaces, than with public ones. The WWC becomes *the* international arena for the water issues where interactions play out, but only on the fringes of public political space: all the categories of actors find themselves either pushed aside or kept out of those spaces, as well as the regulations regarding standard operating procedures and decision-making regulations, which, for example, include neither the official languages of the UN, nor its accreditation system. Groups that fully participate in the WWC, include several private companies, large French water multinationals and especially the Suez group. The WWC also expresses a clear desire to "depoliticize" the debates, which then take on a fundamentally technical and financial dimension.

The WWC has a large number of professional organizations and expertise among its members, including universities and research institutes. Its membership also includes a number of more traditional NGOs such as the Water Supply and Sanitation Collaborative Council, the Foundation for a New Water Culture, Green Cross International and the International Water Secretariat. The WWC, therefore, seems to claim to be substituting itself for public governance, if for the purposes of the analysis, we consider UN institutions to constitute the "public" sphere in the international arena. On their website they claim to be an "international multi-stakeholder platform organization whose mission is to mobilize action on critical water issues at all levels, including the highest decision-making level" (WWC n.d.).

As a result of the role played by the WWC, the UN, for example, released the first edition of its "World Water Assessment Report" (WWAP 2003) at the Third World Water Forum in Kyoto (2003) rather than at the General Assembly, thus excluding many countries. The most important consequence of the high-level governance role of the WWC was that the ministerial declarations at these forums did not recognize access to drinking water and sanitation as a human right but rather as a need.[8] This perception clearly represents a regression when we consider previous conferences and statements in "public" organizations, which, from Mar del Plata to Rio, have always reiterated this right. The WWC focused only on the "economic good" dimension of access to water and used this perspective as a panacea. Indeed, during these forums and ministerial conferences, the confrontation between the consideration of water as economic good or as a human right crystallized.

The creation of the WWC provided a new space for market solutions to be deployed. Sitting side by side in the WWC, representatives of the World Bank and multinational water companies could now propose "solutions," largely framed by the French model of delegated management (a specific kind of Public/Private Partnership known as PPPs or 3P, promoted by the major French private corporations, *Suez-Lyonnaise des Eaux* and *Vivendi/ Veolia*). Several of the major privatization and delegation contracts were put in place during this period. The last decade of the twentieth century marked a turning point in this respect. Statistics show that the share of the population served by the private sector increased from 90 million in 1988 (including 40 million in France) to 250 million in 2000 (Amougou 2001, p. 166). Though the overall proportion remained low, the accelerated increase was indicative of a heavy trend (Gleick et al. 2002, p. 60), and, especially, of the size of the potential markets.

At the First World Water Forum in Marrakech in 1997, the King of Morocco, who hosted this meeting, predicted that water would be the oil of the twenty-first century. Later that year, a report tabled at the UN General Assembly read "It takes a more market-oriented approach to manage water supplies, and water must be a commodity whose price is set by supply and demand" (UN 1997). As a result, the positions of the various organizational actors crystallized, largely around the water as an economic good *or* water as a fundamental human right dilemma.

The terms of the debate remained centered around two principles that would lead to a confrontation in the following years: human right *or* economic good rather than human right *and* economic good, as proposed by the Dublin Conference. This polarization increased at the end of the 1990s and by the beginning of the new millennium, two seemingly oppositional visions appeared: on the one hand, the progressive integration of the 'market-centered' vision among the UN institutions and, on the other hand, a general convergence of NGOs toward the demand to recognize access to water as a human right, despite the differences that persisted between them on other fronts.

Here, we are already witnessing a first stage of the translation process, as conceptualized in the sociology of translation framework, in which states and international institutions are somehow "forced" to take the economic dimension into account. Until then, states, as public authorities, essentially believed that by virtue of their permanent sovereignty over natural resources, remained responsible for the management of water. However, following the 1997 World Water Forum, they were informed that water must be managed according to the principles of the market economy. The second phase of conceptual translation was located between the *or* and the *and*, and came to pass following the polarization and confrontation that occurred at the turn of the new millennium.

Polarization and Confrontation

Following the First World Water Forum, public figures from various countries started to speak out against these orientations. The "Water Manifesto: the right of all to life," which was launched in Lisbon, Valencia, and Brussels in 1998, became the generative document of the World Water Contract, which was chaired by Mario Soares, former President of Portugal. Many groups were already opposed to the dominant water policies, and this initiative would play a catalytic role in rallying participants and developing shared claims. It marks the beginning of a "common front" for the right to water. It is also the same year that the issue of water is nominally taken into consideration within the UN human rights system, with a first report on the issue by the Special Rapporteur Guissé (HRC Sub-commission 1998).

This rallying around the demand for the right to water as a human right quickly marked the strategy of actors from virtually every horizon. From this period onward, despite significant differences in some aspects of water issues, there has been growing evidence of broad international coalitions, ranging from environmental groups, to international trade union organizations, feminist organizations, and an increasing number of traditionally "non-political" charitable NGOs. Thus, for example, the largest Swiss charity NGOs[9] called for an international convention to protect this right, prevent the commercialization and privatization of water, and establish a binding arbitration mechanism in international conflicts.

The following year, in 1999, the social revolt in Cochabamba, Bolivia, became the symbol *par excellence* of this polarization. For the first time, an angry population demanded and obtained the end of a private contract in the water sector. Moreover, this population was predominantly indigenous, which served to expand the "common front" around the right to water. An emblematic example of what was being protested, and what was reversed, is among the conditions for a loan guarantee that were imposed by the World Bank in Bolivia. Those conditions included not only the privatization of the water supply system and the prohibition of subsidizing the poor, but also groundwater exclusivity, which allowed a private consortium to close individual wells if peasants did not pay a fee, in short, they "privatized the rain."[10]

Staging the Confrontation

The Second World Water Forum, at The Hague in 2000, represents a particularly significant moment in these reconfigurations. In addition to the WWC, which convened this international meeting, two other organizations produced documents that were submitted for discussion: (1) "From Vision to Action: Making Water Everybody's Business" which was produced by the Global Water Partnership based on broad consultations and very controversial in several countries (Cosgrove and Rijsberman[11] 2000); and (2) "A Water Secure World," which was prepared by the World Water Commission.[12] Both of these reports presented a largely economic vision of water (Smets 2002, p. 7). This production of analyses and competing proposals indicates that at that moment, the broad coalition, which was originally intended to "bring together all the good will," began to crack, and that while no "stakeholder" denied the importance of the economic dimension of water, all actors did not share the perspective that approaches should be exclusively economic. For example, even though UNESCO and the UNDP were active members of the WWC, they supported activists who were calling for the inclusion of the right to water in the Ministerial Declaration (Taithe 2002, p. 221) at the forum. The Prince of Orange, who hosted the forum, also affirmed that the "vast majority" of forum participants wished to see the right to water included in the Declaration in his first report to the ministerial conference. Even the World Bank Vice-President for Environment, Ismael Serageldin, argued that the right to water is "obvious" at a meeting of NGOs.

Despite this broad rally around a specific claim, the Hague Declaration did not recognize access to water as a human right. This forum, however, was the pivotal moment in which the two poles of the contradiction that cut across the international debate in the field of water are clearly inscribed.

The following year, the Fourth P-7 Summit[13] also focused on "Water, Right of Life in the 21st Century," and clearly contravened the Hague Declaration. The Council of Canadians, for its part, hosted an international meeting in Vancouver[14] called Water for People and Nature that brought together 1000 delegates from 40 countries. In December of that year, the guidelines developed at the Vancouver meeting were adopted in Brussels, by close to 100 NGOs and social movements who participated in the *Our World Is Not for Sale* Network[15] meeting. The battle became concentrated on "the cabal of the world's water oligarchy,"[16] which was accused of denying the right to water as a human right. In other words, as

Satish Kumar, Program Director at the Schumacher College, International Centre for Ecological Studies says: "Capitalism is shrewd enough to use shortages of resources like water to make even more money for the rich" (Leahy 2007). Indeed, the confrontation was clearly established between economic actors and ideas, and human rights actors and ideas.

Resettlement of Water Issues in the "Public" Sphere?

Given the diffidence of the international public institutions that appeared, to some extent, to leave the field open for self-proclaimed and self-appointed organizations to determine how water would be governed globally, as well as the controversy that was made particularly visible at the Forum of The Hague in 2000, non-state actors and some international institutions attempted to bring the issue of water back to the heart of the international public agenda in preparation for the Johannesburg Earth Summit, which was planned for 2002. UNESCO, for example, published an important discussion paper on the ethical aspects of the use of water resources (UNESCO 2000), which clearly affirmed the human right of access to water (UNESCO 2000, p. 39) and drew attention to the dangers of market considerations of this vital resource (UNESCO 2000, p. 32).

As far as non-state actors are concerned, at the turn of the millennium, their declarations multiply[17] and converge around a certain number of principles that brought a certain level of consensus to international civil society, even though some significant differences remained on specific issues.[18] Moreover, in early 2002, the American organization Public Citizens,[19] joined the World Water Contract initiative and began a vast campaign under the title "Defend the Global Commons." They reviewed the struggles to preserve the commonality and collective control of water resources and services that were occurring around the world. Countries included: India, USA, Tanzania, South Africa, El Salvador, Ghana, Bolivia, Zambia, Brazil, Mozambique, Argentina, Ecuador, Nicaragua, Bangladesh, The Philippines, Canada, Uruguay, Mexico, and New Zealand, among others (Public Citizens 2002). In doing so, Public Citizens illustrated the truly global nature of water issues and highlighted the rootedness of this concern.

It should also be noted that this period marked an important ambiguity among the proponents of market solutions for water. In 2000, the International Monetary Fund (IMF) again formally linked its aid to the privatization of water services, to varying degrees, for twelve of the poorest countries,[20] while multinational water companies began to question their interests in this sector in the South:

> Internationalization polices are frozen across the board. Back to the good old days of quick returns on investment in Europe or North America. Suez will reduce its exposure to the difficult climate of the South. The group, present in more than 130 countries, intends to reduce the capital employed in these countries by one third – more than 3 billion euros -, from the 9 billion that has already committed. "This marks the end of a particular idea of globalization that was to provide wealth for everyone," said Gerard Mestrallet, CEO of Suez, in the *Le Monde* newspaper. (Losson and De Filippis 2003)

In November 2002, however, aware of the intensive debate on the international scene, the UN Committee on Economic, Social and Cultural Rights, which was in charge of monitoring the implementation of the covenant of the same name, issued a general comment—No. 15 (EcoSoC 2003)—specifying the nature and scope of the right to water as a human right, and, thus, calling on reluctant governments to respect and protect this right. Nevertheless, despite the appeal made by the High Commissioner for Human Rights on this occasion (Vieira De Mello 2003), the Ministerial Declaration of the Third World Water Forum in Kyoto in March 2003 did not incorporate the explicit recognition of this right.

The emergence of the human right to water has been clearly marked by the four key phases of the "sociology of translation" as described by Callon (1984, 1985, and Chap. 2): (1) problematization, which includes the establishment of the different actors as well as the statements of their respective understanding of problems; (2) interessement, which refers to the stabilization of the actors and interests around a specific issue or problem; (3) enrolment, that is, the transformation of questions/problematizations into affirmations and assured action, which allows resources and alliances to be secured; and (4) mobilization of allies.

Beginning at the end of the first UN Decade for Water (1990) and the conference in Dublin (WMO 1992), and followed by the First (1997) and Second (2000) World Water Forum, water, understood as a resource by the participating actors, was put forth as a fundamentally economic issue. As such, the solutions to this problem had to be sought on the free market. The conference of Dublin represented a form of problematization where water, as an economic good, was posited as such to the different actors; the First and Second World Fora represented the process of interessement in which this specific conception of water was stabilized (Paquerot 2006). At the same time, the privatization of water services furthered the idea of water as a resource and economic good, and structured a form of enrolment for different actors (including private ones, and also many NGOs). It was these actors, as well as some Western States and international organizations, who mobilized this conception of water within the international space, which generated debates and political confrontations supported by the claim of a human right to water.

We may consider that the economic/human right polarization finds a certain "resolution" in 2002 with the formal intervention of the UN Committee on Economic, Social and Cultural Rights: "the access to water, as a human right, is now formally integrated in the UN's human rights system" (Kiefer and Brolmann 2005, p. 183). Since then, virtually all the actors involved in the water debate have recognized that access to water is a human right,[21] which, without completely resolving the contradiction, displaces it.

Reconcile the Irreconcilable: Almost a Decade of Discussion in the System

The international confrontation led to the adoption of Observation no. 15 (EcoSoC 2003) by the UN Committee on Economic, Social and Cultural Rights, which asserted the right to water as a human right, and, thus initiated a second round of confrontation. This time, the confrontation took place within the UN system, where an institutional translation of the sense, scope, and contents of the human right to water was adopted. Following the nomination of Caterina de Albuquerque, an independent expert appointed by the Human Rights Council, and the choice of a liberal definition of this right, the actors fighting against the commodification of water withdrew from the UN system (Veber 2013). The adoption of a resolution by the UN General Assembly (UNGA 2010) and the Human Rights Council in 2010 (HRC 2010) confirmed that the translation of the original claim had occurred from a liberal perspective, which momentarily concluded the translation process at work.

Indeed, while this institutional phase recognized access to water as a human right, that recognition did not solve the political conflict. Even though a resolution on the right of access to water was adopted by the UN

General Assembly on 28 July 2010 and was hailed as a victory by the social movements advocating for this right around the world, the conflict remained. Paradoxically, 41 countries abstained in the vote on this resolution, but none dared vote against it. A few weeks later, on 30 September 2010, the Human Rights Council affirmed the existence of a legal obligation for state parties to the "International Covenant on Economic, Social and Cultural Rights" (ICESCR 1966), with respect to this right.

Yet, in order to understand the very political and conflictual conceptions of the world beyond the institutional recognition of that right to water, it is important to pay special attention to the discourse used during the adoption of this resolution in the General Assembly debate. In a UN Public Information Department document setting out the context of the adoption of the resolution, it is stated:

> The representative of Spain regretted that none of the recommendations of the European Union had been taken into account in the resolution. Nevertheless, he welcomed the amendment which *replaces the word "declares" with "recognizes" in the first paragraph of the operative part.* (UN 2010 – Emphasis added)

If at first glance this distinction appears meaningless, a careful look at the discourse and its legal ramifications demonstrates otherwise: we "recognize" what already exists, which establishes a pre-existing legal basis for the right to water with its limitations. However, the use of the word "declare" by the General Assembly, which has only the power of recommendation and is thus not an established political authority, demonstrates an effort on the part of the proposing state to widen the scope of the rights that already exist, that is, by *declaring* a new right. Spain, along with Germany, was one of the "sponsors" of this subject at the Human Rights Council. Why, one may wonder, would change a single word be so important to a country like Spain that promotes and supports the recognition of this right? The contention is that countries who participated in promoting the right to water have different goals. The resolution brought to the General Assembly in July 2010 was presented by countries for which human rights must be a bulwark against privatization.[22] However, the international human rights instruments, while rendering the States responsible for implementation, have never had the function or the objective of excluding the delivery of the services required for the implementation of rights from the market. *To recognize* rather than *to declare* therefore means to integrate the right to water into the general economy of the instruments that already exist for the protection of rights, and which do not prevent the privatization of infrastructure or the commodification of water resources.

These two speech acts, one could say both political and legal, remain contradictory in some respects. In the first case, it is a question of using human rights as a weapon against privatization and commodification, which has been demonstrated through the analysis of speeches and statements throughout the first decade of the twenty-first century (Veber 2013). However, by moving from the term *declares* to the term *recognizes* in the resolution of the General Assembly, we can discern what Liora Israel aptly distinguishes as "the relative euphemizing of conflictual situations through their introduction into the judicial sphere" (Israel 2009, p. 102).

Indeed, prior to the adoption of the Council Resolution, Catarina de Albuquerque, as an independent expert, made it clear in her 2010 report that privatization is not contrary to the right to water (Albuquerque 2010). As such, the introduction of the human right to water into the human rights system reduces it *through the sociological translation process*, within its effective legal scope, to a dimension deemed acceptable for liberalism, sovereignty, and, more generally, to the principles underlying the dominant international order. This process demonstrates how the dual meaning of justice—as power and as resistance—has contributed to both maintaining order and including marginalized groups in public space (Commaille and Kaluszynski 2007).

Conclusion

The claim to water as a human right has forced international institutional actors, as well as states and even economic actors, to consider the aspirations of national populations on issues pertaining to that right. Human rights, "without which there would be no more principle to support resistance to oppression" (Zarka 2017, p. 8), appear to play two separate roles simultaneously in the expression of conflicts in the confrontation in the field of water. On the one hand, the discourse of human rights legitimizes the challenge: to make a claim in the name of a shared collective value that is at least formally integrated into the international order and the majority of national orders allow the claimant to re-politicize issues that are seen as indisputable in the context of market globalization. Essentially, it can be used to combat political leaders who exclaim "we have no choice" with respect to the rules of trade and international finance. On the other hand, human rights have become the very place of political conflict through the struggle to define the content, scope, and meaning of each right; a conflict highlighted here through the debate on the scope of the right to water as a means to prevent commodification and privatization.

However, because human rights can be interpreted and translated from both the perspective of power and that of resistance, the legitimacy attached to them can also be harnessed by those in power, to their own benefit. Between re-appropriating the "right to have rights" (Nollez-Goldbach 2008) and the instrumentalization of rights to serve the maintenance of order, the effects of human rights on social relations are yet to be entirely understood. Used in many spaces that are monopolized by economic globalization, the discourse of human rights does not necessarily produce the same politicization effects in each case. However, all parties refer to the political function of human rights when interpreted in the light of Article 28 of the Universal Declaration of Human Rights (UN 1948): "Everyone is entitled to a social and international order in which the rights and freedoms set forth in this Declaration can be fully realized."

Notes

1. Except otherwise indicated, the author provided all translations of French quotations.
2. At the time, 23 UN organizations or agencies were working on water issues within the scope of their respective mandates.
3. In 1981 Dutch NGOs founded the International Water Tribunal, which in 1983 held their first session in Rotterdam on water pollution in Western Europe.
4. At their meeting in March 1991, the working group comprised 14 lawyers from Asia, Africa, Latin America, the United States, and the Netherlands.
5. The World Bank relied heavily on this Conference to justify its water policy directions (WB 1994). Contrary to popular belief, it must be emphasized that the Dublin Conference was not a ministerial conference but an expert's conference, and that the state's meeting in Rio a few months later refused to officially endorse the Dublin Declaration.
6. This author classifies the WWC among NGOs. This type of organization is not completely new, as is the case of the International Union for the Conservation of Nature (IUCN), which also includes states and international organizations among its members: out of 1087 members there are

113 governmental agencies, 82 states, and 33 affiliates. (source: http://www.iucn.org/members/).
7. In the sense that the WWC operates on the margins of the UN and its rules and is therefore not accountable to all states but only to its members. It should be noted that until 2003, it was impossible to access the list of members.
8. None of the WWC ministerial conferences recognized the right to water prior to the recognition of that right by the 2010 General Assembly and Human Rights Council. This issue not one of mere discourse because the market responds to needs and political institutions respond to rights.
9. Swissaid, Action de carême, Pain pour le prochain, Helvetas and Caritas.
10. This expression comes from the Indigenous social leader Oscar Oliveira.
11. We can note that the founders of this organization are also at the WWC. The World Bank, the UNDP, and the Swedish International Development Agency (SIDA) are behind this initiative, which dates back to 1996.
12. The World Water Commission was chaired by I. Serageldin, Vice-President Environment, World Bank.
13. P-7 for the poorest countries: the initiative of these summits belongs to the Green Party of the European Parliament.
14. Vancouver, Canada, July 4–8, 2001.
15. http://www.ourworldisnotforsale.org/en/about/.
16. This expression is from Riccardo Petrella, Secretary General of the World Water Contract, who was present at both meetings.
17. The Cochabamba Declaration in December 2000 brought together NGOs around the Bolivian struggle against the privatization of water: http://www.americas.org or http://www.democracyctr.org; the Accra Declaration in May 2001 brought together African NGOs around the same demands. A statement from indigenous peoples, "Water is life: Protect Water Now!" Was also adopted in Vancouver in July 2001 at http://www.canadians.org/blueplanet/protectwaternow-f.html.
18. For example, organizations such as the International Water Secretariat and Green Cross International do not oppose the privatization of services nor do they oppose the Public/Private Partnership put forward by the WWC and the World Bank.
19. It should be noted that the issues of water and food have grown so much that Public Citizens created a new organization entirely devoted to this subject, *Food and Water Watch* that started operating on its own in early 2006.
20. According to data from *Fifty Years Is Enough*: Angola, Benin, Guinea Bissau, Honduras, Nicaragua, Niger, Panama, Rwanda, Sao Tome and Principe, Senegal, Tanzania, and Yemen.

21. One notable exception should be underlined here, that of Peter Brabeck, former CEO of Nestlé.
22. It was sponsored by the Plurinational Republic of Bolivia, among others, which, since the events of Cochabamba, has become a leader of fight against multinational water companies.

References

Albuquerque, Catarina de. 2010. *Human Rights Obligations Related to Non-State Service Provision in Water and Sanitation* (A/HRC/15/31). Geneva: Human Rights Council.

Amougou, Thierry. 2001. L'eau, bien public, bien privé: l'Etat, les communautés locales et les multinationales. (2002). In *L'eau, patrimoine commun de l'humanité, Alternatives Sud*, ed. François Houtart, (vol. III, 4), 147–170. Louvainla-Neuve: Centre tricontinental.

Callon, Michel. 1984. Some Elements of a Sociology of Translation: Domestication of the Scallops and the Fishermen of St Brieuc Bay. *The Sociological Review* 32 (1_suppl): 196–233.

———. 1985. The Sociology of an Actor-Network. In *Mapping the Dynamics of Science and Technology*, ed. M. Callon, J. Law, and A. Rip, 19–34. London: Palgrave Macmillan.

Commaille, Jacques, and Martine Kaluszynski. 2007. *La fonction politique de la justice*. Paris: La Découverte.

Conca, Ken. 2006. Governing Water. In *Contentious Transnational Politics and Global Institution Building*. Cambridge, London: Massachusetts Institute of Technology.

Cosgrove, William J., and Franck R. Rijsberman. 2000. *From Vision to Action: Making Water Everybody's Business*. USA/UK: Earthscan: Global Water Partnership.

Vieira De Mello, Sergio. 2003. *Statement of the High Commissioner for Human Rights*. Kyoto: Third World Water Forum, March.

Declaration of Amsterdam. 1992. *The Case Books Series (vol. 5)*. Netherlands: International Books.

Dellapenna, Joseph, and Joyeeta Gupta. 2008. Toward Global Law on Water. In *Global Governance: A Review of Multilateralism and International Organizations* 14(4): 437–453.

EcoSoC. 2003. *Substantive Issues Arising in the Implementation of the International Covenant on Economic, Social and Cultural Rights, General Comment No. 15 (2002) The Right to Water (Arts. 11 and 12 of the International Covenant on Economic, Social and Cultural Rights)*. Retrieved from: http://tbinternet.ohchr.org/_layouts/treatybodyexternal/Download.aspx?symbolno=E%2fC.12%2f2002%2f11&Lang=en

Gleick, Peter H., Gary Wolff, Elizabeth L. Chalecki, and Rachel Reyes. 2002. The privatization of water and water systems. In *The World's Water 2002–2003: The Biennial Report on Freshwater Resources*, ed. Peter H. Gleick, 57–85. Washington, DC: Island Press.

Human Rights Council [HRC]. 2010. *Les droits de l'homme et l'accès à l'eau potable et à l'assainissement* (Resolution No. A/HRC/15/L.14). Geneva: United Nations.

Human Rights Council Sub-Commission. 1998. *Le droit d'accès de tous à l'eau potable et aux services d'assainissement.* M. El Hadji Guissé, special rapporteur (Publication No. E/CN.4/Sub.2/1998/7). Geneva: United Nations.

ICESCR. 1966. *International Covenant on Economic, Social and Cultural Rights* (Report: 993 UNTS 3, 6 ILM 368,993 R.T.N.U. 3). New-York: United Nations.

Israël, Liora. 2009. *L'arme du droit.* Paris: Presses de Sciences Po.

Kiefer, Thorsten, and Catherine Brölmann. 2005. Beyond State Sovereignty: The Human Right to Water. *Non-State Actors and International Law* 5 (3): 183–208.

Leahy, Stephen. 2007. Thirstier World Likely to See More Violence. *Inter Press Service*, March 16. Retrieved from: http://www.ipsnews.net/2007/03/water-day-thirstier-world-likely-to-see-more-violence/

Losson, Christian, and Vittorio De Filippis. 2003. Suez: le développement durable qui ne dure pas. *Libération*, January 11. Retrieved from: http://www.liberation.fr/futurs/2003/01/11/suez-le-developpement-durable-qui-ne-dure-pas_427542

Margat, Jean. 2000. Vers une nouvelle culture de l'eau. In *Les clés du XXIe siècle*, ed. J. Bindé, 124–128. Paris: UNESCO/Seuil.

Mayrand, Karel. 1999. *Les enjeux stratégiques de l'eau et les initiatives internationales récentes.* Ministère des relations internationales, Direction générale des politiques, Direction des relations interministérielles et des affaires sectorielles.

Nollez-Goldbach, Raphaëlle. 2008. Théorie des droits de l'homme chez Hannah Arendt: le droit d'avoir des droits. In *Lire Hannah Arendt aujourd'hui, Pouvoir, guerre, pensée, jugement politique*, 263–271. Paris: L'Harmattan.

Oxfam-Québec and Secrétariat international de l'eau. 1990. *Charte de Montréal.* Retrieved from: http://www.sie-see.org/fr/articles/charte-de-montreal-sur-leau-potable-et-lassainissement/

Paquerot, Sylvie. 2006. Reconfigurations des acteurs et de l'ordre du jour dans le domaine de l'eau: une gouvernance mondiale en quête de légitimité. In *Jules Duchastel et Raphaël Canet avec la collaboration de Pierre-Paul S t-Onge (dir.), Crise de l'État, revanche des sociétés, Outremont, Athéna éditions/Chaire de recherche du Canada en mondialisation, citoyenneté et démocratie*, 307.

Petiteville, Franck. 2016. Les organisations internationales dépolitisent-elles les relations internationales? *Gouvernement et action publique* 3: 113–129.

Public Citizens. 2002. *Defend the Global Commons: Reports from Organizations Around the World Defending Water as a Common Resource*, February. Retrieved from: http://www.citizen.org/cmep/Water/articles.cfm?ID=10841

Smets, Henri. 2002. *Le droit à l'eau*. Strasbourg: Conseil européen du droit de l'environnement.

Sohnle, Jochen. 2002. *Le droit international des ressources en eau douce: solidarité contre souveraineté*. Paris: La Documentation française.

TAITHE, Alexandre. 2002. Tempête dans un verre d'eau. L'eau: droit, besoin, ou quel bien public? In *Les biens publics mondiaux. Un mythe légitimateur pour l'action collective*, 219–243.

Tien-Duc, Nguyen, and Jean Dausset. 1999. *L'humanité mourra-t-elle de soif?* Paris: Hydrocom.

UN. 1948. *UDHR, Universal Declaration of Human Rights* (General Assembly Resolution No. 217(III)), (UN Document No. A/810, 71). New-York: UNGAOR.

———. 1972. *Declaration of the United Nations Conference on the Human Environment.* [Stockholm Declaration] (Document No. N.U. A/CONF. 48/14/Rév. 1; 11 I.L.M.). New-York: United Nations.

———. 1974. Universal Declaration for the Eradication of Hunger and Malnutrition (1974) Res. 3348 (XXIX) December 17.

———. 1975. *Convening the United Nations Water Conference* (Resolution No. 3513). New-York: United Nations.

———. 1976. The Vancouver Declaration on Human Settlements, A/CONF.70/15, 11 June 1976.

———. 1977. *Report of the United Nations Conference on Water* (Publication No. E/CONF.70/29). Mar del Plata: United Nations.

———. 1980. *Résolution proclamant la période 1981–1990 Décennie internationale de l'eau potable et de l'assainissement* (Resolution No. 35/18). New-York: United Nations.

———. 1992. *Action 21*, (Publication No. A/CONF.151/26/Rev.1). Rio: United Nations.

———. 1997. *Évaluation générale des ressources en eau douce dans le monde : Rapport du secrétaire général des Nations Unies* (Publication No. E/CN.1997/9). New-York: United Nations.

———. 2010. Communiqué, AG/10967 122–0-41, *L'assemblée "reconnaît" le droit à l'eau potable comme un droit fondamental* (28 juillet 2010). New-York: United Nations.

UNESCO. 2000. *L'éthique de l'utilisation de l'eau douce : vue d'ensemble*. Paris: UNESCO.

United Nations General Assembly (UNGA). 2010. *Le droit fondamental à l'eau et à l'assainissement* (Publication No. A/64/L.63/Rev.1; A/64/PV.108). New-York: United Nations.

Veber, Marion. 2013. *Le rôle joué par les ONG agissant au sein du système des droits de l'homme des Nations Unies dans le processus de reconnaissance et de définition du droit à l'eau et à l'assainissement entre 1997 et 2011*. Master's Thesis, IEP, Toulouse.

WMO. 1992. *International Conference on Water and the Environment: Twenty-first Century Development*, (Dublin Declaration). Dublin: WMO.

World Bank. 1994. *Water Resources Management*. Washington, DC: The World Bank Retrieved from: http://documents.worldbank.org/curated/en/940261468325788815/Water-resources-management.

World Water Council (WWC). n.d. *Website: Main Page*, publication date. Retrieved from: www.worldwatercouncil.org/en

WWAP. 2003. *Water for People, Water for Life*. (Publication No. WWDR1). Retrieved from: http://www.unesco.org/new/en/natural-sciences/environment/water/wwap/wwdr/wwdr1-2003/

Zarka, Yves Charles. 2017. Le postcolonialisme ou le crime inexpiable de l'Occident. *Cités* 4: 3–8.

CHAPTER 5

Politics of Neutrality, Human Rights and Armed Struggles: The Turkey Example

Ozan Kamiloglu

Introduction: Hegemony of Human Rights Discourses and Loss of Alternatives

This chapter concentrates on debates that started during 1993 in the Insan Haklari Dernegi[1] (IHD—Human Rights Association) of Turkey regarding the adoption of the extended mandate of Amnesty International (AI) that came out after the 20th International Council Meeting in Yokohama, Japan (referred as Yokohama declaration throughout the debates),[2] and still resonates with many current issues in human rights. By looking at discussions within a local actor (the IHD) surrounding this declaration, which expanded AI's mandate to include work on abuses by armed opposition groups (as well as by the State), this chapter aims to track the appropriation, interpretation and resistance to human rights discourses of AI and other international NGOs. This analysis shows that the debates reflect the broader historical and political context of the immediate aftermath of the collapse of the Soviet Union. It is in this very specific context that the discourses by organizations categorized as "leftist" lost their moral ground

O. Kamiloglu (✉)
Birkbeck, University of London, London, UK
e-mail: o.kamiloglu@bbk.ac.uk

G. Blouin-Genest et al. (eds.), *Human Rights as Battlefields*, Human Rights Interventions,
https://doi.org/10.1007/978-3-319-91770-2_5

for emancipatory politics, and turned instead to an emphasis on rights protection. Thus, the debates within the IHD, triggered by the Yokohama declaration, can be read as a search for a language that can accommodate both, on the one side, the revolutionary ideals and grammar of its participants and, on the other, the depoliticized nature of human rights work in the climate of the 1990s. I argue in this chapter that this endeavor to accommodate often conflicting discourses is the very characteristic of the contemporary politics of human rights: a constant translation and appropriation of its global discourses by local narratives of resistance, and the limitations of this translation after the end of Cold War.[3] As such, Hopgood (2013, p. 178) reminds us about the neo-Westphalian world in which the Human Rights (uppercase) of the West lacks coherence, but where "lowercase human rights, a non-hegemonic language of resistance allied to a variety of causes and motivations" appears to be still operative. Likewise, Upendra Baxi (2006, p. 23) highlights the plurality of human rights made up of "resistances and struggles" against the "dominant and hegemonic" position assumed by a quasi-religious and "universal" human rights. These two different understandings of human rights do not constitute autonomous spaces, but are rather the two sides of a hegemonic struggle, and translations, adoptions, and changes in the meaning of human rights in different time and space is a part of this struggle.

In this respect, this chapter argues that the expansion of the human rights discourses during the 1980s and 1990s from a more 'state-centric' approach to monitoring armed opposition and searching for justice for victims is a symptom of what French philosopher Jacques Rancière (2006) calls 'the ethical turn of aesthetics and politics' in the article with the same name. The debate within IHD reveals that the loss of the political goes side by side with a turn to victims for the political opposition, so that the various discursive encounters within the left over which path to take for emancipation are transformed into debates as to which forms and kinds of violence to be in favor of or against. This turn eventually led to a discussion over the grammar and language of human rights—which includes the meanings of violence, rights, neutrality, and so on—that inevitably carries the legacy of the grammar and language used in the past by revolutionary actors. These debates that divide revolutionary activists over the scope of human rights activism reflect, on the one hand, what Foucault (1988) calls the "modern rationality," which in its extreme leads to loss of the political, and, on the other, an attempt to imagine possible different futures through transmitted meaning of words and political positions from the past.

There is a relatively rich literature on the relations between human rights discourses and Western powers, which also considers de-politicization, or loss of utopias.[4] Also the literature on appropriation, translation and invention of human rights ideals by the 'Third World' has gained volume in recent years.[5] By focusing on an NGO from Turkey, this chapter highlights the dynamism in human rights discourses between the universal and the particular. Human rights discourses are informed by past experiences of local actors and global powers; they are at the same time specifically situated in time and place while still being informed by timeless universal ideas. The article shows that human rights discourses lose their emancipatory potential if they lose their connection to the circumstances of the violation, instead of either focusing on the instant of (bodily) harm or resorting to a vague and abstract universal language. These two alternatives are eventually correlated and inevitably entail de-politicization of human rights discourses.

The first section of the chapter will provide a background to the debates by presenting the history of the IHD and the impact of Amnesty International's Yokohama declaration in relation to that particular history. The second section will focus on the debate that took place in the bulletin of the organization: it shows how some of the arguments reflect the Foucauldian "modern rationality" and advocate for an expansion of human rights activism, while others resist this rationality in different ways by using the revolutionary lexicon. The third section theoretically analyzes this opposition. On the one side, the modern rationality in its extreme form leads to a de-politicization of humanitarian activism, mainly by equating the violation of human rights with bodily harm; on the other side, the human rights grammar and meaning of words are appropriated and embedded into a revolutionary language to resist this de-politicization.

Background of the Yokohama Declaration: History, Context and Debates

The Global Context

The AI's press release following the meeting in Yokohama, Japan in 1991 states that[6]:

> Perhaps the most far-reaching decision taken in Yokohama was to expand Amnesty International's mandate in relation to abuses committed by opposition groups. Amnesty International has for many years condemned the torture or killing of prisoners held by opposition groups. It will now additionally oppose other deliberate and arbitrary killings and hostage-taking by armed political opposition groups. [...] Amnesty International opposes deliberate and arbitrary killings whether the victims are assassinated individually or are killed in indiscriminate attacks.

Furthermore, AI lists (1992) in the first report published after the Yokohama meeting, a wide range of examples of such abuses by armed political opposition groups, such as FARC (Revolutionary Armed Forces of Colombia), ELN (National Liberation Army), Sendero Luminoso (Shining Path) of Peru, the Liberation Tigers of Tamil Eelam (LTTE), the Irish Republican Army (IRA), Euskadi Ta Askatasuna (ETA), and the Kurdistan Workers' Party (PKK). With this declaration, AI stepped into humanitarian action not only against states but also against armed opposition groups through the concept of "deliberate and arbitrary killings and hostage-taking" (Baehr 1994). In addition to the Geneva Convention, customary rules of international humanitarian law by the International Committee of the Red Cross (ICRC) and several UN Security Council resolutions as well as other statements by UN bodies provided a legal framework that made armed groups potentially responsible for human rights abuses (Clapham 2006; Barbara Ann Rieffer-Flanagan 2009; Dudai and McEvoy 2012). Yet, this extension of AI's mandate, together with a similar turn in Human Rights Watch's approach during the 1980s (Goldman 1993), sparked a fundamental discussion among various local human rights groups around the world over the question of violence and especially minorities' right to protect themselves from their oppressors, as well as how human rights should be defined (Dudai and McEvoy 2012). In order to understand the discussion that took place in the Turkish context, a brief overview of the history of the IHD is needed to explain where the association stands historically in the Turkish political landscape.

IHD and the Turkish Context

After the introduction of multi-party elections in 1950, Turkey witnessed three coups: in 1960, 1971, and 1980. During the last coup, the most violent one, more than 650,000 people were detained and thousands were systematically tortured and killed by security forces.[7] Prisoners responded to systematic torture with, among other tactics, hunger strikes, resulting in multiple deaths. After the official end of the coup in November 1983, the Turkish state imposed compulsory prison uniforms, which triggered a wider wave of hunger strikes in 1984 and 1985, predominantly in Diyarbakir, Mamak, Sagmacilar, and Metris prisons (Bargu 2014, p. 181), probably inspired by the 1981 hunger strikes of IRA and INLA (Irish National Liberation Army) prisoners.[8] Prisoners' hunger strike and following fasting unto death led to the founding of the Solidarity Association for the Families and Relatives of the Arrested (TAYAD).[9] Nevertheless, the activities of the group have been suppressed; members have been detained, and harassed by police.[10] Still, they managed to mobilize wider parts of society, which was a factor in the partial success of hunger strikes in prisons: prison clothing was abolished as a result of the continuous struggle of the prisoners and their families. It is important to emphasize the struggle of TAYAD in order to understand the political situation of the country during the years when IHD was founded. IHD is probably today the most important human rights NGO in Turkey, despite the repression it has been subject to. In particular, 23 members have been assassinated, many others faced long sentences, local branches have been closed, and the NGO itself has been demonized by the mainstream media as the common enemy of people during the intense war against the PKK. The main goals of the association are: monitoring human rights violations, preparation of reports about them, and transmission of its findings to the general public. Hüsnü Öndül, head of IHD, defines the IHD as an organization with more "general aims" than TAYAD.[11] According to one of the early activists of IHD, the lawyer Ercan Kanar (1997, p. 5), TAYAD was lacking an outlook based on the universality and indivisibility of human rights, and was not concerned with mobilizing norms on human rights. IHD stated that it had been founded as a response to the state violence of the 1980 coup.[12] It is therefore possible to assert that IHD was founded as a collaboration of prisoners' families and leftist intellectuals and lawyers of the time, as a response to abuses in prisons and widespread torture, and then evolved into a human rights NGO with wider interests. This is the distinctive character of the association: instead of starting with a predetermined human rights agenda and set values and strategies, the association was from the beginning open to discussion over the meanings of human rights. It was a collaboration between grassroots organizations and those who had been subject to violations themselves and those who can use the language of human rights that has been widely accepted in the West, such as lawyers and intellectuals.

The 1991 decision of AI to condemn the abuses of armed political organizations led to turmoil in IHD. Members disagreed over the necessity to adopt AI's position, and the bulletin of the association became the cornerstone of arguments from both sides, which often turned into a discussion over the meaning of human rights.[13] What is common in all these debates was (1) the projection and construction of the neutrality claim of the Western human rights discourses[14]; (2) a linear construction of time and development that flows through and from the West; and (3) the ethicization of the political through universal notions such as individual freedom structured by the West. These debates illustrate how the language of human rights is constantly appropriated, translated, and performed. According to Nicola Perugini and Neve Gordon (2015), the politics of human rights is thus a struggle over different forms of interpretation and translation of their meaning, and it is fundamental to think about how different actors interpret the human rights grammar in their worldviews and how these in turn are informed by this translation. Thus, the meaning of human rights activism is, on the one hand, situated in a particular place and time and, on the other hand, relational to the universal notions invented by the West that inform human rights movements. It is the tension between these two aspects that puts human rights discourses at the same time into the grammar of resistance movements, the lowercase human rights discourses, and into the discourses of the power holders, the uppercase Human Rights. The debates within the IHD, where the question of violence became the focal point, reflected this dynamic of human rights. In this particular case, the principle that requires all forms of violence to be condemned by human rights organizations was challenged, mainly because of the distinctive revolutionary experiences of the organization and its activists.

Yokohama Debates in the IHD

The Yokohama Declaration was published in the bulletin of the association for the first time in March 1993, which launched the discussions.[15] Following the years after the hunger strikes (1992–1994), IHD was trying to take a stand in favor of universal rights for all, with a particular focus on the right to free speech, the right to fair trial, and the right to life. Thus, the Yokohama discussions should be read in parallel with this search of universal norms within the association. For example, Ercan Kanar (1994, p. 28), the head of the IHD Istanbul branch and a well-known human rights lawyer, wrote mostly in favor of "overcoming the dogmas of the 1970s" and embodying a human rights culture in the country.[16] His arguments are supported in articles published the same year by others, such as the head of Izmir branch, Yesim Islegen. Kanar (1994, p. 28) summarizes different positions in the debate over Yokohama Declaration:

> According to one approach, only the violations of states should be targeted [by IHD]. The second approach does not underestimate the violations of alternative power structures, but still mainly targets the State. A third one does not make any distinction between the state and the opposition; and as a demonstration of neutrality, speaks only of the violation itself.

For him, human rights struggles seek to build a tradition and culture of human rights: "Would it be possible to build a culture and tradition of human rights, if we close our eyes to atrocities of the opposition?" (Kanar 1994, p. 28). In this line of argument, the insistence over the subject of human rights is striking: the focus should be the violation itself, instead of the actors in the conflict, their role in the human rights violation and their relative power. In the context of the Yokohama declaration, what is being discussed as violations is killing, given that AI explicitly underlines deliberate and arbitrary killings and hostage-taking by armed political opposition groups. Kanar (1993, p. 34) also makes reference to other forms of bodily violence such as torture, capital punishment, and assassinations. What Kanar highlights as the culture and tradition of human rights is very much informed by the human rights discourses in the West and subsequent adoptions of these discourses by the local activists. Kanar insists upon the need to "find universality in the human rights struggle" (1994, p. 28), and considers international agreements and treaties as triumphs to follow. He is clear about it: "In the way strike actions are being followed by labor agreements, and it is impossible to undermine the importance of them, one has to consider international agreements in this manner" (1994, p. 28). Thus, for him, these agreements have to be followed. His perspective orientated the struggle toward what he calls "free individual, free society," through the universal principles and international agreements, which originated in the West. The rationale for this position can perhaps be reduced to this scheme: the universality of human rights, which can form a tradition and culture of human rights, is possible only by showing neutrality, and the only way of being neutral is to focus on the suffering of the victims. For him, this is the way to change Turkish society for the better, which he encapsulates under the motto of "free individual, free society."[17] Likewise, Yeşim Islegen (1993, p. 40) argues that "the human rights culture is not developed enough in our country" and for a better-developed human rights culture, "we need proportionality, neutrality and transparency, and a human right understanding that does not change with daily politics." In both of the arguments, the notion of development emerges as a motive of human rights struggle, which inevitably sees Western societies as an example of what human right struggles should aim for.

It would be a mistake to consider the position that underlines the need to embrace the international standards as a liberal one. Instead, it is arguably a very modern one. The arguments of Kanar and Işlegen are very much in line with what Foucault (1988, p. 161) called the "modern rationality." Foucault (1988, p. 161) reminded us that

> the main characteristic of our modern rationality in this perspective is neither the constitution of the state, the coldest of all cold monsters, nor the rise of bourgeois individualism. [...] I think that the main characteristic of modern political rationality is the fact that this integration of the individuals in a community or in a totality results from a constant correlation between an increasing individualization and the reinforcement of this totality.

Therefore, focusing on the violation itself, as Kanar and others advocated, led to the individualization and criminalization of historical injustices, by reducing them to acts of victims and perpetrators. It also led to the reinforcement of human rights as totality, through the notion of the human, our shared totality. The Western human rights discourses are thus about the creation of a culture of human rights (totality) and victimization (individualization). Focusing on Amnesty International and Human Rights Watch, Bal Sokhi-Bulley (2016) shows how "the policing technologies are represented by the criteria they must satisfy in order to secure their status as 'suitable' participants to rights discourse" in order to secure attendance at the UN and ECOSOC (The United Nations Economic and Social Council) meetings: that is to be visible and countable. This is, according to Sokhi-Bulley (2016), the policing of International NGOs and humanitarian government through human rights.

However, what we see in the IHD case is the other face of the human rights discourses: they are not only a policing tool, but also an ideological one, whose mechanisms are much more complex than traceable relations of power. Thus, there are different ways of looking at the structure of human rights movements: the first one is the genealogy of dependency through the power relations of the West and the rest (technologies of power). The IHD, for example, does not receive any fund from the UN or other international bodies as a principle. The other one, which is even harder to spot and resist, is how the logic of modernity emanating from Western institutions became the blueprint for thinking about politics (political technology of individuals). What Foucault called modern rationality appropriates its totality (universal principles) and also its individual (individual harm as defined by international agreements and conventions). The more individuals' rights are violated, the more the totality calls for judgment. However, Foucault (1988) does not mention explicitly in "The Political Technology of Individuals" how modern rationality is actually also a Western rationality, which has been adopted by the rest, often in conflict with the history and social and economic dynamics of the society. It is a very complex articulation of power that the human rights discourses of non-Western countries resist, adopt, and translate.

In another essay published in the bulletin of IHD, Ercan Kanar (1993, p. 34) asks for example, "How are you planning to go to further levels if you don't win the people on the street, give them trust, and show a principled decisiveness?" Thus, in connection with the point made earlier about "creating a culture of human rights," the adoption of the Yokohama Declaration would help the IHD to a principled decisiveness, a claim for neutrality, and would allow it to bring citizens to a consciousness of human rights. A linear time line of events is, thus, structured from backwardness to development.[18] This narrative of backwardness and human rights as the means to reach further levels is in line with the Matau Mutua's (2001) terminology of Savages/Victims/Saviors which positions human rights NGOs as Saviors. Further levels in this respect, can be reached only if IHD takes a position against the abuses of the armed opposition forces. Only in this way can it show the "principled decisiveness" which is possible in a position of neutrality, that is, by acting against both parties in a conflict, regardless of the circumstances. It is interesting to observe how a radical lawyer like Kanar reaches what is known as the hydraulic model of human rights, that associates more rights with less domination. In this classic linear model of human rights that can be found in human rights textbooks, global salvation and redemption is achieved through human rights. It is again apparent how Foucault's modern rationality operates: total salvation is only possible with individual rights, thus, "free individual, free society." The correlation between an increasing individualization and the reinforcement of totality is also visible in the instant of the individual harm and the utopian ahistorical totality. As the time becomes instantaneous, focuses on the suffering of the victim and the urgency of the protection of rights at an instant, it becomes simultaneously ahistorical and universal. Human rights embody this tension as a modern political discourse, which demands action because of the urgency to stop the suffering, and concurrently demands an absolute belief in its ahistoricity, therefore its unquestionable universal truth. The correlation between the universality claim and the urgency of the harm, to an extent, explains also why the social and economic rights are never seen as *urgently* requiring action, and thus never able to summon a corresponding accepted universal.

The line of arguments Kanar, Isgoren, and others advocated for has been responded to by a more radical branch of IHD, most of whom define themselves as Marxists and even revolutionaries. The first argument against the adoption of AI's position focuses on the word "arbitrary killings" used in the declaration. In one of the responses to Kanar and others, lawyer Levent Tuzel (1994, p. 25) invites them to look at what Yokohama declaration exactly says:

> It is obvious that no one would support arbitrary killings of civilians, torture or kidnappings. What constitutes an arbitrary killing will give rise to further discussions, since it is impossible to have a standard or criteria for this. Forget about declaring support for political actions, it seems it will be impossible to even stay silent for them. I would have accepted the declaration if it was not all violent acts, but only the arbitrary ones that will be criticised by AI, in struggles for rights and class wars. But when AI gives examples from countries like Turkey in this declaration, it is possible to find traces that arbitrariness is considered subjectively for the actions of armed militant organisations.

Tuzel emphasizes the notion of arbitrary since it is set as the standard of acceptability of the violence, according to Amnesty. In a similar manner, another participant in the debate, Ayhan Erkan (1994, p. 24) asks:

> It is not possible to show a single human rights activist, who doesn't raise his voice against arbitrary killings, torture or kidnapping. [...] Why has AI come up with this lapalissade [tautology]? [...] Apart from few criminal psychopaths who are the products of class society, is it possible to imagine someone committing such a crime [arbitrary killings]? Which criteria will decide on what is an arbitrary killing? [...] Imperialists are holding all humanity as hostages with the system of paid slavery [labor markets], and colonialism. What if it is necessary to take some people hostage in order to stand against this taking of the masses as hostage? Are we supposed to say let humanity stay hostage?

These striking lines, which perhaps sound partisan to the ears of the Western human rights activists, clearly oppose the idea of defining an imaginary place built upon the term *neutral*. This is what international law has experienced, particularly in the context of the Geneva Convention (Clapham 2006). The convention underlines the proportionality of means to ends, namely physical suffering inflicted in modern warfare is acceptable as far as the ends it serves and the strategic advantage it brings, are worth it. Talal Asad (2003, p. 117) emphasizes, for example, this point, asking "how can the calculated cruelties of modern battle be reconciled with the modern sensibility regarding pain? Precisely by treating pain as a quantifiable essence." In this respect, the arbitrariness of the violence as the standard of the Yokohama Declaration is an attempt to quantify the killings. As Asad (2003, p. 117) underlines, "Only necessary punishment of noncombatants should be used. But given the aim of ultimate victory the notion of "military necessity" can be extended indefinitely. Any measure that is intended as a contribution to that aim, no matter how much suffering it creates, may be justified in terms of military necessity." In a similar manner, the violence of the armed organizations would fall into the category of arbitrary since there cannot be any justification in the military or public sense that can justify the killing. Various commentators in the Yokohama debates warned of the danger of establishing a category of killings that can cover only the atrocities of the armed groups, as a consequence of the structure of these conflicts.

These justifications are in close relation to the technological advancement of the parties. Insurgent groups use relatively less controllable and less precise weapons compared to technologically advanced states:

> There is no question that technological asymmetry erodes the persuasiveness of the "all bound by the same rules" idea. It should not be surprising that forces with vastly superior arms and intelligence capacity are held to a higher standard in the court of world public opinion than their adversaries. As persuasion, the law in force has indeed become a sliding scale. (Kennedy 2006, p. 139)

Particularly because of these technological advances, the division of violence as arbitrary and deliberate produces, as commentators in IHD highlight, an asymmetry also in the legitimation of the act in public and international law. Kennedy (2006, p. 139) adds that "by internalizing human rights and humanitarian law, you will make your force interoperable with international coalitions, suitable for international peacekeeping missions. […] Most importantly, we insisted, humanitarian law will make your military more effective—will make your use of force something you can sustain and proudly stand behind." This indicates another basis of the arguments of the party opposing the Yokohama declaration in IHD, which states that such an adoption would lead to positioning *with* the state. Furthermore, formation of such a category by Amnesty would also serve to categorize killing as civilized (which has an objective, a detailed and deliberate plan that can be seen by the international law) or barbarian (i.e. arbitrary and aimed at terrorizing the society) (Mbembe 2003).

Another important critique of the first position is related to the aims of the association, and more generally to the meaning of the human rights struggle. Levent Tüzel (1994, p. 25) continues in the same article:

> Originally it was declared that the Association (IHD) was founded against the violations of rights by the state, that other rights violations were subject to trials by state courts, and security institutions were already fighting against those crimes; that is why there was no need for the association to condemn every instance of violence. […] In recent years, a new understanding of human rights, which takes sides with the "free individual and free society" is coming to prevail in our headquarters. In this understanding, everything is explained by *human rightsism* and it is argued that the utopic end of a free society is no longer relevant. A kind of denial of class society without denying the classes.

Tuzel argues that the aim of IHD should be documenting the violations of the state since it is these violations that are not documented, not visible, or not being taken to the courts. According to him, the aim of IHD has always been to use international treaties and pressure or public opinion to counter abuse of power by state. What now makes IHD responsible for the violations of other armed groups? This is a significant question particularly in the context of a claim of neutrality. As we have seen, one part of the discussion highlighted the importance of neutrality since it is also a way to convince and win the trust of ordinary people and therefore to foster a human right culture among citizens. This is only possible by what Tuzel later in the article calls "taking sides with the state." This example shows that to make the claim of neutrality is actually to get into a negotiation about the meaning of human rights struggle for public acceptance of the association and the human rights culture *in general.* In this sense for Tuzel, there is a danger of having an NGO "taking sides with the state": if they condemn the armed groups with human rights language, this would eventually legitimize the state itself. It would also mean that the state is taking sides with the respectable human rights discourses, next to the respected NGO. This is a concession for Tuzel, since those armed groups are already chased by the state forces, and any abuse they have committed is already documented by state institutions. Moreover, courts are also prosecuting them according to the criminal law of the state, mostly with the aggravated sentences attached to terrorism charges.[19] Therefore, on the basis of this argument, the rationale behind the human rights NGOs that aim to protect individual rights against the State cannot be imported to the violations by armed groups. This argument demonstrates that the claim of neutrality is actually the very politics of rights struggles. Neutrality becomes the term for the de-politicization of this very political relationship. In this particular context, neutrality means also to make the language of human rights available to states and thus to support their claims to legitimacy for their actions in the public and international arena.

Ayhan Erkin (1994, p. 24) also points in the same direction as Tuzel:

> The world crushed socialism, now, it seems, the target is revolutionary movements in the less developed countries. [...] But how come Yokohama becomes an issue in the IHD? Here is why: 1) Since the human rights struggle is not being considered with a class perspective, which classes AI represents is obscure. 2) Not being able to look with the lens of class resonates with a 'beyond class' approach. The AI's approach that says, "we are against both this and that" goes together with the worry about falling into double standards. And eventually, the state and state supporting media's side prevails. 3)

> In the same way as the private law of bourgeoisie hides the property relations of the bourgeoisie, international norms and agreements hide the reign of the imperialists.

The claim of universality (beyond classes) and neutrality of human rights discourses hides the conflictual character of human rights behind the clarity of meaning of neutrality. As Fitzpatrick (2014, p. 125) states, human rights "claim explicitly, and foundationally, an operative universality whilst being, and inevitably being, a particularity." The universality and the particularity of human rights are interconnected by being ahistorical in universal principles but always urgent in the need to intervene. The argument Ayhan Erkin develops here is against the mainstream lexicon on human rights that "speak only of the violation itself"; in other words, uncovering instances of violation instead of structural underpinnings of the violent situation.

In an article from 1994, Özcan Sapan (p. 22), another activist lawyer from IHD, in relation to Yokohama declaration, asks the question,

> Does Amnesty International think they are the *Institute of Standardisation of Human Behaviours* that decides what fits to it and what doesn't? [...] AI is interested not in the processes through which human becomes a victim, but the notion of victim itself. It can be said that it highlights the violence of opposition. [...] It equates the violence of a local group with that of the State. [...] If we push the reading of the Yokohama declaration a bit more, we face with this notion that is not directly in the text: Terrorist! [...] Although it is not mentioned in the text, Amnesty International says 'there is no just war', and in this way it closes its eyes to institutions of the state like the judiciary, the police, interrogation centers, and prisons that take the shape of headquarters of dissuasion for those in opposition. It misses the fact that revolutionary violence is in the form of a self-defense against the state violence, although it seems to restrict itself with arbitrary violence for now.

The claim of neutrality and exclusive emphasis on the suffering caused by violations by the human rights lawyer inevitably avoids a more systematic critique. The use of violence becomes the only yardstick giving meanings to the political. This moving away from a structural critique, according to Perugini and Gordon (2015, p. 45), manifests itself as, "the constitution of the violation as a case and the appeal to the violating state to correct the violation, constitution of the violation as a routine to be administered in the human rights standards and reduction of structural colonial violence to a series of symptoms." Özcan Sapan foresees the fact that this reduction would eventually create the use of the term terrorist for the combatants of armed movements.

Between the Universal and the Particular

While considering the particularities of the Turkish context, it is interesting that both parties in these discussions turn to writings of Marx in order to justify their arguments. One can even say that peculiarly, the discussion over human rights and violence is translated into a discussion over different Marxist interpretations throughout Yokohama debate, since both parties are able to translate their arguments into a Marxist lexicon.

As some of the actors complain, the debate actually turns to a discussion over utopias, and how to reach them. If human rights discourses claim to solve all problems of the world, they have to widen their territory of influence, and this is how ultimately the ethics of violence takes the place of the politics of violence. This is what Jacques Rancière discusses in his article "The Ethical Turn of Aesthetics and Politics" (2009). For Rancière, ethical turn "signifies the constitution of an indistinct sphere" which is the elimination of the distinction that separates moral judgments and politics; or, in other words, the elimination of the distinction between "*what is* and *what ought to be*." Rancière refers to it as the distinction of fact and law. This creates, according to Rancière, the inclusion of "all forms of discourse and practice beneath the same indistinct point of view." For Rancière (2009) the ethical turn is also the conjunction of two phenomena: "On the one hand, the instance of judgment, which evaluates and decides, finds itself humbled by the compelling power of the law. On the other, the radicality of this law, which leaves no alternative, equates to the simple constraint of an order of things." In parallel with what Foucault called the modern rationality that correlates more individual rights (i.e. more instantaneous, particularly in this context by focusing on the urgency of reacting to bodily violence) with founding of a community (humanity, nation), Rancière also underlines the moment of instantaneous judgment and the universal law. After the ethical turn, the moment of judgment becomes more instantaneous, and in this way, supports the totality, the law, that informs the judgment (and vice versa). Turning the rights violation into instantaneous bodily violence leaves less chance for alternatives, since it eventually takes its justification from the unquestionable universal law that it claims to reflect. This eventually leads to the labeling (with labels such as terrorist) of those who are not within the reach of its universals, its law. As the human rights discourses expand the kinds of problems they can solve and consequently their reach, being outside of that border becomes even more dreadful, since the universal law that informs the discourse is even more absolute (in this case "you shall not kill").

The discussions in the IHD of Turkey during 1990s carry the legacy of the line that has been inherited from the revolutionaries and the left of parliamentary politics in the Turkish political scene of 1970s. That line seems to be translated into thc landscape of human rights discourses: while both parties are appropriating humanitarian approaches to limit the state power, one wants to keep the instance of judgment open to evaluation and decision by considering many different factors, and other calls on human rights law to solve "many problems of the world." The Yokohama declaration shows how human rights discourses expand their influence over politics. As Rancière (2004) states: "if those who suffer inhuman repression are unable to enact human rights that are their last recourse, then somebody else has to inherit their rights in order to enact them in their place." If this argument is considered in parallel with the claim of neutrality, the place of the neutral always belongs to an outside. This outside is a troublesome place, in which one has to look from the point of view of the victim. The neutral is in the outside, therefore, the adoption of AI's position, simultaneously demands human rights activists to be outside the history they are part of, social and economic relations they are part of, inequalities they observe, and their ideas over the sources of violations. The neutrality claim inevitably demands of activists alienation from themselves. If IHL provides justification for Western states to "bring democracy" in the form of military interventions, concurrently it demands that human rights activists, in the rest of the world, step out of their own history that shaped their identity.[20]

Samuel Moyn (2012) calls human rights "the minimalist utopia of antipolitics" in the times of its breakthrough, the late 1970s. In a similar manner, Jacques Rancière (2004, p. 307) summarizes this dilemma neatly: "When [rights] are of no use, you do the same as charitable people do with their old clothes. You give them to the poor. These rights that appear to be useless in their place are sent abroad, along with medicine and clothes, to people deprived of medicine, clothes, and rights. [...] They become humanitarian rights, the rights of those who cannot enact them." The debates over the adoption of Yokohama declaration in the IHD show that the picture is more nuanced than this. Receivers of the human rights discourses engage with them, transform them, and use them in different ways than their original intention. The poor, or those who need the protection of their basic rights, are not as passive as the uppercase human rights discourses imagine them. The debates in the IHD didn't end up with the adoption of AI's position but the contrary, IHD members refused to implement this position in their 1992 and 1994 meetings. In the same way, human rights discourses are strangled with the absolute law, that reflects the universals of the rulers, they also can affect those universals, by taking legitimacy from field work and risks, they can hold their positions, their past, and their respective ideologies, and consequently disrupt the moment of judgment. The past of the human rights defenders' shared value systems and their imagined universals are sometimes not easy bedfellows, and self-coherence is possible only with a critical interrogation of the given value systems. This indicates not the end of human rights, but many lives of human rights discourse.

Conclusion

In her book *In Defence of the Terror* Sophie Wahnich (2012, p. 48) asks "how could the agents of a public vengeance that led to the spilling of blood claim the sentiment of humanity?" She analyzes September Massacres during the French Revolution and highlights a conflict over human sentiments, between the sentiments of natural humanity and political humanity, which also determined the political camps. One of these sentiments is (p. 52)

> committed to saving bodies indifferently (those of friends, enemies, accomplices, traitors, slaves) so as not to injure its sentiment of natural humanity, was attached above all to the life of each human being *as such*, while other was attached to preserving the meaning a person wishes to give to life, to the common wellbeing.

If one of these sentiments that is driven by one set of universals is dedicated to saving bare lives, the other sentiment is dedicated to protecting mutual liberty. Humanity thus is not any more a natural sentiment but a political one, not a descriptive one but a prescriptive one. Although not as sharp as this example, the debates in IHD is one of those times in which these two sentiments find themselves in a conflictual position. While one party demands an understanding of human rights taking into consideration the violation and victims, and aims to dream of a utopia which is born out of these individual rights, the other sees it as one of many struggles, and tries to combine those different struggles with the aim of mutual liberty. The ironic part in this picture is the way that the moral authority of human rights discourses that is gained through a history of protection of minorities and individuals from state violence is easily converted to a violence/non-violence—victims/perpetrators question. After the ethical turn, since the harm is reduced to that of instantaneous bodily harm, it is difficult to separate the law from the fact. The political motives behind the judgment are indistinguishable from the ethical ones, which are absolute. Revolutionary human rights defenders complicate this established understanding of rights and utopia, by making visible the politics behind it, only by resisting the lure of acceptable narratives, via unexpected translations of revolutionary lexicon to human rights discourses.

Notes

1. Most of the work of the association and its structure can be seen from http://en.ihd.org.tr/. Unfortunately, the bulletins that are the main material of this chapter are not digitalized and published only in Turkish. All translations in this chapter are mine.
2. For more information on the results of this meeting, see Amnesty International Report. 1992. Available at: https://www.amnesty.org/en/documents/pol10/0001/1992/en/.
3. Steven L. Robins (2008, p. 2), in the South African context focusing on the struggle between the emancipatory politics and rights speech over the same period of time, states that "[r]adical keywords and concepts such as socialism, national liberation, class struggle, people's revolution, resistance to racial capitalism and colonialism-of-a-special type, were replaced with tamer words such as rights, citizenship, liberal democracy, nation-building, transformation, black economic empowerment (BEE) and so on."
4. Some of the seminal works are Costas Douzinas (2007), *Human Rights and Empire: The Political Philosophy of Cosmopolitanism,* Samuel Moyns (2012), *The Last Utopia,* and Wendy Brown (1995) *States of Injury.*
5. Some relevant examples of literature on the human rights and the Third World are Upendra Baxi (2006) *The Future of Human Rights,* José-Manuel Barreto (2013) *Human Rights from a Third World Perspective: Critique, History and International Law,* Martti Koskenniemi, "Colonization of the 'Indies': The Origin of International Law?" in *La idea de América en el Pensamiento Ius Internacionalista del Siglo XXI,* ed. Yolanda Gamarra

(Zaragoza: Institución Fernando el Católico, 2010) and "Empire and International Law: The Real Spanish Contribution," *University of Toronto Law Journal* 61 (2011), and also Arturo Escobar, "Imperial Globality and Anti-Globalisation Movements," *Third World Quarterly* 25 (2004): 210.

6. Statute of Amnesty International is amended by the 20th International Council meeting in Yokohama, Japan, August 31–September 7, 1991, and defined a *mandate* that is for either the promotion of certain goals or opposition to certain practices. The points raised in this press release found place in the *mandate* of AI.
7. The number is approximate and taken from the Parliamentary Research Committee Report, Cilt 2, September 2012. See also Info-Turk, Monthly Bulletin, October 1988, and Kayasu v Turkey, no. 64119/00, ECHR 2008.
8. For information about hunger strikes before held by Kurdish independence movement particularly. See: Bargu, B. (2014). *Stave and Immolate*, Colombia Unıversity Press, New York.
9. For a full list of hunger strikes and death fasts in this period, Ertugrul Mavioglu Asılmayip da Beslenenler: Bir Eylül Hesaplaşması [Those Who Were Not Hanged but Fed: Settling Accounts with September 12]. Istanbul: Babil Yayinları, 2004. And Bargu, B. (2014). *Stave and Immolate*, Colombia Unıversity Press, New York.
10. Lois Whitman (1989, p. 114) states "The group has been indicted ten times, charged with violations of the Associations Law because of its press conferences, statements and conferences. (...) In 1987, for example, a case was brought against 18 TAYAD directors in connection with a demonstration in front of Sagmalcilar Prison."
11. This is the expression used by Hüsnü Öndül, Akademi Notları, presented in the Human Rights Academy Diyarbakır Branch seminars, 2016. Available at: http://www.ihd.org.tr/akademi-egitim-notlari-dort-insan-haklari-konusu/. Accessed Dec 18, 2017.
12. Thousands of people gathered for IHD's first meetings in Istanbul, Diyarbakir and Izmir, and this mobilization was directed toward the goals of ending torture, calling for a general political amnesty and the abolition of death penalty (IHD. 2008). For more information see "History of Human Rights Association (IHD)." Available at: http://en.ihd.org.tr/index.php/2008/12/08/history-of-human-rights-association-ihd/. Accessed Dec 18, 2017.
13. The bulletin has been published whenever possible, commonly two or more each year. Also, there was a special edition for Yokohama debates in this period.
14. Drawing borders of 'Western human rights discourses' is always difficult, given that, as this chapter tries to show, there is a constant translation and

(re)appropriation of human rights discourses between actors and institutions. I follow definition and descriptions of José-Manuel Barreto (2013). He highlights "the Eurocentric theory of human rights presents itself as objective and universal and, while it assumes exclusive authority and legitimacy, it condemns a Third World approach to impossibility or silence. [...] This predisposition is accompanied by a tendency to give a notorious and unfair weight to the events occurring in Europe. This is the case in Hegel's philosophical notion of "universal history," from which Asia, Africa and the Americas are excluded. By framing human rights in conceptions of history based exclusively on European milestones the theory of rights remains within a Eurocentric horizon of understanding. Having been born out of the experience of bourgeois revolutions, European theories of human rights deal mainly with relations between state and society, or between governments and individuals, putting aside the problematic of interactions between empires and colonies." In this sense, what 'Western' corresponds is not necessarily geographical, but about narrations of history, universals and eventually power.

15. First publication of the Yokohama Declaration was in the IHD Bülteni (Bulletin of Human Rights Association). 1993. Sayı 49–50.
16. Kanar makes reference to a general dogmatism of the left, rather than any particular one.
17. Bulletin of Human Rights Association, 1994, pp. 56–57.
18. Arturo Escobar (2011) in *Encountering Development*, on the notion of development underlines, "Perhaps no other idea has been so insidious, no other idea gone so unchallenged."
19. How to define the actions of armed groups (human rights abuses, or breaches of local or international criminal law) is an important and relevant discussion (Dudai and Mcevoy 2012).
20. For an application of how the ethical turn has been reflected to transitional justice processes see Robert Meister (2011).

References

Amnesty International Press Release. 1991. Though Stand Against Killings, Hostage-Taking by Violent Groups, ORG 50/14/91, Sep 7.

Amnesty International Report. 1992. London: Amnesty International Publications.

Asad, Talal. 2003. *Formations of the Secular: Christianity, Islam, Modernism.* Stanford: Stanford University Press.

Baehr, Peter R. 1994. Amnesty International and Its Self Imposed Limited Mandate. *Netherlands Quarterly of Human Rights* 12 (1): 5–21. https://doi.org/10.1177/016934419401200102.

Barbara Ann Rieffer-Flanagan. (2009). Is Neutral Humanitarianism Dead? Red Cross Neutrality: Walking the Tightrope of Neutral Humanitarianism. *Human Rights Quarterly* 31 (4): 888–915. https://muse.jhu.edu/. Accessed 19 June 2018.

Bargu, Banu. 2014. *Stave and Immolate*. New York: Colombia University Press.

Barreto, José-Manuel, ed. 2013. *Human Rights from a Third World Perspective : Critique, History and International Law*. Newcastle-upon-Tyne: Cambridge Scholars Publishing.

Baxi, Upendra. 2006. *The Future of Human Rights*. New Delhi: Oxford University Press.

Brown, Wendy. 1995. *States of Injury: Power and Freedom in Late Modernity*. Princeton: Princeton University Press.

Clapham, Andrew. 2006. Human Rights Obligations of Non-State Actors in Conflict Situations. *International Review of the Red Cross* 88 (863): 491–523.

Douzinas, Costas. 2007. *Human Rights and Empire. The Political Philosophy of Cosmopolitanism*. Abingdon: Routledge-Cavendish.

Dudai, Ron, and Kieran McEvoy. 2012. Thinking Critically About Armed Groups and Human Rights Praxis. *Journal of Human Rights Practice* 4 (1): 1–29. https://doi.org/10.1093/jhuman/hus014.

Erkan, Ayhan. 1994. Yokohama Bildirgesi. *IHD Bülteni*, Sayı 53.

Escobar, Arturo. 2004. Imperial Globality and Anti-Globalisation Movements. *Third World Quarterly* 25 (1): 207–230.

———. 2011. *Encountering Development: The Making and Unmaking of the Third World*. Princeton: Princeton University Press.

Fitzpatrick, Peter. 2014. The Revolutionary Past: Decolonizing Law and Human Rights. *International Studies in Phenomenology and Philosophy* 2 (1): 117–133.

Foucault, Michel. 1988. The Political Technology of Individuals. In *Technologies of the Self: A Seminar with Michel Foucault*, ed. Luther H. Martin, Huck Gutman, and Patrick H. Hutton, 145–162. London: Tavistock Publications.

Hopgood, Stephen. 2013. *The End Times of Human Rights*. Ithaca: Cornell University Press.

Insan Hakları Derneği. 1993. Yokohama Bildirgesi. *IHD Bülteni*, Sayı 49–50.

İşlegen, Yeşim. 1993. Yokohama Bildirgesi Üzerine. *IHD Bülteni*, Sayı 49–50.

Kanar, Ercan. 1993. Uluslararası Af Örgütünün 1991 Yokohama Bildirgesinin Düşündürdükleri. *IHD Bülteni*, Sayı 49–50.

———. 1994. Sorun tek başına Yokohama bildirgesi mi, yoksa insan hakları mücadelesinin uzun erekli kendine özgü politikalarının gerekliliği sorunu mu? *IHD Bülteni*, Sayı 56–57.

———. 1997. Insan Haklari Mucadelesinde Insan Haklari Dernegi, Insan Haklari Yazilari. *Ozel Sayi* 1: 3–15.

Kennedy, David. 2006. *Of War and Law*. Princeton: Princeton Press.

Kogod Goldman, R. 1993. International Humanitarian Law: Americas Watch's Experience in Monitoring Internal Armed Conflicts. *American University Journal of International Law and Policy* 9 (1): 49–94.

Koskenniemi, Martti. 2010. Colonization of the 'Indies': The Origin of International Law? In *La idea de América en el Pensamiento Ius Internacionalista del Siglo XXI*, ed. Yolanda Gamarra. Zaragoza: Institución Fernando el Católico.

———. 2011. Empire and International Law: The Real Spanish Contribution. *University of Toronto Law Journal* 61: 1–36.

Mavioglu, Ertugrul. 2014. *Asılmayip da Beslenenler: Bir Eylül Hesaplaşması*. Babil Yayinları: Istanbul.

Mbembé, J.-A. 2003. Necropolitics. Trans. Libby Meintjes. *Public Culture* 15 (1): 11–40 https://muse.jhu.edu/. Accessed 3 Apr 2018.

Meister, Robert. 2011. *After Evil: A Politics of Human Rights*. New York: Colombia University Press.

Moyn, Samuel. 2012. *The Last Utopia*. Cambridge: Belknap Press/Harvard University Press.

Mutua, Makau W. 2001. Savages, Victims, and Saviors: The Metaphor of Human Rights. *Harvard International Law Review* 42 (1): 201–245.

Öndül, Hüsnü. 2017. Akademi Eğitim Notları: Dört İnsan Hakları Konusu. http://www.ihd.org.tr/akademi-egitim-notlari-dort-insan-haklari-konusu/. Last accessed 30 Jan.

Perugini, Nicola, and Neve Gordon. 2015. *The Human Right to Dominate*. New York: Oxford University Press.

Rancière, Jacques. 2004. Who Is the Subject of the Rights of Man? *South Atlantic Quarterly Spring/Summer* 103 (2–3): 297–310. https://doi.org/10.1215/00382876-103-2-3-297.

———. 2006. The Ethical Turn of Aesthetics and Politics. *Critical Horizons* 7 (1): 1–20.

———. 2009. *Aesthetics and Its Discontents*. London: Polity.

Robins, Steven L. 2008. *From Revolution to Rights in South Africa*. South Africa: University of KwaZulu-Natal Press.

Sapan, Özcan. 1994. Yokohama Bildirisi İnsan Hakları Kavramı ve Sol içi Şiddet. *IHD Bülteni*, Sayı 54–55.

Sokhi-Bulley, Bal. 2016. *Governing (Through) Rights*. Oxford: Hart Publishing.

TBMM. 2012. Parliamentary Research Committee Report. Cilt 2.

Tüzel, Levent. 1994. Uluslararaı Af Örgütü – Yokohama birdirisi ve İHD. *IHD Bülteni*, Sayı 53.

Wahnich, Sophie. 2012. *In Defence of the Terror, Liberty or Death in the French Revolution*. Trans. D.Fernbach. London: Verso.

Whitman, Lois. 1989. *Paying the Price: Freedom of Expression in Turkey*. New York: International Freedom to Publish Committee of the Association of the American Publishers.

PART II

Overcoming the Frontiers of Discrimination and Structural Violence: Intersectional Struggles of Human Rights from Below and Transformations of Political Space

CHAPTER 6

Child Prisoners, Human Rights, and Human Rights Activism: Beyond 'Emergency' and 'Exceptionality'—An Australian Case Study

Judith Bessant and Rob Watts

Introduction: Youth Justice and Human Rights

In 2006 when the Victorian Parliament passed the Charter of Human Rights and Responsibilities Act 2006, Victoria became the first and only major jurisdiction in Australia to enact a statutory 'bill of rights'.[1] This was a significant moment given that Australia, even though a signatory to the International Covenant on Civil and Political Rights (1966), remains unencumbered by a national bill of rights.

That Charter faced a very severe test in the last months of 2016 and the first months of 2017. After years of complaints about abuse and brutality by staff, young inmates in Victoria's youth justice system rioted in Victoria's Parkville Youth Justice Centre. Claiming that this was a surprise and an 'emergency', the government ordered heavily armed police to intervene using CS gas and batons to subdue the children. The Andrews

J. Bessant (✉) • R. Watts
RMIT University, Melbourne, VIC, Australia
e-mail: judith.bessant@rmit.edu.au; rob.watts@rmit.edu.au

G. Blouin-Genest et al. (eds.), *Human Rights as Battlefields*, Human Rights Interventions,
https://doi.org/10.1007/978-3-319-91770-2_6

government claiming it faced an emergency indicated that the offending children would be transferred to an adult prison. The Minister for Children, Jenny Mikakos, was reported as saying, 'Enough is enough, these perpetrators of this damage will face serious consequences' (Houston et al. 2017). A number of children including indigenous children, and many of them on remand, were removed to Barwon, a high security adult prison where they were held for several months in many cases in solitary confinement for up to 23 hours a day (Marks 2017). This was not an isolated situation either in Australia or internationally nor was this response which breached many international children's rights conventions all that unusual (Cunneen et al. 2016; Bessant 2014a, b, pp. 597–612).[2]

A network of community groups reacted swiftly. The network included faith-based groups like the Brigidine Order of nuns, indigenous rights groups like the Victorian Aboriginal Legal Services, and well-resourced human rights advocates like the Human Rights Legal Center. Hugh de Kretser, the executive director of the Human Rights Law Centre, said the Government's claim that it had few choices when dealing with an 'emergency' like this had always had other options: 'It defied belief that the only place the Victorian Government could find to house some 12, 15, at its most 28 children … was a unit within the maximum security adult Barwon Prison' (Young 2017).

Drawing on some formidable legal experience and resources, the network briefed two of Australia's leading human rights lawyers and mounted two successful cases in Victoria's Supreme Court. Twice the Victorian Supreme Court ordered the release of the boys. On the first occasion, on 21 December 2016 the Supreme Court ordered the release of the boys. The government, without waiting to appeal the decision, sidestepped the Court's ruling by simply reclassifying the unit in Barwon Prison as a 'Youth Justice Centre'. On the second occasion, on 11 May 2017, Victoria's Supreme Court Justice John Dixon found that transferring and holding teenagers in an adult prison was contrary to section 38(1) of the Victoria's Human Rights Charter. As the judge explained: 'The impact of [Barwon Prisons] built environment on youths who are children detained there was, and remains immutably that of a maximum-security adult jail' (Younger 2017). This result, it seemed, was a landmark case which used the Victorian Charter to force the government to remove the children from Barwon prison.

As we will argue here, this case reveals the potential for well-resourced community and civil society groups to intervene and begin to rebalance the unequal power relations that currently define the relations between many states, including liberal-democratic states, and their citizens. This is especially the case for children who are best understood as 'denizens' rather than 'citizens'.

Most, if not all young Australians lack basic legal protections, entitlements, and civic rights associated with being a citizen that most other citizens have long been taken-for-granted.

Apart from the legal age of voting, which is generally 18, the right to participate in other democratic practices or basic rights to freedom of expression, of association, and to assembly or the right to privacy are all restricted on an age-based discrimination.

In this respect, children and young people in Australia experience an ambiguous, if not paradoxical socio-legal status (Bessant and Watts 2017, pp. 3–23). As 'denizens' children and young people (aged 12–25) are also one of the most governed groups subjected to many kinds of prohibitions on activities citizens typically can engage without restriction.

They are also subject to extreme institutional and legally sanctioned discrimination justified on the grounds that it is in their 'best interest'. It is currently lawful, for example, for Australian employers to discriminate against 16 to 21 year olds on the basis of age by paying them lower wages than other employees for work of equal value (in the form of the 'youth wag'). This happens in the context of legislation that renders age-based discrimination unlawful for any other citizens. In some municipal and state jurisdictions, for example, children and young people are also subject to police move-on powers and curfews (Morgan 2007, pp. 11–19). Added to this are practices that deem certain quasi-public spaces like some public university campuses as children free and shopping centers and certain other public spaces to be 'youth free' zones, or at least zones where young people are tightly managed. These practices are typically justified by restrictive public insurance liability provisions that children and young people ought to be protected from certain kinds of information and/or that they disrupt normal business. Young people are also largely excluded from knowledge-making about themselves with the requirement for parental or guardian consent for their participation in research. Finally, many young people and children continue to be subject to forms of parental 'discipline' or punishment, which if other citizens were subjected to, would constitute criminal assault.

While all of this may be known or acknowledged, it is also considered by many adult Australians to be normal and proper, even desirable. This judgment rests on long-standing assumptions and prejudices about certain 'natural' deficits that are assumed to characterize children and young, deficiencies usually ascribed to their position in biological and social life-cycle stages, that mean children and young people are naturally 'dependents'. These ideas play a key role in ensuring that young Australians continue to be subject to prejudicial and unfair treatment.

This case raises a number of significant issues. One issue is about the extent to which states take their responsibility to uphold and protect human rights of vulnerable groups like children and young people seriously. As this chapter argues, successive Victorian governments had accepted as normal, a pattern of official neglect and abuse of children and young people in its statutory youth justice system. This has been done persistently and with little regard for the human rights of children and young people. Second, it raises the question of how far and how effectively civil society organizations and activists can go in undoing often deeply unequal power relations between, in this case, a vulnerable group of children, and a state intent on using its sovereign power to the fullest effect. As we will argue, this case offers some cause for limited optimism. Thirdly, however, and most fundamentally, the case points to some problems about the legitimacy of the state and its legal system that arise in a liberal-democratic polity that *ostensibly* operates according to rule of law principles.

As we demonstrate in this chapter, what initially looks to be a contest between a government committed to tough 'law 'n order' using legalist techniques to defend its response, and human rights activists concerned with promoting the human rights of young inmates, opens up some serious and intractable problems.

We begin by describing the circumstances in the decade before several major 'riots' or protests staged by young inmates in the Parkville Youth Justice Centre in 2016–17. We document how the Victorian Andrews government sought to solve the emergency by transferring 16 children to a unit (Grevillea) inside a maximum-security adult prison. We then describe the role played by a network of community-based human rights activists and the political and legal significance of a landmark legal case heard in Victoria's Supreme Court in May 2017 that saw the Supreme Court order the immediate removal of the children from that adult prison. We situate that decision and the successful use made by the Supreme Court of the Victorian Charter in a number of intractable problems to do with the relations between law and the political.

State of Emergency in Juvenile Justice, 2016–17

What the Andrews government described as an 'emergency' ostensibly began over two nights on 13–14 November 2016 (Gough and Dmytryshchak 2016). About 40 inmates were involved in two days of rioting at the Parkville Youth Justice Centre reportedly damaging property and setting off the center's fire alarms. Heavily armed riot police backed by a dog squad overcame the inmates. The government's claim to have been taken by surprise cannot be taken seriously. There had been a series of 'incidents' running back through 2016 including a serious riot in March 2016.

There was no 'sudden emergency' but rather an enduring pattern of abuse and neglect in a slowly crumbling system that had targeted hundreds of vulnerable children. Evidence that Victoria's juvenile justice system was in trouble had been apparent for decades. The Victorian state government, for example, was repeatedly informed by the state Ombudsman of its serious concerns for over a decade. One Ombudsman (Dr. Barry Perry) commented extensively in his 2002 annual report on how he had verified allegations of staff trafficking drugs and mistreating young people (Victorian Ombuds 2002). In 2004, his successor George Brouwer, reported on cases of young inmates being injured by staff during incidents at one youth justice center (Victorian Ombuds 2004). In 2010, Brouwer reported that the conditions in Victoria's juvenile justice facilities were appalling and unacceptable on a number of grounds (Victorian Ombudsman 2010, pp. 3–6). The problems included the design and location of the Precinct which he judged inappropriate for a custodial facility housing vulnerable children. His report highlighted the dirty, unhygienic and ill-maintained conditions 'that reflected poorly on the management and staff at the Precinct' (Victorian Ombuds 2010, p. 6). This was exacerbated by the overcrowding that meant, for example, that mattresses were placed in isolation rooms, with young people having to go to the toilet in buckets. Worse, the number of beds in the facility was not sufficient for the number of either remanded or sentenced detainees that the facility was required to accommodate. As a result, remanded detainees were being unlawfully placed in units with sentenced offenders, which section 22(2) and 23(1) of the *Charter of Human Rights and Responsibilities 2006* and section 482(1)(c) of the *Children, Youth and Families Act 2005* prohibited.

That report also confirmed various allegations by inmates of systemic abuse and violence directed at them. The Ombudsman found that staff had incited physical fights between detainees, assaulted detainees, used excessive force during restraints on detainees, introduced contraband into the Precinct, falsified records, stole goods and consumables, and slept during night shift (Victorian Ombuds 2010, p. 9). The Ombudsman concluded that while management was aware of the staff misconduct, it failed to take appropriate action:

> In my view, the department's failure to address improper conduct, particularly conduct which impacts on the health and safety of detainees, contravenes the department's statutory obligations and human rights provisions. This shortcoming is compounded, in several instances, by the department's failure to take decisive action when these issues have come to light. (Victorian Ombudsman 2010, pp. 9–10)

A subsequent report by Victoria's Commissioner for Children and Young People (2017) also reported that inmates were routinely placed in solitary confinement. In theory Victoria's *Children, Youth and Families Act 2005* only permitted use of isolation in limited circumstances and never as a form of punishment. The United Nations Special Rapporteur of the Human Rights Council made it clear that the solitary confinement of juveniles—defined as the physical and social isolation of individuals being confined to their cells for 22–24 hours a day—constituted cruel, inhumane, and degrading treatment (Commission for Children and Young People 2017, p. 5). This report however (using data provided by Department of Human Services and Health) indicated that isolation, separation, and lockdown practices in Victorian youth justice facilities, between February 2015 and July 2016 were used on average nearly nine times a day during the primary review period, while during December 2016, the average increased to 42.4 isolations per day. Departmental data indicated many recorded isolations were for short periods of one hour (23%), but also that some children and young people were isolated for weeks at a time. Young people were also denied access to fresh air, exercise, meaningful activities, education, support programs, and visits, sometimes for extended periods.

Finally, the government had been warned as recently as mid-2016 of a serious crisis. The confidential Muir report prepared in May 2016 blamed the March 2016 riots on factors like the overzealous use of 'lockdowns'—where the children. many of whom were on remand and so had not been convicted of any crime, were locked in their cells for very long periods due to endemic staffing problems and due to the inconsistency in practice caused by the lack of permanent, experienced, and competent staff (Mckenzie et al. 2017).

> Unconstrained by a concern for truth, the Andrews Labor government responded by removing children some of whom were on remand awaiting trial, to the Barwon maximum security prison. Premier Andrews said "The behaviour that we have seen at Parkville is completely unacceptable. I am sick ... and the Victorian community is sick of it. Those inmates will be going to adult prison and I make absolutely no apology" (Houston et al. 2017). Minister for Families and Children Jenny Mikakos declared that a 'significant number' of the inmates would be temporarily transferred to an adult prison while the damaged facility was 'strengthened'. The Minister said the centre was no longer 'fit for purpose' because the infrastructure was 'letting us down' and the facility would be redeveloped (ABC News 2016). This action was justified endlessly on the grounds of public safety: 'We took the steps necessary to ensure that the community was kept safe, that our staff was kept safe and the young offenders themselves were kept safe' (Younger 2017). Premier Andrews argued for the primacy of a regard for public safety. There has been some criticism of the Government's decision to relocate those prisoners to that facility but we make no apology for doing that. I don't think you could see a more powerful demonstration of our resolve to keep our staff safe and to keep the community safe than our decision to relocate these offenders who have behaved appallingly to Barwon Prison (Cited in Edwards 2016).

This in turn underscored the use of the idea of emergency. In its initial decisions to send the children to Barwon, the Victorian government published a number of Orders in Council in Victorian Government Gazette S354, which effectively excised the Grevillea Unit from Barwon Prison, and established it as 'a remand centre for emergency accommodations' and 'a youth justice centre for emergency accommodation'.

Important in supplying a semblance of legitimacy was the implicit connection between the official talk of emergency and summary action taken by the government, and the Murdoch tabloid press 'describing' a system out of control and being run by 'young thugs' (Buttler 2016; Buttler and Dowling 2016).[3] Talk by the Opposition emphasized that young criminals were taking advantage of the government's lack of action following previous riots at the center—even though the center was holding a significant number of children on remand who had not faced any court (Roberts 2017). Pointing to the extensive body of evidence of systemic abuse, maltreatment, and neglect cut little ice with the tabloid press which maintained that the Andrews' government needed to stop pussy footing around inmates' rights and take a tough approach 'law 'n order' approach. One major media outlet, for example, argued that:

> [...] while young offenders should be treated differently than adult offenders, a therapeutic health response to youth crime must not take priority over law and order and the protection of the public. (Herald-Sun 2017)

Undeterred by the media-sponsored 'moral panic' a network of community groups reacted quickly in the days after the initial riots and the government's announcement of its response. Awareness of persistent, general, and systemic abuse of children's human rights in systems ostensibly committed to youth justice, played an important part in the response by human rights advocates in Victoria to the Andrew government's claim that an urgent response was needed to deal with an emergency. Groups like the Human Rights Law Center had routinely advocated the idea that young people require clear-sighted and rigorous protection of their human rights (National Children's and Youth Law Center 2007; Copeland 2004, pp. 40–45).

Hugh de Kretser, the executive director of the Human Rights Law Centre, for example, made it clear from the start that the Andrews' Government's claim that it had few choices when facing an emergency like this, had always had other options: 'It defied belief that the only place the Victorian Government could find to house some 12, 15, at its most 28 children ...was a unit within the maximum-security adult Barwon Prison' (Young 2017).

On 23 November, the Victorian Aboriginal Legal Service launched a Supreme Court challenge to the Andrews' Government's decision to place some 40 children involved in the Parkville riot in Barwon a maximum-security prison. Wayne Muir, chief executive of the service explained this decision saying his staff received 'phone calls from panicked children who were about to board the prison transfer bus on Monday, saying they were afraid of being sent to Barwon' (Edwards 2016).

The legal campaign action taken against the Victorian government drew together a coalition of highly talented and experienced people working in a network of community organizations. Key figures in this network could point to decades of activism, campaigning, and the use of litigation to protect the human rights of asylum seekers, women, young people, and indigenous people. The network included faith-based groups like the Brigidine Order, indigenous rights groups like the Victorian Aboriginal Legal Services and well-resourced human rights advocates like the Human Rights Legal Center. Drawing on some formidable legal resources, the network mounted two court cases in Victoria's Supreme Court, briefing two of Australia's leading human rights lawyers.

Because some of the children removed to Barwon were Aboriginal children, the Victorian Aboriginal Legal Services (VALS) undertook to mount the first Supreme Court action challenging the legality of detaining children in Barwon prison. VALS is an independent Aboriginal community-controlled organization operating across Victoria, providing community justice services and legal practice services to the Victorian Aboriginal community. It has a long record of providing culturally competent services and for highlighting the appallingly disproportionate rates of criminal conviction and imprisonment affecting indigenous Australians. The Aboriginal Legal Service movement had its origins in growing anger about police harassment of Aborigines living in the Sydney suburb of Redfern in the late 1960s.

A group of activists including Paul Coe, Isobel Coe, Gary Williams, Gary Foley and Tony Coorey gathered enough evidence to persuade Hal Wootten, then Dean of Law at the University of New South Wales, to assist them in setting up the Aboriginal Legal Service of New South Wales in October 1970. In Victoria soon after, activists from the Aborigines' Advancement League working with Melbourne and Monash University law students and academics helped to establish the Victorian Legal Service in June, drawing on the pro-bono services of over 100 lawyers (Faine 1993, pp. 24–6). These law students were committed to human rights in general and aboriginal rights in particular and had already established a legal advice service at the Melbourne Citizens Advice Bureau in 1971. Its founders included leading human rights lawyers like Robert Richter QC, Ron Merkel QC and Ron Castan QC—who played a major role in the Mabo case that confirmed the existence of aboriginal land rights in Australian law in 1990. VALS made it plain from the start that the fact that children were being kept in solitary confinement for more than 23 hours a day in Barwon was utterly unacceptable. Wayne Muir chief executive of VALS said: 'Putting kids in an adult jail is dangerous.'

The public face of the campaign to get the children out of Barwon was Sr. Brigid Arthur, an 83-year-old Sister of the Brigidine Order who acted as the litigation guardian in the court proceedings. An ironic indicator of the denizen status of the children in Barwon, she had to take on this role because, under Victorian law, a person under 18 years of age (or a 'handicapped person') is not able to initiate legal action: the law required that an adult be appointed under court rules, enabling that person or people to conduct the litigation. The Brigidines had been in Victoria since 1886 engaging in education and social justice. Sr. Brigid Arthur has been a key player in campaigns going back several decades run by various Christian NGOs to support asylum seekers and to promote public discussion about the Australian government's asylum-seeker policies and the abuse of human rights those policies have made possible. She had co-founded the Brigidine Asylum Seeker Project in 2001, a project committed to providing hospitality and practical support for people seeking asylum and to actively network with like-minded individuals and groups who are working for justice for asylum seekers (BASP 2017). She was also a board member of the Asylum Seeker Resource Centre and vice-chairwoman of the Australian Churches Refugee Taskforce. She has also been involved in *Love Makes a Way*, a religious organization that organizes peaceful sit-ins at the offices of prominent politicians to protest asylum-seeker policies. As she made plain in testimony given to the National Inquiry into Children in Detention (2014), she has long been opposed to the detention of children under any circumstances pointing out she had been arrested on a number of occasions during sit-ins at politicians' offices.

The Human Rights Law Centre was also involved from the moment the Victorian government moved a number of aboriginal and non-aboriginal children from Parkville to Barwon Prison. Ruth Barson, the center's director of legal advocacy, declared the center 'would be doing everything we can' to get children released from Barwon. The center established as the first independent, not-for-profit, non-government human rights organization in Australia in January 2006 has been a major site of human rights education advocacy and litigation. It was established by the Public Interest Law Clearing House (Vic) Inc. and the Victorian Council for Civil Liberties with support from leading human rights academics like John Tobin and Lee-Ann Basser, leading law firms like Allens, Arthur Robinson, Blake Dawson Waldron, Mallesons Stephen Jaques, Clayton Utz and Maddocks Lawyers led by key members of the Victorian Bar like Brian Walters SC, Ron Merkel QC, and Michael Pearce SC.

The center used an integrated strategic combination of legal action, advocacy, research and professional development. It can legitimately claim major achievements including running a case to the High Court establishing the constitutional protection of the right to vote, improved access to healthcare for prisoners, human rights training to over 15,000 people and consistently holding Australian governments to account for their human rights obligations on the international stage. It had a special focus on ensuring prisons, youth justice centers, and police cells comply with human rights. It has been well-resourced from its inception. The HRLC has some 19 major law firms providing pro-bono legal support as well as substantial corporate financial support. For the first court hearing, the HRLC briefed Brian Walters QC a leading peace activist, human rights advocate and Greens Party candidate with a long background representing trade unions and environmental activists in court actions. For the second of the two Supreme Court cases, it briefed Dr. Ian Freckelton QC a leading legal scholar with many major law texts to his credit and an extensive and successful pattern of advocating in leading major human rights cases. The success enjoyed by this coalition undoubtedly contributed to the fact that Freckelton, the Human Rights Law Centre, the Victorian Aboriginal Legal Service, Fitzroy Legal Service and barristers Brian Walters QC, Ian Freckelton QC, Matthew Albert, Sarala Fitzgerald and Adam Macbeth were awarded the Tim McCoy award in 2017.

A Human Rights Victory?

In appreciating the significance of this action, it's worth noting that Australia does not have a national bill of rights and that Victoria is the only major Australian government which has one. Yet it also needs to be noted that unlike many other liberal jurisdictions that have introduced significant human rights provisions, the Victorian Charter of Human Rights is relatively weak in this regard.

The Victorian Charter is an act of Parliament which identifies 24 civil and political rights, and declares these rights will be protected. There are, however, a number of unusual features about this Charter. Saunders (2002) identifies three distinguishing features:

- the reliance on a statutory basis for identifying human rights rather than embedding them in a constitution;

- the inability of judges to strike down legislation or to award damages to people whose rights have been breached; and
- the retention by Parliament of the power to ignore, amend, alter, or even abolish the bill of rights.

Neither Victoria's courts nor the Parliament are defined as 'public authorities' and so are *not* required to comply with the Charter. Further as per s 39 of the Charter, no citizen can take action under the Charter to seek remedy if they believe their rights have been abrogated, though they can pursue a remedy using other legislation. Instead this Charter relies on a 'dialogue model' which calls on the government to dialogue with those who believe it is not conforming with the Charter rather than relying on the courts or a body like Victorian Human Rights and Equal Opportunity Commission to declare the legislation, policy, or practice either illegal or non-compliant with the Charter (Evans and Evans 2008).

Finally, the Parliament is required merely to *consider* the impact of all new legislation on those human rights specified in the Charter. This is done by requiring Members of Parliament (MP) or departments drafting legislation, to prepare and table Statements of Compatibility for each new bill introduced into Parliament. This statement is required to establish the effect that the Bill is, or is not compatible with the Charter, accompanied by a statement outlining the ways in which the Bill is, or is not compatible. The Charter, for example, requires in (Part 1 (2) (d)) that 'statements of compatibility with human rights … be prepared in respect of all Bills introduced into Parliament and enabling the Scrutiny of Acts and Regulations Committee to report on such compatibility'. The government has spoken about the 'requirement' that all of the existing array of statutory provisions represented by current Victorian laws and regulations need (as per s 32 of the Charter) to be interpreted as far as possible in ways that are compatible with human rights, international law as well as relevant court judgements. That is, s 32 of the Charter provides that 'so far as it is possible' all legislation must be interpreted in a way that is compatible with human rights, but that notwithstanding this requirement, any legislation that is not compatible with human rights is still valid law.

Here we see a plethora of exceptions defined into law, which have the effect of nullifying any effective protection of human rights.

There is also the matter of the rights of the child. Australia is a signatory to the United Nations Convention on the Rights of the Child (CRC). That Convention (at Article 4) requires States Parties to:

> [...] undertake all appropriate legislative, administrative, and other measures for the implementation of the rights recognized in the present Convention. With regards to economic, social and cultural rights, States Parties shall undertake such measures to the maximum extent of their available resources [...]

Yet, Australia like many other societies has decided not to incorporate the entirety of the United Nations Convention on the Rights of the Child (CRC) into its domestic legislation. This is a legally valid response since the implementation of the CRC is mandatory following ratification; the measures used to implement the Convention are understood to legally fall within each state's discretion. That is, the measures used to implement the Convention are each state's discretion. The UNICEF Innocenti Research Centre (2007) established that, at that time, the Convention on the Rights of the Child had been directly incorporated into national law in two-thirds of the 52 countries covered by the study although it was found that full and direct incorporation of the Convention had taken place in only 3 countries of the 12 examined (Belgium, Norway, and Spain) (Lundy et al. 2013).[4] However, like a number of other jurisdictions, Australian governments have incorporated only a small number of elements of UNCROC like the best interest principle (under Article 3) and the right of the child to be heard (under Article 12).

All this suggests that the human rights activists representing the children who had been relocated into the Barwon prison would face some serious difficulties in using the Charter of Human Rights, a problem conceded in the first major review of the Charter (Young 2015, pp. 117–36).[5]

This seemed to be the case when Judge Dixon rejected the litigant's argument that the government did not have the power to establish a youth justice center at Barwon prison. The Judge also found that the Secretary of Department of Human Services and Health was empowered to transfer persons from one facility to another under s 484 of the Children, Youth and Families Act, and that the government was entitled to exempt a class of persons pursuant to s 8B of *the Control of Weapons* Act (Josev 2017). Finally, and most alarmingly Dixon found that the Secretary of the Department of Human Services was *not* required to accord procedural fairness to two inmates before they were removed to Grevillea (Supreme Court of Victoria 2017).

What became a central issue, however, was whether the litigants could use the *Charter of Human Rights and Responsibilities* 2006 at all. Here the litigants and their lawyers were successful. Judge Dixon accepted the arguments put by the litigants that the Charter was relevant and made this case by relying on the conventional style of legal reasoning favored by Australian legal practitioners within a legal field of practice that has evolved as an Australian version of legal positivism called 'legalism'.

On the face of it, the ethos of Australian law and politics can be characterized as 'legalist' or even 'hyper-legalist' (Inder 2010; Josev 2017). In this sense, Australian 'legalism' is part of a larger number of approaches that include legal positivism, literalism, formalism, textualism, and, in the United States, constructionism. These are traditions that share or promote the idea that the legal judgments of judges are apolitical or value free, or *ought* to be free from 'contamination' by ethical or political considerations. There is a large literature addressing the question of how well, for example, Australian judges conform to the legalist model, where a substantial argument has been made that judges do actually rely on various ethical and political commitments (Sawer 1967; Galligan 1987; Craven 1992; Goldsworthy 2006; Josev 2017).

In the case of 'Certain Children by their litigation guardian Sister Marie Brigid Arthur v Minister for Families and Children & Ors (No. 2)' Judge Dixon used the legalist device of grounding his findings in certain 'jurisdictional facts'. As Dixon noted in his judgment, he relied on a number of High Court definitions of a jurisdictional fact: a '[jurisdictional] fact must exist, objectively, before an administrative jurisdiction to exercise a power is enlivened'. The critical issues with respect to the statutory powers under consideration are firstly what facts, if any, must exist before the power is enlivened. Secondly, the question is to determine who decides whether those facts exist? These issues are resolved partly by 'the proper construction' of the relevant legislation' (ie., an accurate interpretation of the purpose of the relevant legislation). Whether the exercise of a statutory power is conditioned by the existence of certain facts is a question of statutory construction according to 'ordinary principles'—'the proper approach is to look to the text, context and purpose of the statute read as a whole (Supreme Court of Victoria 2017, paragraphs 40–43). It is then up to the Court to determine whether the facts existed at the relevant time and do this by 'finding those facts' in the usual way because these jurisdictional facts must exist before any jurisdiction is enlivened.

Using this mode of legal rationality, Dixon found that the government's decisions did abrogate the human rights of the children. He found the children were held in lockdown for up to 23 hours a day, were handcuffed when released from their cells and had been tear-gassed. Dixon argued these actions were not demonstrably justified as 'reasonable in a free and democratic society based on human dignity, equality and freedom as required by section 7(2) of the Human Rights Charter'. Accordingly, Dixon found that pursuant to ss. 17 and 22(1) and s 38(1) of the Human Rights Charter, the government acted unlawfully in classifying Grevillea as a youth facility and transferring children into that facility, or exposing them to tear gas and the use of batons.

These determinations reflected Dixon's capacity and willingness to use the dominant mode of legal reasoning operating in Australia, that is, 'legalism'. This stipulates the requirement that judges demonstrate their capacity to provide objective and principled elaboration to support their decisions (McHugh 1987). In this case, Judge Dixon established the point and purpose of legislation like the *Charter of Human Rights and Responsibilities* and the *Children, Youth and Families Act 2005* by identifying certain governing principles said to 'animate' this legislation (McQuigg 2012). Those principles, for example, require the Secretary and the Children's Court, among other relevant decision makers, to have regard to the *best interests of children*. This means that 'When determining whether a decision or action is in the best interests of the child, the need to protect the child from harm, to protect his or her rights and to promote his or her development (taking into account his or her age and stage of development) must always be considered.' As Dixon explained:

> The Court must have regard to the principles set out in this Part [of the Children, Youth and Families Act] (where relevant) in making any decision or taking any action under this Act, [just as] the Secretary must have regard to the principles set out in this Part (where relevant) in making any decision or taking any action under this Act or in providing any service under this Act to children and families. (Supreme Court of Victoria 2017)

This is not, however, all that needs to be said. Rather we see in the relevant legislation and in Dixon's judgment certain substantive contradictions and repeated instances of exercises in ignoring the rule of law *by various legal means*. This highlights a problem about the credibility of liberal claims that the rule of law matters. This in turn affects any judgment about the capacity of human rights activists in Australia to use the legal system to re-weigh the asymmetric relations of power between state and citizens, let alone between the state and denizens like young people.

The Rule of Law, Liberal Polities and Legal Exceptions

The question of legitimacy is: on what does the authority and rightness of law rest? In the Victorian case of 'Certain Children v Minister for Families and Children & Ors' (No. 2) [2017] we see major tensions and contradictions in respect to the sources and authority of legal and political legitimacy. In the western tradition, the question about the authority of the law was posed by Plato (2012) in his dialogue *Crito* which has Socrates' pondering whether he is obligated to accept the death sentence imposed on him by the law of the Athenian *polis.* Socrates posed an early version of a modern question when he asked what he should do if he doesn't like a legal decision (like the imposition of the death sentence on us) when he has agreed to obey the law and has generally benefitted in the past from that obedience? In modern times, the legitimacy of government decision-making is said to rest on the sovereignty of the people, that is, the democratic principle. If so, doesn't the practice of judges overturning legislation or decisions made by a democratically elected government raise a major difficulty for any idea about the sovereignty of the people? Referring to the liberal idea that legitimacy rests on the rule of law principle, however, opens other problems. Australian governments, for example, like to promote the idea they are committed to the rule of law principle and also to the idea that law itself is somehow 'above' politics because it is:

> [e]ndowed with its own discrete integral history, its own 'science', and its own values which are all treated as a single block sealed off from general social history, from general social theory, from politics and from morality. (Shklar 1986, p. 2)

Does this case suggest that legitimacy is grounded in the sovereignty of law located, for example, in a norm like a constitution or in the fact that a statute like the Charter of Human Rights and Responsibilities provides certain protections for vulnerable groups? (Kelsen 1945).

The answer to these questions in this specific case is that, the litigants could rely on the *Charter of Human Rights and Responsibilities* 2006 and on the *Children, Youth and Families Act 2005* to persuade the Supreme Court to order the release the children from Barwon prison. It was a result depending on the court choosing not to 'see' how contradictory the critical legislation actually was, which may point to the meaning of the blindfolded goddess of Justice sitting on the roof of Victoria's Supreme Court.

As we saw, Justice Dixon highlighted the 'best interest of the child' principle embedded in the *Children, Youth and Families Act 2005* when ordering the release of children from Barwon Prison. Dixon read the *Children, Youth and Families Act 2005* as 'welfare legislation' concerned to promote and protect the welfare of the child and their families including a system of 'child protection'. Read that way, especially in conjunction with the Charter of Human Rights, the court ordered the release of children from Barwon prison. However, to do this Dixon had to repress the other part of the very same legislation, that part that establishes the apparatus of Victoria's 'juvenile justice', enabling the administration to impose custodial sentences.

The *Children, Youth and Families Act 2005* is a legislation which translates into the twenty-first century, the long-standing conflation of a welfare logic *with* a criminal justice logic. That conflation was installed in Victoria's first child welfare-juvenile justice legislation evident in the very title of the legislation, the *Neglected and Criminal Children's Act 1864* (Jaggs 1986). Its contemporary incarnation (i.e., the *Children, Youth and Families Act, 2005*) establishes the Children's Court requiring that this court address the welfare needs of children based on the best interests of the child principle while imposing custodial sentences on children should they engage in criminal conduct. The same statutory legislation not only mandates welfare interventions oriented to ensuring the best interests of the child while also enabling governments to establish what are called 'corrective services' like remand centers and youth justice centers.

How this authorizing legislation keeps faith simultaneously with the 'best interests of the child' principle while allowing for children to be subjected to custodial sentences is unclear. This contradiction could not be blanked out even though Dixon went to great lengths to stipulate the relevance of the 'best interest of the child principle' without but asking the question: when, if ever, is it in the best interests of a child that they be given a custodial sentence?

This authorizing legislation is at odds with the abundant body of research demonstrating the many serious negative consequences for children who are incarcerated as well as with international law.

There is now a large established body of international research evidence that shows that incarceration is extremely damaging to children in the short term and impedes their healthy development over the longer term

(Willow 2015). The research on youth corrections shows that detention has a profoundly negative impact on young people's mental and physical wellbeing, their education, and their future employment (Holman and Zeidenberg 2001). Other studies show that for one-third of incarcerated youth diagnosed with depression, the onset of the depression occurred after they began their incarceration (Mace et al. 1997). Imprisonment is also not an effective mechanism for preventing youth crime (Bateman 2016, p. 1). In Victoria, of the 5385 children and young people sentenced in the Children's Court in 2008–09 (the 'study group'), 61% reoffended within six years of their 2008–09 sentence. Many offenders reoffended more than once (44%), with 15% sentenced on five or more occasions within the six-year follow-up period (Sentencing Advisory Council 2016, p. 1). Worse, 52% of the study group (2789 offenders) had progressed to the adult criminal jurisdiction by the end of the study period (30 June 2015). The 2789 offenders who continued offending into the adult criminal jurisdiction represented the majority of the 3261 people in the study group who reoffended (86% of reoffenders) (Sentencing Advisory Council 2016, p. 3). Of course, in this particular case, there never was nor could there ever be any consideration of the legitimacy of placing children in prison-like settings called youth justice centers let alone in a unit in an adult prison that has been arbitrarily reclassified as a youth justice center at the stroke of the Executive's pen.

Indeed the 'normal' recourse to custodial sentences in Victoria is also clearly at odds with Article 37 of the UN Convention on the Rights of the Child that proscribes the use of child imprisonment other than as a 'measure of last resort'. The obligation on jurisdictions like Australia as a signatory to the Convention, to uphold principles like 'the best interest of the child', has not had any effect on the administration of juvenile justice in Victoria because UNCROC has not become domestic legislation.

However other contradictions in this legislation are illustrated when the *Children, Youth and Families Act 2005* declares that certain actions are prohibited in relation to a child detained in a remand center or a youth justice center. The actions prohibited include the use of isolation as a punishment and the use of physical force like tear gas or batons. However, in privileging security and 'public safety', that prohibition is abolished. The Act allows that 'the officer in charge of a remand center, youth residential center or youth justice center may cause a person detained in the center to be isolated in the interests of the security of the center'. In effect if the use of isolation as a punishment and the use of physical force 'is reasonable and is necessary for the security of the center or police gaol' or 'is otherwise authorized by or under this or any other Act or at common law' then officials can use these otherwise prohibited actions.

In summary, we see in the drafting of the Victorian Charter of Human Rights and the *Children, Youth and Families Act 2005* and in the continuing attempts by the Andrew's government to fix the problem of children acting up in juvenile detention centers, exercises designed to ignore the rule of law *using various legal means*. This is the idea that states routinely use what Dyzenhaus (2006) and Vermeule (2009) call legal 'black holes' and 'grey holes'.

Legal 'Black Holes' as Exceptionality

Legal black holes arise when statutes or legal rules 'either explicitly exempt [...] the executive from the requirements of the rule of law or explicitly exclude [...] judicial review of executive action' (Dyzenhaus 2006, p. 3). Grey holes, which are 'disguised black holes', 'arise when there are some legal constraints on executive action – it is not a lawless void – but the constraints are so insubstantial that they pretty well permit government to do as it pleases' (Dyzenhaus 2006: 3). 'Grey holes' thus present 'the façade or form of the rule of law rather than any substantive protections' (Dyzenhaus 2006: 3). When resorting to these devices, governments typically point to an emergency that needs to be dealt with. This points to a deeper crisis in the public administration of juvenile justice, certainly in Victoria—and in many other liberal-democratic jurisdictions. Arguably the use of these legal gray and black holes is one of the ways ostensibly democratic societies create a legal form of exceptionality mandated by law and at the cost of genuine democratic sovereignty and of human rights. As Dyzenhaus and Vermeule argue, we need to acknowledge the dark shadow cast by Carl Schmitt's theory of sovereignty which has fundamental implications for any account of political legitimacy.

In Schmitt's extended conceptualization of the political and the nature of sovereignty in his *Political Theology* he (1985, p. 5) declared the 'Sovereign is he who decides on the state of exception'. This was supplemented by his account of the political (1976) as the relation between friends and enemies.

Schmitt argued that the possibility for legality and legitimacy is always open to being rendered suspect by the political act that suspends it (1985; 1996). This is Schmitt's account of sovereignty as the state of exception:

'sovereign is he who decides on the state of exception'. What Roman law called *iustitium* is the 'state of exception', that circumstance when the operation of the law, or constitution is suspended by the state.

Schmitt made the constitution and the processes of erstwhile liberal political practices dependent on the political will of those running the state. In Schmitt's terms, politics and the framework of law-making were necessarily subservient to the capacity of the state. At issue here is the sovereignty of the state and the question of legitimacy.

Simon Critchley observed that central to Schmitt's theory of the political is the claim that the true subject of the political is the state, and that the state must always stand higher than the law—or the citizen (Critchley 2011, p. 105). For Schmitt, the nature of state power (or sovereignty) is revealed when a state decides to suspend the rule of law. This argument and the empirical evidence supporting it presents a problem for those arguing for a distinction between 'legitimate' state actions and 'illegitimate' state actions based on whether the action is grounded in the law or not. The problem is whether legitimacy rests on the idea that laws are made by popularly elected governments (i.e., sovereignty grounded in the people), or that law is law and so always legitimate (which is the legal positivist claim). What if law itself grounded (e.g., in a constitution) allows for the suspension of the law but allows for this as part of the normal processes of legislation?

What Schmitt called 'the exception' presents an insuperable problem for the aspiration of liberal democracies to govern on the basis of the rule of law principle (Vermeule 2009).

As Dyzenhaus (2006) and Vermeule (2009) also argue, we do need not focus on major emergencies to see that normal public administration provides for legal 'black' and 'grey holes'. In this respect, administrative law in jurisdictions like the United States and Australia is already Schmittian not because of a suspension of the rule of law but because states now so regularly use the legislative process to suspend the rule of law.

Australia provides a helpful case study that highlights the way administrative law is Schmittian. There may, for example, be conventions that specify executive actions will always be reviewable in court for conformity with law, except when legislators or judges decide that an exception is necessary (Vermeule 2009). Alternatively, a convention may allow that executive action is always reviewable when it fails to conform to the dictates of legal rationality and reason (i.e., it is 'arbitrary'). Or a given statute might specify that government must follow a set of procedures, but also specify that agencies can dispense with those procedures when they have reason ('good cause') to do so. As we saw above, the *Children, Youth and Family Act 2005* prohibits the use of isolation of physical punishment except when what is deemed 'safety or security' requires the use of what is otherwise prohibited.

Conclusion

This chapter documented the role played by a network of activist advocacy and human rights groups when they learned that the Victorian government had authorized the use of armed police and gas against children and the relocation of some 16 boys, most of them on remand, into adult maximum-security prisons in 2016–17. It then traced out the way the activists were able to use Victoria's Human Rights Charter to protect the human rights of young children who had been transferred into an adult jail.

We focused on a landmark legal case heard before the Victoria's Supreme Court in 2017 where human rights lawyers successfully used the Victorian Charter of Rights to persuade the court to order the government to remove the children from an adult prison. Seen historically, this Supreme Court decision was significant because it overturned a decision made by a democratically elected government, (something that is usual in Australia). It was also significant because it rejected the recourse by media and politicians to a vocabulary of 'emergency' and 'exceptionality'. On this occasion the government was unsuccessful in making the case that an 'emergency' had justified the suspension of certain rule of law principles, while human rights activists successfully invoked human rights principles. Yet this victory for human rights cannot be taken at face value. The deeper contradiction operating in legislation providing simultaneously for the application of welfare *and* criminal justice rationalities is another way of thinking about how, what critical scholars call legal 'black' or 'grey' holes, now work (Dyzenhaus 2006; Vermeule 2009; Bessant 2014a, pp. 329–348).

This case highlights the intertwined nature of the relations between the political and the law, and indicates why appreciating this helps those wanting to secure human rights. As Koskenniemi argued, modern liberal, social, and political organization rests on the promise that freedom, equality, and the rule of law are critical if we are not to succumb to the political 'understood as a matter of furthering subjective desires and leading into an international anarchy' (1990, p. 5). Yet, as he also recognized, politics is an inevitability in the profession of law (Koskenniemi 2009, p. 7). Given that paradox, it seems human rights activists will always have their work cut out for them.

Notes

1. The smaller territory which is the capital of Australia called the Australian Capital Territory had earlier passed a Human Rights Act 2004.
2. Anyone familiar with youth justice in Australia and internationally will see in this a distressingly familiar story. In July 2016 ABC-TV's *Four Corners*, Australia's leading current affairs show, used official video footage to highlight the abuse of six, mostly indigenous teenage boys serving a sentence in the Northern Territory's Don Dale youth detention center. A Royal Commission set up to investigate Don Dale subsequently confirmed that conditions in solitary confinement were appalling and inhumane. Inmates were routinely locked in cells for nearly 24 hours a day with no running water, little natural light, as well as being denied access to schooling and educational material. They were also regularly stripped, beaten, locked down, hooded, and shackled. Similar patterns of violence targeting young people are found internationally. Juvenile justice facilities in England and Wales, for example, have been the focus of concern about the increased use of force against inmates and evidence that many children in these facilities feel unsafe (Redmond 2015). This led Taylor (2016) in a major review of English juvenile justice to call for a radical shift in policy. American juvenile justice facilities have also been the object of complaints about systemic abuse since the late 1970s (McCarthy et al. 2016). Likewise in 2009, the US Department of Justice concluded that too many staff at facilities across America:

   > routinely used uncontrolled, unsafe applications of force, departing both from generally accepted standards and [departmental] policy … This one-size-fits-all control approach has, not surprisingly, led to an alarming number of serious injuries to youth, including concussions, broken or knocked-out teeth, and spinal fractures.

   More recently Mendel revealed evidence of systemic or recurring maltreatment in all but five American states' youth prisons between 1970 and 2015 (Mendel 2015).
3. Buttler (2016) and Buttler and Dowling (2016), for example, emphasized how young inmates acting as 'a band of young thugs' or members of the Apex gang (which existed in the minds of these tabloid reporters) had taken over the Parkville center.

4. In Norway the parliament decided to incorporate the CRC in full into domestic legislation in 2003, four years after the enactment of the Human Rights Act of 1999 which incorporated the International Covenant on Economic, Social and Cultural Rights (ICESCR), the International Covenant on Civil and Political Rights (ICCPR), and the European Convention of Human Rights (ECHR) into Norwegian law.
5. Victoria's courts especially the Supreme Court only recently began to use the Charter to reshape the terrain of human rights in Victoria (McQuigg 2012). Between 2008 and 2015 the Charter was cited in at least 70 published decisions by courts.

References

ABC News. 2016. Melbourne Youth Justice Centre: Police Negotiating with Young Rioters Holed Up in 'Inaccessible Area. *ABC News*, November 14. http://www.abc.net.au/news/2016-11-14/melbourne-youth-justice-centre-riot-police-called-second-time/8022206.

Bateman, Tim. 2016. *The State of Youth Custody*. London: National Association for Youth Justice.

———. 2014a. Criminalizing the Political in a Digital Age. *Critical Criminology* 23 (3): 329–348.

———. 2014b. In Pursuit of El Dorado: In Pursuit of *El Dorado*: Notes on an of an Encounter with Youth Policy in Terra Incognita. In *A Critical Youth Studies for the 21st Century*, ed. A. Kamp and P. Kelly, 597–612. Leiden: Brill Academic Publishers.

Bessant, Judith, and Rob Watts. 2017. History of Children and the Law, Children and the Law in Australia. In *Children and the Law in Australia*, ed. L. Young, M.A. Kenny, and G. Monahan, 2nd ed., 3–23. Chatswood: LexisNexis.

Brigidine Asylum Seekers Project (BASP). 2017. About Us, Brigidine Asylum Seekers Project. http://basp.org.au/about-us.

Buttler, Mark. 2016. Young Thugs Involved in Justice Centre Riots Now Put Parole at Risk'. *Herald-Sun*, November 16. http://www.heraldsun.com.au/news/law-order/young-thugs-involved-in-justice-centre-riots-now-put-parole-at-risk/news-story/34d80aef2adbb8b89a8b1fdc486ed8b2.

Buttler, Mark, and Jason Dowling. 2016. Inside the Anarchy in Melbourne's Youth Jail Riots. *Herald Sun*, November 15. http://www.heraldsun.com.au/news/law-order/inside-the-anarchy-in-melbournes-youth-jail-riots/news-story/084c36cf3d837ffa5b2128b6445c542b.

Commission for Children and Young People. 2017. *The Same Four Walls: Inquiry into the Use of Isolation, Separation and Lockdowns in the Victorian Youth Justice System*. Melbourne: Commission for Children and Young People and Victorian

State Government. file:///Users/judithbessant/Documents/CCYP_-_Inquiry_Report_-_The_Same_Four_Walls_L1NNtqzB.pdf 5.

Copeland, Anna. 2004. Public Space: A Rights Based Approach. *Youth Studies Australia* 23 (3): 41–45.

Craven, Gregory. 1992. The Crisis of Constitutional Literalism in Australia. In *Australian Constitutional Perspectives*, ed. H.P. Lee and George Winterton, 1–32. Sydney: Law book Company.

Critchley, Simon. 2012. *The Faith of the Faithless: Ethics of Commitment Politics of Resistance*. London: Verso.

Cunneen, Chris, Goldson Barry, and Sophie Russell. 2016. Juvenile Justice, Young People and Human Rights in Australia. *Current Issues in Criminal Justice 23* 28(2): 173. http://www.austlii.edu.au/au/journals/CICrimJust/2016/23.html.

Dyzenhaus, David. 2006. *The Constitution of the Law: Legality in a Time of Emergency*. New York: Cambridge University Press.

Edwards, Jean. 2016. Victorian Government's Decision to Send Youth Rioters to Adult Prison to be Challenged in Court. *ABC News*, November 23. http://mobile.abc.net.au/news/2016-11-23/decision-to-send-youth-rioters-to-adult-prison-to-be-challenged/8050922?pfmredir=sm.

Faine, Jon. 1993. *Lawyers in the Alice: Aboriginals and Whitefella's Law*. Annandale: Federation Press.

Galligan, Brian. 1987. *Politics of the High Court*. St Lucia: UQP.

Goldsworthy, Jeffrey, ed. 2006. *Interpreting Constitutions A Comparative Study*. Oxford: Oxford University Press.

Gough, Deborah, and Goya Dmytryshchak. 2016. Melbourne Youth Justice Centre Hit by Fresh Riot, Officer Hurt at Second Jail. *The Age*, November 13. https://www.theage.com.au/national/victoria/melbourne-youth-justice-centre-hit-by-fresh-riot-officer-hurt-at-second-jail-20161113-gso268.htm.

Herald-Sun. 2017. Youth Jail Overhaul. February 7. http://www.heraldsun.com.au/news/opinion/youth-jail-overhaul/news-story/b3e9bced22400fe-a6176f4fa702fc6f2.

Holman, Barry, and Jason Ziedenberg. 2001. *The Dangers of Detention: The Impact of Incarcerating Youth in Detention and Other Secure Congregate Facilities*. Baltimore: Annie E. Casey Foundation.

Houston, Cameron, Chris Vedelago, and Josh Gordon. 2017. New Youth Detention Centre for Victoria. *The Age*, January 31. https://www.theage.com.au/national/victoria/new-youth-detention-centre-for-victoria-20170131-gu-2jgu.html.

Inder, Claire. 2010. International Migration Law: Hyper-Legalism and Migration Management: The Pacific Solution. In *The Politics of International Migration Management*, ed. Martin Geiger and A. Antoine Pecoud, 220–251. London: Palgrave Macmillan.

Jaggs, Donna. 1986. *Neglected and Criminal: Foundations of Child Welfare Legislation in Victoria*. Melbourne: Centre for Youth and Community Studies: Phillip Institute of Technology.

Josev, Theodore. 2017. *The Campaign Against the Courts: A History of the Judicial Activism Debate*. Annandale: Federation Press.

Kelsen, Hans. 1945. *General Theory of Law and State*. Madison: University of Wisconsin Press.

Koskenniemi, Marti. 1990. The Politics of International Law. *European Journal of International Law* 1 (1): 4–32 http://ejil.org/pdfs/1/1/1144.pdf.

———. 2009. The Politics of International Law-Twenty Years Later. *European Journal of International Law* 20 (1): 7–19.

Lundy, Laura, Kilkelly Ursula, and Bronagh Byrne. 2013. Incorporation of the United Nations Convention on the Rights of the Child in Law: A Comparative Review. *International Journal of Children's Rights* 21 (3): 442–463.

Mace, David., P. Paul Rohde, and V. Ginny Gnau. 1997. Psychological Patterns of Depression and Suicidal Behavior of Adolescents in a Juvenile Detention Facility. *Journal of Juvenile Justice and Detention Services* 12 (1): 18–23.

Marks, Russell. 2017. Call for Backup: How Authorities Lost Control of Juvenile Detention. *The Monthly*, March. https://www.themonthly.com.au/issue/2017/march/1488286800/russellmarks/call-backup.

McCarthy, Patrick, Vincent Schiraldi, and Miriam Shark. 2016. *The Future of Youth Justice: A Community-Based Alternative to the Youth Prison Model*, New Thinking in Community Corrections. no. 2. Harvard Kennedy School. https://www.ncjrs.gov/pdffiles1/nij/250142.pdf.

McHugh, Michael. 1987. The Law-making Function of the Judicial Process. In *Presented at the Ninth National Conference of Labor Lawyers at Perth*, 1–58. September 19.

McKenzie, Nick, Farrah Tomazin and Richard Baker. 2017. Youth Justice Chief Moved as Secret Report Reveals Chaos in System. *The Age*, January 25. https://www.theage.com.au/national/victoria/youth-justice-chief-moved-as-secret-report-reveals-chaos-in-system-20170124-gtxrmv.html.

McQuigg, Ronagh. 2012. The Use of the Charter of Human Rights and Responsibilities in the Courts of Victoria. *Journal of Commonwealth Law and Legal Education* 8 (2): 22–40.

Mendel, Richard. 2015. *Maltreatment of Youth in U.S. Juvenile Corrections Facilities: An Update*. Baltimore: Annie E. Casey Foundation.

Morgan, George. 2007. Curfew, Children, Class and Colonialism. In *Outrageous! Moral Panics in Australia*, ed. Scott Poynting and George Morgan, 11–19. Hobart: ACYS.

National Children's and Youth Law Centre and Youth Law. 2007. *Preliminary Report of the Implementation Status of the Seen and Heard Reports*, Discussion Paper. NCYLC & Youthlaw.

National Inquiry into Children in Immigration Detention. 2014. Melbourne Public Hearing Wednesday, 2 July: Testimony of Sr Brigid Arthur. https://www.humanrights.gov.au/.../Mr%20Karapanagiotidis%2C%20Ms%20Curr%20.

Plato. 2012. *Crito*. Trans. C. Woods and R. Pack. http://www.pitt.edu/~mthompso/readings/crito.pdf.

Redmond, Alissa. 2015. *Children in Custody 2014–15, An Analysis of 12–18-year-olds' Perceptions of Their Experiences in Secure Training Centres and Young Offender Institutions.* London: Ministry of Justice. http://www.justiceinspectorates.gov.uk/hmiprisons/wp-content/uploads/sites/4/2015/12/HMIP_CP_-Children-in-custody-2014-15-FINAL-web-AW.pdf.

Roberts, Brendan. 2017. Teen Prisoners Riot Again at Parkville Detention Centre. *7 News*, November 13. https://au.news.yahoo.com/a/33193853/teen-prisoners-riot-again-at-parkville-detention-centre.

Saunders, Cheryl. 2002. Protecting Rights in Common Law Constitutional Systems: A Framework for a Comparative Study. *Victoria University of Wellington Law Review* 83. http://www5.austlii.edu.au/nz/journals/VUWLawRw/2002/21.html.

Sawer, Geoffrey. 1967. *Australian Federalism in the Courts.* Canberra: ANU Press.

Schmitt, Carl. 1985. *Political Theology: Four Chapters in the Concept of Sovereignty.* Trans. G. Schwab. Chicago: University of Chicago Press.

———. 1996. *The Concept of the Political.* Trans. G. Schwab. Chicago: University of Chicago Press.

Sentencing Advisory Council. 2016. Reoffending by *Children and Young People in Victoria,* Melbourne: Sentencing Advisory Council.

Shklar, Judith. 1986. *Legalism: Law, Morals, and Political Trials.* Cambridge: Harvard University Press.

Supreme Court of Victoria. 2017. 'Certain Children by Their Litigation Guardian Sister Marie Brigid Arthur v Minister for Families and Children & Ors no 2, VSC 251.May 11.

Taylor, Charlie. 2016. *Review of the Youth Justice System in England and Wales.* London: Ministry of Justice. http://www.yjlc.uk/wp-content/uploads/2016/12/Review-of-the-Youth-Justice-System.pdf.

UNICEF. 2007. *Innocenti Research Centre. Law Reform and Implementation of the CRC.* Florence: UNICEF.

Vermeule, Adrian. 2009. Our Schmittian Administrative Law. *Harvard Law Review* 122: 1095–1149.

Victorian Charter of Human Rights and Responsibilities Act, (Victorian) Act 43/2006. 2006. http://www.legislation.vic.gov.au/Domino/Web_Notes/LDMS/PubStatbook.nsf/f932b66241ecf1b7ca256e92000e23be/54D73763EF9DCA36CA2571B6002428B0/$FILE/06-043a.pdf.

Victorian Ombuds. 2002. *Whistleblowers Protection Act 2001* Investigation into Conditions at the Melbourne Youth Justice Precinct, October, Melbourne: Victorian Government Printer.

———. 2004. *Whistleblowers Protection Act 2001* Investigation into Conditions at the Melbourne Youth Justice Precinct, October, Melbourne: Victorian Government Printer.

———. 2010. *Whistleblowers Protection Act 2001* Investigation into Conditions at the Melbourne Youth Justice Precinct, October, Victorian Parliamentary Paper no. 388, Session 2006–10, Melbourne, Victorian Government Printer.

Willow, Carolyne. 2015. *Children Behind Bars: Why the Abuse of Child Imprisonment Must End*. Bristol: Policy Press.

Young, Michael. 2015. *From Commitment to Culture: The 2015 Review of the Charter of Human Rights and Responsibilities Act 2006*. Melbourne: Victorian Government Printer.

Younger, Emma. 2017. 'Barwon Prison: "Teens Moved After Court Rules Children Should not be Held in Adult Jail". *ABC News*, May 11. http://www.abc.net.au/news/2017-05-11/teens-moved-from-victorias-adult-jail-barwon-prison/8514310.

CHAPTER 7

Who Is a Child? The Politics of Human Rights, the Convention on the Right of the Child (CRC), and Child Marriage in Nigeria

Olabanji Akinola

Childhood, like gender, is a sociohistorical construct. However, unlike gender, which is more fluid and flexible, childhood is defined by the rigid parameters of age. At every point in time in the history of societies, what makes a "proper" or "good" childhood is framed by families, communities, and the machinery of the state in accordance with social transformations.
– Aderinto (2015, p. 2)

Introduction: Who Is a Child?

Twenty-seven years after the United Nations Convention on the Rights of the Child (CRC) defined a child as "every human being below the age of eighteen years, unless under the law applicable to the child, majority is

O. Akinola (✉)
University of Guelph, Guelph, ON, Canada
e-mail: oakinola@uoguelph.ca

G. Blouin-Genest et al. (eds.), *Human Rights as Battlefields*,
Human Rights Interventions,
https://doi.org/10.1007/978-3-319-91770-2_7

attained earlier" (Convention on the Rights of the Child 1989, Article 1), the battles over "who is a child" is still very much alive in many countries. While these battles may be traced to the different sociohistorical constructions/definitions of childhood by various state and non-state actors and institutions as suggested in the quote above, the battles reflect continuous opposition to the CRC's chronological definition of a child as anyone below 18 years. However, from a conceptual perspective, these "battles" broadly reflect the "politics of human rights" in general (Blouin-Genest and Paquerot 2016). Indeed, in countries like Nigeria where different stakeholders, including religious and traditional leaders, politicians, women, and human rights activists argue for and against child marriage, these battles have become more salient over time. With a plural legal system that comprises civil law (English common law), Islamic/Sharia law, and customary law in different parts of the country (Durojaye 2013), the battle over definitions of "who is a child" is arguably one of the most contentious issues surrounding the domestication of the CRC in Nigeria. Although the CRC has been domesticated at the national level in Nigeria through the Child Rights Act (CRA) of 2003, the definition of 18 as the age of marriage has been resisted at the subnational level where some of Nigeria's 36 federating states have refused to pass the enabling laws giving effects to the CRC/CRA. The implication of the impasse is visible in the battles over the promotion and protection of the human rights of children as vulnerable members of society, especially with regards to the human rights of young girls.

Consequently, in seeking to understand the politics of human rights in relation to the CRC and CRA broadly—and child marriage and rights specifically—this chapter examines the battles over the definitions of who qualifies as a child for the purpose of marriage in Nigeria. In particular, it examines how different religious, traditional, political, and human rights actors advocate for and against child marriage, that is, the marriage of persons below 18 years of age in Nigeria. This is done through an examination of the definitions of a child in the CRC/CRA on the one hand, and the arguments in support of early marriage based on extant religious and customary practices and laws that permit the marriage of anyone that has attained puberty, on the other hand. For clarity, and as used here, attaining puberty includes, but is not limited to, biological development such as the experience of menarche for girls and the growing of pubic hairs for boys. In all, the chapter mainly addresses the following question: how does the politics of human rights in Nigeria influence the definitions of who qualifies as a child? Based on analysis of past and current debates on child marriage issues, and drawing mainly on secondary sources and publications of the battles surrounding child marriage in Nigeria, the chapter argues that the current battles over the definitions of a child for marital purposes represent a major fault line in the politics of human rights in Nigeria. The chapter proceeds in the following three sections. Section "The Politics of Human Rights: An Overview and Conceptual Framework" provides the conceptual framework applied in this chapter. Section "The CRC and Battles over the Definitions of a Child" provides a much-needed analysis of the CRC and its contributions (or otherwise) to defining the age of a child with regards to marriage. Section "The CRC, Child Marriage, and the Politics of Human Rights in Nigeria" engages in a critical analysis of the battles over the question of who is a child in Nigeria, and engages the discourses and processes relating to the domestication of the CRC into national law. This is followed by a brief concluding section.

The Politics of Human Rights: An Overview and Conceptual Framework

Perspectives vary considerably on what constitutes the politics of human rights (see, for instance, Vincent 2010; Ingram 2008; Isaac 1996). Although an elaborate coverage of the varying perspectives goes beyond the scope of this chapter, it is worthwhile to examine two interrelated perspectives on the politics of human rights. For the purpose of this chapter, these are (1) the politics of universalism in human rights discourses and practice, and (2) human rights as a battlefield for political contests and confrontations among stakeholders. As discussed below, the review of these perspectives relates to discourses of politics at the local and international levels.

To begin with, it is not uncommon to read about the universal nature of human rights or, put differently, about how human right claims have universal appeal across the globe given that the history of humanity is replete with claims and counterclaims to a shared humanity. But in the aftermath of the Second World War, human rights discourses have often referred to the creation of the United Nations and the 1948 Universal Declaration of Human Rights (UDHR) as a testament to commitments by nations across the globe as a leveling field for humanity as a whole. However, as Ignatieff (2001) notes, claims to the universality of human rights before and after the adoption of the UDHR have always been challenged on cultural grounds from three main sources: resurgent Islam, Western postmodernism, and East Asian cultures. Tellingly, for Ignatieff (2001), in seeking to defend and promote their religious and cultural mores and milieus against what is mostly considered Western attempts to impose individualistic, liberal human rights claims, on the rest of the world, supporters from these three sources have often challenged how the language of human rights is framed. In this context, Ignatieff argues that the UDHR itself represents a political compromise, especially with respect to accommodating the religious and cultural objections raised against the universalizing language of the UDHR. For example, Ignatieff explains that "[w]hen the Universal Declaration of Human Rights was being drafted in 1947, the Saudi Arabian delegation raised particular objection to Article 16, relating to free marriage choice, and Article 18, relating to freedom of religion" (2001, p. 102). He goes on to add that, "In Islamic eyes, universalizing rights discourse implies a sovereign and discrete individual, which is blasphemous from the perspective of the Koran" (ibid.).

Yet, notwithstanding the compromises involved in the politics of human rights, including those relating to the UDHR, Ignatieff argues that it is the politics of human rights that allows the existence of a language of universality with respect to human rights claims. As he puts it,

> The language of human rights is the only universally available moral vernacular that validates the claims of women and children against the oppression they experience in patriarchal and tribal societies; it is the only vernacular that enables dependent persons to perceive themselves as moral agents and to act against practices – arranged marriages, purdah, civic disenfranchisement, genital mutilation, domestic slavery, and so on – that are ratified by the weight and authority of their cultures. These agents seek human rights protection precisely because it legitimizes their protest against oppression. (Ignatieff 2001, p. 109)

While it is difficult to argue against the (non-)universality of human rights, and even though Ignatieff maintains that the politics of human rights entails trades and compromises that sometimes involve conflicts and cooperation with religious and traditional belief systems, Brown (2004) questions Ignatieff's (2001) argument about how the universal language of human rights liberates individual agents. As Brown explains, "it is not at all clear that human rights discourse actually secures the autonomy and agency Ignatieff promises; rather, this discourse offers a form of protection for individuals that may trade one form of subjection for another." For Brown, this may mean "an intervention by an external agent or set of institutions that promises to protect individuals from abusive state power in part by replacing that power" (2004, p. 455). Indeed, what Brown alludes to is sometimes illustrated by the fact that with different states seeking to interpret the claims to the universality—or otherwise—of human rights, support or opposition to universal claims of human rights are most of the time contingent on national interests of each state, with some invoking claims to the principles of national sovereignty and non-interference. To be sure, with special reference to defending their own domesticate human rights records when accused of gross violations of such rights, the inconsistency on the support or defense of allies and friends as opposed to foes and enemies is a consistent feature in (global) human rights politics. It is such practices that lead Moynihan (1977, p. 19) to argue that the "selective morality of the United Nations in matters of human rights threatens the integrity not merely of the United Nations, but of human rights itself."

Extending the criticism of the selective nature of human rights discourses and practice beyond the arena of games played by nation states, Evans (2001, 2005) argues that the global politics of human rights has a predetermined end in promoting global liberal capitalism, which is advanced by Western states and multinational corporations. Evans believes that under the guise of promoting human rights for everyone, the forces of global capital have teamed up to support the unequal relations among states in the global north and global south (Evans 2005). The fact that neoliberalism and the globalization of capitalism have favored more people and countries in the global north than those in the global south provides the evidence for the negative results that the politics of human rights engenders in Evans's opinion. However, for Gready (2003), Evans's position ignores the significant and positive roles that the politics of human rights permits, especially in engendering and emancipating other non-state actors such as non-governmental organizations, human rights activists, community organizations, and citizens, to challenge the powers of neoliberalism at the global and local levels. Indeed, Gready (2003) maintains that the politics of human rights can be "principled," and this "principle politics" can allow a multitude of actors and institutions to manifest and take part in shaping the outcomes of human rights debates. At the heart of Gready's argument is the emphasis on the fact that it is inaccurate to identify a single politics of human rights, especially when it is assumed that the politics of human rights inevitably always leads to negative outcomes. For Gready, therefore, the "politicization of human rights and its role, use and misuse in international politics, indicates that to an ever-increasing degree human rights cannot be seen as non-political, and human rights actors need to develop responses to this reality" (2003, p. 752).

Essentially, from the above, it is clear that human rights discourses and practice do not take place in a vacuum. Put differently, any discussion of human rights outside a system of politics where actions and institutions give meaning to rights is "quasi-tautological" (Balibar 2013, p. 18). But to understand the politics of human rights requires acknowledging the role that multiple actors and institutions play in seeking to interpret and translate rights in any political system, whether at the international or local levels. Here, and borrowing from actor-network theory (Law 1992), to understand the "mechanics of power" in any society, it is necessary to examine the heterogeneity of networks of actors whose interactions determine the translations of social order into practice. In other words, as different actors and institutions engage in processes and actions aimed at translating their own preferences into practice within any given society, understanding how they mobilize resources for their own purposes, while preventing or challenging other networks of actors, is crucial to explaining the kinds of outcomes or results they generate or gain (Law 1992). With regards to the politics of human rights, this is akin to a scenario where different actors are involved in a political battlefield as they seek to influence the interpretation and translation of their knowledge and actions into practice (Blouin-Genest and Paquerot 2016). According to Blouin-Genest and Paquerot (2016, p. 135), "the emergence of rights as a political battlefield" was aided by the limits imposed on sovereignty and the evolution of political confrontation in the international system. But the political confrontations go beyond the international arena to manifest at the local level, which combined illustrates the multilayered sociological space of contest over human rights.

To place Blouin-Genest and Paquerot's (2016) position into perspective, particularly given its relevance as a conceptual framework in this chapter, human rights as political battlefield recognizes the presence of various actors and institutions acting as networks to translate and interpret human rights in different international and local domains. By acknowledging the interplay of actors and institutions in any given network(s), human rights are recognized as "spaces for dispute over power, as places of claims and productive confrontations" (Blouin-Genest and Paquerot 2016, p. 139). Consequently, as used in this chapter, human rights as a political battlefield is understood as "the social and political space through which different human rights actors become organized and mobilized in order to claim a specific understanding/practice of these rights through a logic of emancipation from their original context and objectives" (Blouin-Genest and Paquerot 2016, p. 140). As discussed in the following paragraphs, the attempts by different actors/stakeholders, especially religious and traditional actors in Nigeria, to resist the definition of a child—and by extension the rights of children and young girls—as anyone below 18 years for the purpose of supporting child marriage constitutes a major political battleground in the grand narrative of who is a child. But before elaborating on these battles, an understanding of the CRC and its contributions or otherwise to protecting children generally, and the girl child specifically, against child marriage is necessary as the next section demonstrates.

The CRC and Battles over the Definitions of a Child

The Convention on the Rights of the Child was passed and adopted by the UN General Assembly on November 20, 1989, and till today arguably remains one of the most comprehensive bodies of international treaty relating to children's rights (Doek 2009; Santos Pais and Bissell 2006). With more than 190 state party signatories, it also currently ranks as one of the most signed and ratified international treaty (Mauras 2011). As a comprehensive body of law relating to child rights, the CRC covers a wide range of issues, including, but not limited to, civil and political rights as well as social, economic, and cultural rights. Central to the issues of children's rights as contained in the CRC is the imperative of promoting the following four principles: (1) non-discrimination (Article 2); (2) adherence to the best interests of the child in all matters (Article 3); (3) the right to life, survival, and development (Article 6); and (4) the right to be heard (Article 12) (CRC 1989).

Yet, despite its significance as a key international treaty on children's rights, the definition of a child as "every human being below the age of eighteen years, unless under the law applicable to the child, majority is attained earlier" in Article 1 of the CRC is highly controversial. The areas of contention not only relate to the chronological age threshold of 18 years and under but also to the complexities surrounding the qualifying statement that 18 years should be the limit "unless under the law applicable to the child, majority is attained earlier." With regards to the definition of a child in the CRC, therefore, a criticism of the CRC often relates to the fact that the CRC's definition of a child is ambiguous and serves as an avenue for state and non-state actors and institutions opposed to a firm definition of a child as anyone under 18 years to avoid adhering to the chronological age limit (Warner 2011; Askari 1998). Along this line, Warner (2011, p. 251) argues that even though the CRC is intended to be a comprehensive treaty that promotes and protects the best interest of the child, the lack of a clear definition of "majority" in Article 1 leaves the interpretation and translation to local laws at the national level, which among other things is problematic for the protection of children, in practice. However, it can be argued that the ambiguous reference to the word "majority" in the definition of a child in Article 1 was intended to recognize the definition of a child in many societies based on "social age" constructions. As Clark-Kazak (2009, p. 1309) argues, it is a common practice in many non-Western cultures to define a child based on social age constructions, that is, based on the "social meaning and roles ascribed to different stages in the human life cycle." For Clark-Kazak, it is important that definitions of a child should acknowledge both the chronological and social age of a child. Thus, it may have been the intention of the drafters of the CRC to accommodate both social and chronological age definitions of a child, even though the implications of defining a child based on social age definitions, especially in relation to issues of child marriage, has proven to be difficult.

Another criticism of the CRC relates to what critics consider a glaring omission of any article or text that explicitly prohibits child marriage (Warner 2011). This omission, critics maintain, illustrates how the CRC does not specifically address and protect the girl child like it does with the explicit mention of "child soldiers" that mostly relates to the experience of the boy child in Article 38 of the CRC (Askari 1998). As Askari (1998, p. 124) notes, "Despite its comprehensiveness, the CRC does not adequately protect and promote the rights of girl children… The absence of a provision against the child marriage will be used as the basis for the conclusion that the CRC does not apply to boys and girls equally." But notwithstanding the criticisms of the CRC's definition of a child and omission of any Article explicitly prohibiting child marriage, critics and advocates of the CRC acknowledge that the CRC was intended to refer to all children, and when read in relation to the full weight of all its Articles, the CRC provides relevant protection for all children (Warner 2011; Askari 1998; Mauras 2011; Onyango and Lynch 2006). At the same time, the contents of its two optional protocols on the involvement of children in armed conflicts and sexual exploitation, respectively, address issues that involve all children, males and females alike. In addition, advocates believe that since the adoption of the CRC, all children have ceased to be considered simply as "objects of protection" but are also considered as "subjects of rights" (Mauras 2011, p. 52). Moreover, building on the protection and promotion of children's rights in other international treaties, supporters of the CRC maintain that the Articles of the CRC significantly complement those contained in other conventions and treaties enacted before and after the adoption of the CRC in 1989 (Mauras 2011; Onyango and Lynch 2006). For instance, the CRC draws inspiration from, and echoes relevant rights that are similar to those found in the UDHR (1948), the International Covenant for Civil and Political Rights (ICCPR 1966), the International Covenant on Economic, Social, and Cultural Rights (ICESCR 1966), the Convention on Consent to Marriage, Minimum Age of Marriage, and Registration of Marriages (Marriage Convention 1964), and the Convention on the Elimination of all Forms of Discrimination Against Women (CEDAW 1979). It has also inspired the development of other children rights' treaties such as the African Charter on the Rights and Welfare of the Child (ACRWC 1990) and other regional, international, and national laws regarding children's rights. Notably, however, on the issue of the definition of a child and child marriage, the ACRWC, which essentially builds on the CRC, specifically defines a child as "every human being below the age of 18 years" (Article 2), and explicitly prohibits "child marriage and the betrothal of girls and boys" (Article 21).

Putting all the above into perspective, and taken on its own merits, it can be argued that the CRC represents a major contribution to the advancement of children's rights, but admittedly, its definition of a child as anyone under 18 except "majority is attained earlier" opens an avenue for different actors and institutions to challenge one another at the local level over who is old enough to marry. Here, and based on the conceptual framework adopted in this chapter, it is clear that the politics of human rights, understood as a political battlefield, lends the definition of a child in the CRC to various interpretations and translations by different actors and networks at the national level. As discussed below, in the case of Nigeria where the practice of child marriage is sometimes justified in the name of religious and customary laws and practice, actors and institutions have justified the practice of child marriage according to the attainment of "majority." Conversely, human rights campaigners and activists who oppose child marriages have also sought to prohibit child marriages with reference to the CRC. Tellingly, and despite the challenges faced in their battles over how to define the age of a child, the continuous efforts of women and human rights activists and civil society networks to combat the throes of religious and traditional practices like child marriage, as well as the battle against the promoters and defenders of these practices, constitute one of the defining aspects of the politics of human rights in Africa, which combined reflects how violations of the rights of women and girls continue to unravel on the continent (Okafor 2007; Ibhawoh 2001; Odinkalu 2001; Mahmud 1993). The next section analyzes the realities of these battles in the Nigerian context with regards to defining the age of a child and child marriage.

The CRC, Child Marriage, and the Politics of Human Rights in Nigeria

Nigeria signed and ratified the CRC in January 1990 and April 1991 respectively (Braimah 2014). Yet, even though the country finally domesticated the CRC in 2003 after the Child Rights Act (CRA 2003) was signed into law, the CRA has not been fully adopted by all 36 federating states in Nigeria. Following its signing and ratification of the CRC in the early 1990s, efforts by the Federal Government of Nigeria under the former military regimes of Generals Ibrahim Babangida (1985–1993) and Sani Abacha (1993–1998) to promulgate the CRC into law was rejected and resisted by opponents, mostly religious and traditional leaders, who argued that the CRC was incompatible with Nigeria's customs and traditions (Alemika et al. 2004). According to Alemika et al. (2004, p. 6), "A first Bill on Children's rights had already been elaborated in 1993, but could not be passed into law by the military government because of opposition from religious groups and traditionalists. A special committee was subsequently set up to 'harmonize the Children's Bill with Nigerian religious and customary beliefs.'" The military did not succeed in domesticating the CRC before the restoration of democratic rule in 1999. The return of democratic governance to Nigeria reopened the space for (re)introducing a bill to domesticate the CRC, and in 2002, an attempt was made by supporters of the CRC to pass a draft bill titled the Child Rights Bill in the national parliament. But due to opposition by some legislators who argued that the bill, especially its definition of a child as anyone under 18, is incompatible with the religious and traditional customs of Nigeria, the bill was defeated (Braimah 2014; Alemika et al. 2004).

With the local and international condemnation that followed the parliament's failure to pass the Child Rights Bill in 2002, the bill was reintroduced in the parliament and was successfully passed and signed into law as the Child Rights Act in 2003. Notably, although the passage of the CRA was a significant achievement for advocates of child rights in Nigeria, not least because the CRA's definition of a child as anyone below 18 years old was retained and because the CRA explicitly follows the trend of the ACRWC in banning child marriage and betrothal of children, opposition to the CRA still continues. It is equally important to note that the compromise reached by the Nigerian legislators hitherto opposed to the CRA can be seen as reflecting their knowledge of the fact that the CRA is not effective until passed at the subnational level. This is because the Nigerian constitution empowers and authorizes the subnational parliaments in each of the 36 states to legislate on child-related issues in their jurisdictions as part of items in the residual legislative list (Federal Government of Nigeria (FGN) 1999, Section 4(7a)). Hence, many of the national legislators opposed to the CRC, many of whom were from the conservation northern states where Sharia law is practiced as part of the plural legal system at the subnational level, and where child marriages are quite common, understood that shifting the battle to the subnational level might take away focus at the national level. Indeed, partly due to the refusal to adopt the definition of a child as anyone less than 18 years old, 11 of Nigeria's 36 federating states have not passed the enabling laws to give effect to the CRA in their own jurisdictions, 14 years after the passage of the CRA at the national level.

To be sure, while the domestication of the CRA at the subnational level has been slow, the battles over "who is a child" has been mainly prominent among actors who argue in favor of Sharia and customary laws that sometimes serve as justification for marriages of persons below 18 years. Ten of the 11 states that have not passed the CRA are Sharia practicing states in northern Nigeria where early marriage is common. Tellingly, in Jigawa State, which is also a Sharia practicing state that has domesticated the CRA, the CRA was domesticated without the adoption of 18 years old as the legal age for a child to marry; instead, it opted for a definition of a child as anyone that has not reached puberty (Ogunniran 2011). Worse still, some other non-Sharia practicing states where the CRA has been domesticated also did not adopt the definition of anyone under 18 years as a child, not least due to some customary practices supporting the marriage of persons under 18. For instance, Iguh and Nosike (2011, p. 98) observe that "In the process of adapting [the CRA], some states have changed the definition of a "child". In some states, a child is a young person under age of thirteen years. In other states like Akwa Ibom State, he/she is a young person under the age of sixteen years." Consequently, the

CRA has faced a myriad of interpretations and translations. But to understand the battles that have led to multiple interpretations and translations of the CRC/CRA in Nigeria, it is necessary to analyze the arguments of key actors. In particular, considering the plural legal system in operation in Nigeria, understanding the position taken by key actors, especially in relation to Islamic law and jurisprudence, and the arguments of local and international child/women and human rights activists, is imperative.

To begin with, to accommodate its religious and cultural diversity, and building on its colonial foundation as a former British colony with an English common law legal system, Nigeria operates a constitutionally sanctioned plural legal system. As the main legal document of the country, Nigeria's 1999 constitution recognizes and makes provision for a common law legal system alongside Islamic and customary laws at the subnational levels. Thus, Chapter VII of the Nigerian constitution of 1999 makes provision for the application of a common-law system across the federation and specifies the hierarchy of courts, both at the federal and state levels, but with clear mention of the Supreme Court of Nigeria as the highest court of the land (FGN 1999). But the constitution does not explicitly define who qualifies as a child in Nigeria. Yet, with regards to eligibility for citizenship renunciation, Section 29(4a) states that such person must be of "full age," meaning a person of 18 years above, and Section 29(4b) states that "any woman who is married shall be deemed to be of a full age." Although the latter section primarily concerns citizenship, it raises the question about how marital rights are set in relation to chronological and/or social age definitions. Without a clear definition of who qualifies as a child in the constitution, and with the prerogative of setting the age of marriage falling on the subnational states, it is not uncommon to find different ages in the laws of various states in Nigeria. Although the CRA's definition of a child as anyone below 18 years (FGN 2003, Section 274) was intended to clarify the age of a child as applicable in Nigeria, the application of that age limit is only to the extent that states adopt the CRA without making changes to the definition of the age of a child in their jurisdictions.

Consequently, even though the federal government continues to advocate for the adoption of the CRA without alterations to the definitions of a child at the state level, such advocacy has sometimes been resisted at the federal and subnational level by religious and traditional leaders and politicians opposed to the definitions of a child in the CRA. For example, Imam Sani, a notable Islamic cleric in Nigeria, once declared that "if the [Federal] government imposed the CRA, there will be violent conflicts from some Muslims to the extent that some will even die in the process" (Iman Sani, quoted in Ogunniran 2011, p. 92). Perhaps a more notable example of such resistance comes from a renowned Nigerian Senator, Ahmed Yerima, who not only resisted attempts to expunge Section 29(4b) of the Nigerian constitution in 2013 (Ekott 2013) but who also put up a religious-based defense in response to condemnations of marrying a 13-year-old Egyptian girl in 2010 (Braimah 2014; Ogunniran 2011). According to Senator Yerima, "any Muslim who marries a girl of nine years and above is following the teaching and practice of Prophet Muhammad (SAW). If there is anyone who will tell me that what you did contradict Islam, I will say I will submit, and I will do whatever they ask me to do" (Senator Yerima, quoted in Braimah 2014, p. 486). It should be added that after Nigeria returned to democratic rule in 1999, Senator Yerima was a major champion of extending Sharia law beyond Islamic personal law to criminal laws, and was the Governor of Zamfara State, the first state to pass state legislation extending the jurisprudence of Sharia law to criminal matters in 2000 before the other 11 Sharia practicing states did same (World Watch Monitor 2013).

It is quite instructive to note that religious arguments in support of respecting Islamic/Sharia laws are often advanced as expression of religious freedom and rights as guaranteed by the Nigerian constitution. In fact, Islamic clerics and advocates of Sharia in Nigeria sometimes allude to Section 38 of the 1999 constitution that guarantees the "right to freedom of thought, conscience, and religion" (FGN 1999; see also Kendhammer 2013; Suberu 2010; Paden 2005). Moreover, as Braimah (2014) notes, arguments in support of the legality of child marriages can equally be defended by religious and traditional actors based on the contents of the Second Schedule, Part 1, item 61, of the 1999 Nigerian constitution, which limits the powers of the federal government in nullifying marriages contracted under religious and/or customary laws. As part of items under the exclusive legislative list that the federal government can solely legislate upon, Section 61, Part 1 of the Second Schedule of the 1999 constitution states as follows: "[t]he formation, annulment and dissolution of marriages other than marriages under Islamic law and customary law including matrimonial causes relating thereto." Hence, despite the fact that the CRA clearly states in Section 21 that "[n]o person under the age of 18 years is capable of contracting a valid marriage, and accordingly, a marriage so contracted is null and void and of no effect whatsoever," such marriages may be considered valid with respect to Section 61, Part 1 of the Second Schedule of the 1999 constitution. The same validity arguments may be advanced to trump the contents of Section 22 of the CRA, which states that "[n]o parent, guardian or any other person shall betroth a child to any person" (FGN 2003) if based on religious and customary grounds.

At issue is the fact that regardless of the rather ambitious and progressive contents of the CRC and the CRA, which combined should protect the rights of children generally, and those of young girls and women in particular against early marriage (Mauras 2011; UNICEF 2007), the ambiguous and sometimes contradictory provisions of the Nigerian constitution regarding (child) marriage provide ample space for different actors to battle over the definition of a child. Yet, local and international human rights opponents of child marriage have also tried to advocate for children's rights in Nigeria based on the contents of the CRC, the CRA, and the Nigerian constitution of 1999. Noting that the CRC, the CRA, and the Nigerian constitution contain relevant provisions on fundamental human rights such as the right to health and protection against harmful religious and cultural practices, women and human rights activists continue to argue against child marriages in Nigeria (Tajudeen 2015; Obiechina 2014; Akwara et al. 2005). Citing the detrimental effects of child marriages on children, including the high rates of maternal mortality and the cases of Vesicle Vagina Fistula (VVF) and Rectum Vagina Fistula (RVF) as common problems experienced by young mothers, human rights activists continue to battle advocates of child marriages in Nigeria (Ogunniran 2011; Para-Mallam 2010; Jacob and Dosunmu 2014). The unenviable position of Nigeria as one of the countries where child marriage is still prevalent, and the fact that the practice of child marriage often leads to social exclusion of young girls, many of whom are often times denied access to education once married at a young age, have also been put forward to oppose the practice of child marriage in Nigeria (National Bureau of Statistics and UNICEF 2017; Ekpe et al. 2014; Makama 2013; Staveren and Odebode 2007). Thus, when interpreting extant laws regarding the age of a child, human rights activists often seek to draw on the CRC, the CRA, and the fundamental human rights such as the right to life and dignity of the human persons as provided for in the Nigerian constitution but also on other rights that are at stake especially for girls—right to health and right to education mainly.

More so, in cases where children who are (forcefully) married at young ages by their parents and/or guardians are accused of committing crimes, human rights activists have often defended such children with references to laws like the CRA. For example, during a highly publicized case involving Wasila Tasiu, a 14-year-old child who was accused of poisoning her 35-year-old husband and three of his friends in Kano State in 2014, Hussaina Ibrahim, a lawyer, human rights activist, and member of the International Federation of Women Lawyers, defended Tasiu (Rahman 2014). Even though the CRA makes provision for anyone under 18 years to be tried for criminal offenses in a Child Justice Administration system, which would require that Tasiu be treated as a minor as her lawyer argued, she was remanded in a prison during the trial and charged in a regular court because the CRA does not apply in Kano State, a Sharia practicing state where the CRA is yet to be domesticated. Facing the death penalty if convicted and with evidence by the prosecutor alleging her confession to the crime (Stein 2014), local and international attention was drawn to Tasiu's case. Although Tasiu's case was discontinued in 2015 after the state prosecutor withdrew the charges against her and requested that the case be closed, many observers attribute the withdrawal of the case to pressures from both local and international human rights groups (Hart 2015; Sandler Clarke 2015). Indeed, it was reported that part of Tasiu's confession to the crime included statements regarding her intention to leave a marriage she was forced into by her parents, and one where she did not love the man she was forced to marry (Rahman 2014; Stein 2014). The attention generated by the case brought unwanted focus on the institutionalized practice of child marriage in Nigeria, and Tasiu's case also highlighted the vulnerability of young girls to the powers of the state as well as harmful religious and cultural practices that continue to violate the rights of young girls in Nigeria.

Conclusion: Slow Winds of Change

This chapter focused on the battles surrounding the definition of a child and specifically examined the battles between supporters and opponents of child marriage in Nigeria. It examined the justifications and arguments put forward by actors such as religious and traditional leaders (religious freedom) as well as politicians and human rights activists (child rights, women's rights) with regards adhering to the age limits set out by the CRC and CRA for marriages in Nigeria. As discussed above, the battle over the age of a child for marital purpose in Nigeria is a complicated one that highlights how the politics of human rights in Nigeria is a political battleground for different actors to confront one another and justify their own positions, sometimes drawing from similar legal sources like the Nigerian constitution. Despite setting the age of 18 years as the age of marriage in the CRA, the lack of such a definition in the 1999 constitution of Nigeria, and the fact that the constitution contains provisions that can be drawn upon to justify child marriages on religious and customary grounds, creates a challenge for many opponents of child marriage in Nigeria.

However, human rights activists have continued their advocacy against child marriages and continue to demand for the age of marriage of persons below 18 years to be upheld as illegal across Nigeria. On its part, the government has continued to emphasize its advocacy around ending child marriage, and in 2016, the government of Nigeria launched a National Strategy to End Child Marriage by 2030 (FGN 2016). It is also important to note that while still at an early stage, and despite the resistance from religious and traditional leaders and institutions in the northern part of Nigeria, the Emir of Kano, Sanusi Lamido Sanusi, has become a strong opponent of child marriage and an advocate for ending the practice. According to the Emir, who ascended the headship of the Kano Emirate in 2014, "[t]here is an idea in the north [of Nigeria] that child marriage is Islamic, but it is not an article of faith, it is something societies decide for themselves" (Emir Sanusi, quoted in Akinwotu 2017). Hence, the Emir has made it a part of his reform agenda to end child marriage in his Emirate, a strong religious and political institution with great influence in northern Nigeria. If the Emir's efforts to reform the system of child marriage in Kano State succeed, at least to some extent, it may serve as an inspiration for other states in the north of Nigeria to follow in curbing the practice of child marriage. But while it will take some time to change the minds of religious and traditional actors to end the practice of child marriage, it is necessary to end by noting that the battles over the definition of a child will require strong networks and partnerships among state and non-state actors and institutions opposed to the practice.

References

Aderinto, Saheed, ed. 2015. *Children and Childhood in Colonial Nigerian Histories*. New York: Palgrave Macmillan.

Akinwotu, Emmanuel. 2017. "Lamido Sanusi, Kano's 'Progressive Fraud,' Takes Aim at Child Marriage in Nigeria." *The Guardian*, August 25. https://www.

theguardian.com/global-development/2017/aug/25/lamido-sanusi-emir-kano-end-child-marriage-nigeria.

Akwara, Azalahu Francis, Adekunle G. Soyibo, and Michael S. Agba. 2005. Law and Children's Rights Protection: The Nexus for a Sustainable Development in Nigeria. *Canadian Social Science* 6 (2): 26–33.

Alemika, E.E.O, Innocent Chukwuma, Donika Lafratta, Daniel Messerli, and Jarmila Souckova. 2004. *Rights of the Child in Nigeria: Report on the implementation of the Convention on the Rights of the Child by Nigeria*. A Report Prepared for the Committee on the Rights of the Child. 38th Session—Geneva, June. https://www.scribd.com/document/87272302/Nigeria-Ngo-Report-OMCT.

Askari, Ladan. 1998. The Convention on the Rights of the Child: The Necessity of Adding a Provision to Ban Child Marriages. *ILSA Journal of International Comparative Law* 5 (1): 123–138.

Balibar, Etienne. 2013. On the Politics of Human Rights. *Constellations* 20 (1): 18–26.

Blouin-Genest, Gabriel, and Sylvie Paquerot. 2016. Environmental Human Rights as a Battlefield: A Grammar of Political Confrontation. *Journal of Human Rights and the Environment* 7 (1): 132–154.

Braimah, S. Tim. 2014. Child Marriage in Northern Nigeria: Section 61 of Part I of the 1999 Constitution and the Protection of Children Against Child Marriage. *African Human Rights Law Journal* 14: 474–488.

Brown, Wendy. 2004. "The Most We Can Hope For...": Human Rights and The Politics of Fatalism. *The South Atlantic Quarterly* 103 (2/3): 451–463.

Clark-Kazak, Christina Rose. 2009. Towards a Working Definition and Application of Social Age in International Development Studies. *The Journal of Development Studies* 45 (8): 1307–1324.

Committee on the Rights of the Child. 1996. *Consideration of Reports Submitted by States Parties Under Article 44 of the Convention*. Geneva: United Nations.

———. 2010. *Consideration of Reports Submitted by States Parties Under Article 44 of the Convention*. Geneva: United Nations.

Convention on the Rights of the Child. 1989. *Convention on the Rights of the Child*. New York: United Nations.

Doek, E. Jaap. 2009. The CRC 20 Years: An Overview of Some of the Major Achievements and Remaining Challenges. *Child Abuse and Neglect* 33 (11): 771–782.

Durojaye, Ebenezer. 2013. 'Woman, but Not Human': Widowhood Practices and Human Rights Violations in Nigeria. *International Journal of Law, Policy and the Family* 27 (2): 176–196.

Ekott, Ini. 2013. Yerima Makes Senate Back Underage Marriage, as Lawmakers Oppose Local Government Autonomy. *The Times*, July 17. https://www.

premiumtimesng.com/news/141117-yerima-makes-senate-back-underage-marriage-as-lawmakers-oppose-local-government-autonomy.html.

Ekpe, E. Dickson, Alobo Eni Eja, and Egbe Inyang John. 2014. Women, Gender Equality in Nigeria: A Critical Analysis of Socio-economic and Political (Gender Issues). *Journal Research in Peace, Gender, and Development* 4 (1): 15–20.

Evans, Tony. 2001. *The Politics of Human Rights: A Global Perspective.* 1st ed. Ann Arbor: Pluto Press.

———. 2005. *The Politics of Human Rights: A Global Perspective.* 2nd ed. Ann Arbor: Pluto Press.

Federal Republic of Nigeria. 1999. *1999 Constitution of Nigeria.* Abuja: Federal Republic of Nigeria.

———. 2003. *Child Rights Act.* Abuja: Federal Republic of Nigeria.

———. 2016. *National Strategy to End Child Marriage.* Abuja: Federal Republic of Nigeria.

Gready, Paul. 2003. The Politics of Human Rights. *Third World Quarterly* 24 (4): 745–757.

Hart, Beth. 2015. Killer Bride: Prosecution Drops Charges Against Wasila. *Naija News*, May 20. https://www.naija.ng/64073.html.

Ibhawoh, Bonny. 2001. Cultural Relativism and Human Rights: Reconsidering the Africanist Discourse. *Netherlands Quarterly of Human Rights* 19 (1): 45–62.

Ignatieff, Michael. 2001. The Attack on Human Rights. *Foreign Affairs* 80 (6): 102–116.

Iguh, Nwamaka Adaora, and Onyeka Nosike. 2011. An Examination of the Child Rights Protection and Corporal Punishment in Nigeria. *Nnamdi Azikiwe University Journal of International Law and Jurisprudence* 2: 97–111.

Ingram, D. James. 2008. What Is a "Right to Have Rights"? Three Images of the Politics of Human Rights. *The American Political Science Review* 101 (4): 401–416.

Isaac, C. Jeffrey. 1996. A New Guarantee on Earth: Hannah Arendt on Human Dignity and the Politics of Human Rights. *American Political Science Review* 90 (1): 61–73.

Jacob, Ogunniyi Olayemi, and Akinola George Dosunmu. 2014. Historical and Cultural Implications of Immunodeficiency Virus (HIV) and Women's Rights in Nigeria: A Contextual Clarification. *European Scientific Journal* Special Edition: 321–326.

Kendhammer, Brandon. 2013. The Sharia Controversy in Northern Nigeria and the Politics of Islamic Law in New and Uncertain Democracies. *Comparative Politics* 45 (3): 291–311.

Law, John. 1992. Notes on the Theory of the Actor-Network: Ordering, Strategy, and Heterogeneity. *Systems Practice* 5 (4): 379–393.

Mahmud, S. Sakah. 1993. The State and Human Rights in Africa in the 1990s: Perspectives and Prospects. *Human Rights Quarterly* 15 (3): 485–498.

Makama, Godiya Allanana. 2013. Patriarchy and Gender Inequality in Nigeria: The Way Forward. *European Scientific Journal* 9 (17): 115–144.

Mauras, Marta. 2011. Public Policies and Child Rights: Entering the Third Decade of the Convention on the Rights of the Child. *The Annals of the American Academy of Political and Social Science* 633: 52–65.

Moynihan, P.Daniel. 1977. The Politics of Human Rights. *Commentary* 64 (2): 19–26.

Mulinge, M. Munyae. 2010. Persistent Socioeconomic and Political Dilemmas to the Implementation of the 1989 United Nations Convention on the Rights of the Child in Sub-Saharan Africa. *Child Abuse and Neglect* 34: 10–17.

National Bureau of Statistics (NBS) and United Nations Children's Fund (UNICEF). 2017. *Multiple Indicator Cluster Survey 2016–17*, Survey Findings Report. Abuja: National Bureau of Statistics and United Nations Children's Fund.

Obiechina, O. Georgy. 2014. Violation of Child's Rights in Nigeria: Implications for Child Health. *Academic Research International* 5 (1): 151–159.

Odinkalu, Anselm Chidi. 2001. Analysis of Paralysis or Paralysis by Analysis? Implementing Economic, Social, and Cultural Rights Under the African Charter on Human and People's Rights. *Human Rights Quarterly* 23 (2): 327–369.

Ogunniran, Iyabode. 2011. Child Bride and Child Sex: Combating Child Marriages in Nigeria. *Nnamdi Azikiwe University Journal of International Law and Jurisprudence* 2: 85–96.

Okafor, C. Obiora. 2007. *The African Human Rights System, Activist Forces and International Institutions.* Cambridge: Cambridge University Press.

Onyango, Philista, and Margaret A. Lynch. 2006. Implementing the Right to Child Protection: A Challenge for Developing Countries. *Lancet* 367: 693–694.

Paden, N. John. 2005. *Muslim Civic Cultures and Conflict Resolution: The Challenge of Democratic Federalism in Nigeria.* Washington, DC: Brookings Institution Press.

Para-Mallam, J. Funmi. 2010. Promoting Gender Equality in the Context of Nigerian Cultural and Religious Expression: Beyond Increasing Female Access to Education. *Compare: A Journal of Comparative and International Education* 40 (4): 459–477.

Rahman, Sophia. 2014. Child Bride Aged 14 'Killed 35-Year-old Husband with Rat Poison and Signed Confession with Thumbprint'. *Mirror*, December 23. http://www.mirror.co.uk/news/world-news/child-bride-aged-14-killed-4867292.

Sandler Clarke, Joe. 2015. Child Bride Freed by Nigerian Authorities Looks to New Beginnings. *The Guardian*, June 11. https://www.theguardian.com/global-development-professionals-network/2015/jun/11/child-bride-threatened-with-death-freed-nigeria.

Santos Pais, Marta, and Susan Bissell. 2006. Overview and Implementation of the UN Convention on the Rights of the Child. *Lancet* 367: 689–690.

Stein, Chris. 2014. When She Was Barely a Teen, Wasila Tasiu Became a Wife. Seventeen Days Later, She Was an Accused Killer. *Al Jazeera America*, December 3. http://projects.aljazeera.com/2014/child-marriage/.

Suberu, Rotimi. 2010. The Sharia Challenge: Revisiting the Travails of the Secular State. In *Encountering the Nigerian State*, ed. Wale Adebanwi and Ebenezer Obadare, 217–241. New York: Palgrave Macmillan.

Tajudeen, Ojo Ibraheem. 2015. Legal Framework for the Protection of Child Rights in Nigeria. *AGORA International Journal of Juridical Sciences* 3: 46–52.

United Nations Children Fund. 2007. *Information Sheet: Child Rights Act*. Abuja: UNICEF.

Van Staveren, Irene, and Olasunbo Odebode. 2007. Gender Norms as Asymmetric Institutions: A Case Study of Yoruba Women in Nigeria. *Journal of Economic Issues* 41 (4): 903–925.

Vincent, Andrew. 2010. *The Politics of Human Rights*. Oxford: Oxford University Press.

Warner, Elizabeth. 2011. Behind the Wedding Veil: Child Marriage as a Form of Trafficking in Girls. *Journal of Gender, Social Policy and the Law* 12 (2): 233–271.

World Watch Monitor. 2013. *Former Nigerian Governor Allows 'Under-Age' Marriage Loophole into Constitution*, July 23. https://www.worldwatchmonitor.org/2013/07/former-nigerian-governor-allows-under-age-marriage-loophole-into-constitution/.

CHAPTER 8

Forcibly Sterilized: Peru's Indigenous Women and the Battle for Rights

Ñusta Carranza Ko

Toward the summer of 2016 when Peru's presidential race headed for a runoff, a human right story that had been previously sidelined surfaced as an emblematic case of impunity against indigenous people's rights: the forced sterilization of indigenous women during the period of the internal armed conflict in Peru (1980–2000). Referred to as a "crime against humanity" by then presidential candidate Pedro Pablo Kuczynski (El Comercio 2016), forced sterilizations are "surgical procedures of sterilization performed on a person against their will or without their free and informed consent" (MINUS 2017). In Peru, forced sterilization represented "the trashing of indigenous women's rights."[1] Despite the public's attention brought on this case during the presidential elections and the claims to justice from indigenous non-governmental organizations, in the months following the presidential race the Public Prosecutor's Office put aside a total of 2074 cases of forced sterilization for insufficient information and "definitively" shelved a separate set of 77 cases of forced sterilization on grounds of no state responsibility (La República 2016). The challenges facing accountability for indigenous women and the violence of

Ñ. Carranza Ko (✉)
Ohio Northern University, Ada, OH, USA
e-mail: n-carranzako@onu.edu

G. Blouin-Genest et al. (eds.), *Human Rights as Battlefields*, Human Rights Interventions,
https://doi.org/10.1007/978-3-319-91770-2_8

forced sterilization they suffered shed light to the status of indigenous women's rights in Peru, as a battlefield, that is constantly debated and contested by the state.

This chapter examines the current status of indigenous people's rights in Peru as it relates to human rights violations from the internal armed conflict period. Particularly, it focuses on the forced sterilization of women of indigenous and poor economic backgrounds under the name of the *Programa de Salúd Reproductiva y Planificación Familiar* (Program of Reproductive Health and Planned Parenthood or PSRPF) (1996–2001) that represents a culmination of violence against indigenous people and women's rights. According to Article 7(I)(g) of the Rome Statute of the International Criminal Court, forced sterilization is a crime against humanity (ICC 2002). Despite the gravity of the crime, indigenous women victims of forced sterilization have had to accept the state's non-recognition of their suffering, including the human rights community's failure to include the violations in the Final Report of the Truth and Reconciliation Commission, released in 2003. However, in Peru, forced sterilization has been invoked during every presidential election period since 2006 by political parties and presidential candidates and swayed voters in favor of Pedro Pablo Kuczynski in the 2016 election (El Comercio 2016).

Nevertheless, the forced sterilization issue has been neglected by the truth-seeking process (2001–2003)[2] and as of 2017 has not been brought to trial. Relying on interviews with prominent human rights practitioners and archival sources collected by domestic and international advocacy groups on forced sterilization, this chapter analyzes the current status of Peru's indigenous people's rights. It proposes an intersectional human rights analysis for understanding the case of forced sterilization of indigenous women. The analysis is rooted in the perspective that human rights violations may have overlapping categories of rights violations based on gender, race, ethnicity, and class. To this approach, individuals who carry "more than one stigmatized characteristic" (Fried 2002, p. 88), be that of an ethnic minority and of a marginalized gender, are more likely to be targets of discrimination and human rights violations. The intersectional framework has been employed to examine sexual violence in Peru's internal armed conflict (Boesten 2016) but not to analyze the precise case of forced sterilization of indigenous women. This perspective helps to understand why no progress has been made within the Peruvian institutions on such a revolting issue as is the forced sterilization of hundreds of thousands of indigenous women, despite strong activism and international support for these claims.

The chapter first uses intersecting normative markers from international human rights agreements to draw a broad picture of the status of state compliance with international norms on the protection of indigenous peoples and women. The legal instruments address discrimination on the basis of indigenous rights and gender, and capture intersectional linkages between racial (indigenous peoples) and sexual violence. These include the protection against all forms of discrimination and eradication of violence against indigenous women, enshrined in the United Nations Declaration on the Rights of Indigenous Peoples (2007), International Labor Organization's (ILO) Convention 169, the Inter-American Convention on the Rights of Indigenous Peoples (2016), and the Inter-American Convention on the Prevention, Punishment, and Eradication of Violence Against Women (1994). Considering the case of forced sterilization, this chapter finds limitations in state compliance with adopted international norms on respecting indigenous people and women's rights.

This chapter argues that such limitations of norms compliance and the resulting case of forced sterilization are perpetuated by the intersecting set of domestic oppressive forces of sexism, racism, and class-based discrimination directed at an economically marginalized population, who are also a vulnerable group in Peru's patriarchal society. The crime of forced sterilization reflects the structural inequality embedded in historical power relationships between the dominant white society and the marginalized indigenous sectors. As such, the sparks of interests toward indigenous people, particularly indigenous women's rights for instance during presidential elections, only serve to reaffirm the differences in power, the multiple layers of discrimination, and how indigenous people's rights are contested and manipulated as a political tool to advance elite political interests as will be argued.

Debates in Human Rights

In the last two decades, the scholarship on human rights has moved away from analyzing human rights violations toward women as a single category of discrimination, to include other relevant categories such as race, ethnicity, class, religion, and sexual orientation. Scholars have suggested the building of a "framework for a reconceptualization of human rights" and changes to the structure of "human rights institutions" that will allow an "intersectional human rights analysis" (Bond 2003, p. 52). This intersectional perspective borrows heavily from critical race studies, with scholars such as Crenshaw (1991) who theorizes how the "experiences of women of color are frequently the product of intersecting patterns of racism and sexism" and that their "intersectional identity as both women and of color" marginalizes them further (1991, pp. 1243–1244). Such views are now echoed in human rights work on how discrimination and "human rights abuses" against women are shaped by intersecting layers of hierarchies based on "religions, races, classes, ethnicities, sexualities" (Bond 2003, p. 80).

Related to Peru's internal armed conflict, scholars have discussed the possible relationship of race, class, and gender in human rights violations. In her study on sexual violence during armed conflict, Boesten explains that the profile of the majority of the victims of sexual violence showed how "race, class, and gender are interlinked to the formation of hierarchies in Peru" (2016, p. 18). She argues how given the marginalization of the indigenous population, economically and racially, it was inevitable that the most vulnerable population in society would become targets of human rights violations. Within this victim group, in particular, indigenous women accounted for the majority of victims as the subaltern group in a patriarchal society who also belonged to a socially undermined racial group (Boesten 2016, p. 18).

Using a comparative study of Peru, Guatemala, and Colombia's experiences of sexual violence during internal armed conflict, Kravetz provides a similar observation to Boesten's on the importance of gender, class, and race. These dimensions "played a key role in rendering certain communities" more vulnerable than others in all three states (Kravetz 2017, p. 709). For Peru and Guatemala in particular, this included women from "indigenous and rural communities" (Kravetz 2017, p. 711). Kravetz's work is substantiated by Bueno-Hansen (2015), who has also examined gender-based violence from an intersectional perspective. She argues how "ethnicity, language, and gender" may have interacted to affect the Andean Quechua-speaking women peasants to be vulnerable targets of violence (2015, p. 3). Expanding the intersections, Bueno-Hansen brings insights from de-colonial feminism that studies "the way that colonial relations of exploitation and domination function and persist to the present day" (2015, p. 3). In doing so, she explains how exclusions based on geography, language, and identification from the colonial era have been crucial for "understanding the embedded layers of violence" (Bueno-Hansen 2015, p. 13).

Within the framework of sexual violations, forced sterilizations represent a unique case of women's reproductive rights and indigenous people's rights violations. Getgen (2009) critically evaluates the role of Peru's Truth and Reconciliation Commission (CVR) in not documenting the forced sterilization of indigenous women.[3] She argues that the CVR's voluntary omission of the state's forced sterilization of indigenous women "without informed consent through the State's Family Planning Program" in the Final Report (2003), revealed the limitations of the Commission in presenting an overarching picture of human rights crimes during the internal armed conflict (2009, p. 4).[4] Moreover, the exclusion of these particular human rights violations in the CVR's Final Report made it significantly more difficult for victims, predominantly poor indigenous Quechua-speaking women, to seek accountability (Getgen 2009, p. 4).

Mantilla Falcón analyzes forced sterilization from a more legalistic standpoint. Noting how the case represented more of a violation of reproductive rights, she argues how a male-centered approach in international law has made reproductive rights invisible (Mantilla Falcón 2016, p. 11). In the case of Peru, she argues it is important to recognize international documents that protect women's rights and for the state to acknowledge the different rights that have been violated as a result of forced sterilizations. These include the right to reproductive health, right to life without discrimination and violence on the basis of gender, right to education, and the right to liberty and personal security (Mantilla Falcón 2016, pp. 17–20).

Other scholars focus more on what the sterilization campaign represented in Peru. Ewig analyzes the economic and structural societal factors associated with this human rights violation, looking at how forced sterilization was justified on grounds of population control for Peru's economic advancement (2014, p. 53). She explains that Fujimori launched his campaign stemming from Thomas Malthus's idea of overpopulation, resource depletion, and economic downturn. The President used the fight against poverty as a justification for a family planning campaign which included forced sterilization (Ewig 2014). On a related note, Del Aguila (2006) discusses how the sterilization campaign reflects Peruvian society's unequal treatment of the indigenous population. Referring to the historic roots of racial inequality and urban-rural divide from the Spanish colonial period, he discusses how Fujimori's discourse was used to manipulate indigenous peoples in the rural areas. He documents malpractices of government health practitioners coming from urban areas, speaking Spanish, and who were of mixed European heritage who subjugated and forced with false information indigenous women to accept sterilization (Del Aguila 2006, p. 115). Such societal interactions were made possible in the context of Peru's society where indigenous peoples in rural areas were treated as inferiors in comparison to those coming from the urban centers with a lighter skin complexion.

This chapter aims to complement these existing human rights research on sexual violence, while also introducing a new scholarship of an intersectional human rights analysis to the case of forced sterilization of indigenous women. This is accomplished through the use of international and regional instruments of human rights that address indigenous people's rights and women's rights. The overlapping layers of rights categories define a new intersectional normative marker that assesses the Peruvian state's protection of indigenous people's rights in the case of forced sterilization. The marker is complemented by a domestic intersectional exploration of ethnicity, gender, and class that provides the reasons why indigenous people's rights and indigenous women's rights have become a political battlefield (and are still currently contested) in Peru. Ultimately, these findings bring to light the limitations of international instruments in influencing domestic states toward respecting indigenous people's rights in Peru and the continued prevalence of domestic historical roots of racism, sexism, and class-related discrimination that shape state behavior toward human rights.

Human Rights in Peru

Peru's modern history of massive human rights abuses and internal armed conflict began on May 17, 1980, when the leftist guerrilla group *Sendero Luminoso* (Shining Path) announced its "popular war from the countryside to the city" (Comisión de la Verdad y Reconciliación 2003, p. 54). During the two decades from 1980 to 2000, Peru experienced three periods of authoritarian rule with a significant military presence in Belaúnde Terry (1980–1985), Alan García (1985–1990), and Alberto Fujimori's governments (1990–2000). Political repression against *Sendero Luminoso* resulted in 7995 deaths and disappearances during Terry's government (Comisión de la Verdad y Reconciliación 2003). Violations increased with García to the extent that respect for human rights virtually evaporated

(Roberts and Peceny 1997, p. 199). And with Fujimori, Peru endured an even more heightened period of repression. From 1990 to 2000, the state carried out the "gravest breaches of human rights" (Cassese 1999, p. 162), marked by a rule of human rights abuses from the state against insurgency groups and suspected government opponents. Human rights violations became commonplace, with the emblematic cases of violations in the 1991 *Barrios Altos* massacre of civilians and the forced disappearance and extra-judicial execution of students and professors at *La Cantuta* University in 1992 by state-sponsored death squads.

Long after the official dismantlement of *Sendero Luminoso* in 1992, Fujimori's resignation in 2000 signaled the end of the internal armed conflict. With the incoming interim government of Valentín Paniagua (2000–2001), Peru's CVR began its mandate to investigate past human rights abuses. In the Final Report (2003), the CVR calculated a total of 69,000 Peruvians killed or disappeared from 1980 to 2000 (Transfer Commission of the Truth and Reconciliation Commission of Peru 2014, p. 12). The Commission established state responsibility for 37 percent of the deaths and disappearances and *Sendero Luminoso* for 54 percent of the deaths and disappearances. Of the victims, the Commission concluded that the majority were civilians who spoke Quechua or other indigenous languages as their mother tongue and lived in Andean provinces and the Amazon region. These victims were caught between the political war of the leftist guerrilla movements (such as *Sendero* and the *Movimiento Revolucionario Túpac Amaru* [Revolutionary Movement of Tupac Amaru]) and the state, and they faced persecution from both groups. The characteristics of the victims of violence pointed to possible roots of racism and inequality within Peruvian society against indigenous peoples that played a part in the violence (Hayner 2001, p. 37; Lerner 2004, p. 208).

After the CVR released its findings, moments of justice followed with prosecutions of human rights violations that involved indigenous populations (e.g., Accomarca Massacre sentence issued in 2016). And in 2011, Peru became the first state to fully implement the ILO Convention 169 (ratified in 1993) via Law No. 29785 which recognizes tribal people's land ownership and the right to prior consultation for indigenous peoples. As part of a follow-up to the new law, the government established a multisectoral commission to implement prior consultation in 2016 via Supreme Decree No. 052-2016-PCM. During the same year, Peru also adopted the Inter-American Convention on the Rights of Indigenous Peoples.

Yet, despite successes in accountability and adoption of new norms respecting indigenous populations' rights, the situation of indigenous people's rights in Peru today continues to be politically contested. Indigenous peoples are marginalized and lack protection of their rights from the Peruvian government (Amnesty International 2017). Struggles for justice against impunity continue in unfinished cases of human rights violations directed at indigenous populations from the internal armed conflict and also in recent cases of indigenous rights violations. For instance, as of 2017, no state officials have been prosecuted for their role in the 2009 Bagua Massacre when police clashed with indigenous Amazonian people protesting against the US-Peru Free Trade Agreement provisions on occupation of indigenous people's land and exploitation of natural resources in Bagua, a northeastern city in the Department of Amazonas (Amnesty International 2017).

Sexual Violence

The status of indigenous rights in cases dealing with sexual violence committed during the internal conflict and periods of authoritarianism has also not fared better over the years. According to the Truth and Reconciliation Commission, sexual violence was a persistent practice during the internal armed conflict that affected women of low economic status from rural areas, 75 percent of whom were Quechua speakers (CVR 2003, p. 276). Many of these indigenous women lack government-issued identifications, which has made their violations virtually non-existent for the state (APRODEH 2008, p. 32). Most importantly, the state has failed to take responsibility for sexual violations that were disguised as a government family planning policy and targeted indigenous women. Alberto Fujimori's government implemented the PSRPF from 1996 to 2001. To promote the family planning program, the Ministry of Health began a national campaign holding Health and Fertility Festivals across rural and poor communities where the majority of the population were of indigenous descent. The festivals originally were to promote the use of various contraceptive methods, including voluntary surgical sterilization.

According to government documents, health officials performed 272,028 sterilizations on a majority of poor, rural, indigenous Quechua-speaking women.[5] While it is true that there were some voluntary sterilizations, in other cases, coercion and manipulation of information were commonplace.[6] Practices of forced sterilization were in part due to the obligatory sterilization quotas health officials were required to meet. The pressure exerted on health officials to meet their obligations, even involved monetary incentives when quotas were met (CLADEM 1999, p. 41).

Nonetheless, these pressures do not explain why, specifically, women predominantly of rural, poor indigenous communities were not provided the consent form, nor informed of other contraceptive options, intimidated to commit to surgery, and even deprived of liberty and locked in the waiting room prior to the surgery (CLADEM 1999, p. 41; Mogollón 2008, p. 40). Luisa Pinedo Rango, an indigenous woman from Shipibo of Ucayali, recalls how on two different occasions government health officials came to her native Amazonian community to inform her about family planning. Then, on the second visit, they urged her to undergo surgery, put her on a boat, and took her and other indigenous women to the health center. After giving her anesthesia without any information as to what was going on, she recalls, "I woke up and they told me that I could go back home…but I felt pain and I did not know what to do…they did not even give me a pill."[7] Luisa's story is corroborated by CVR's President Salomón Lerner who observed cases where after coerced tubal ligation there was no postoperative follow-up which increased the possibilities of infections and life-threatening conditions.[8]

The most emblematic case of forced sterilization was of María Mamérita Mestanza Chávez in 1998. Government health officials threatened to denounce María and her husband Jacinto Salazar Suárez to the police, claiming that they had violated the law by having more than five children (Corte Interamericana de Derechos Humanos 2003). Coerced by false information, María agreed to undergo a tubal ligation procedure on March 27, 1998. The surgery resulted in a series of health complications and her death on April 5, 1998. At the petition of various human rights organizations demanding justice for María from the Peruvian government, in 2003 the Inter-American Commission on Human Rights (IACHR) intervened to reach an amicable agreement of truth, justice, and reparations between María's family and the state. However, despite this agreement, as noted in press releases most recently on May 26, 2017, the Peruvian government failed to follow-up with the IACHR's recommendations (La República 2017b).

María's case is not the only one facing impunity. Other cases against the state and the former President Fujimori, totaling 2074 have been put aside by the Public Prosecutor's Office for insufficient information and are not being considered as a case of crimes against humanity (La República

2016). These include the stories of Quechua-native Dionicia Calderón Arellano who suffered multiple human rights violations, such as illegal detention by military forces, disappearance of her husband, and forced sterilization.[9] Despite the gravity of the crime, forced sterilization has faced difficulty in achieving accountability. The explanations related to this case point to the intersection of ethnicity, gender, and class that permeates Peruvian society today and impedes the state's compliance with international norms toward respecting indigenous people's rights.

Intersection of International Norms

Forced sterilization transcends a single category of human rights violation. The discussion on this particular crime thus extends to the intersection of norms from various international human rights agreements that complement one another on women's rights and indigenous people's rights. Such analysis of intersection from international human rights norms is especially relevant as Peru's legal system is based on a monistic system of law, where international and internal legal systems form a unity. Under Article 55 of Peru's 1993 Constitution, international law in Peru has an automatic effect once the state becomes a party to international commitments (Tribunal Constitucional 1993). All norms enshrined in treaties ratified by the state thus form a part of national law.

However, the case of forced sterilization shows that the de jure international legal norms ratified by Peru did not hinder the state's noncompliance with the norms. For instance, regarding women's rights, Peru ratified the Convention on the Elimination of Discrimination Against Women (CEDAW) on September 13, 1982, and the Inter-American Convention on the Prevention, Punishment, and Eradication of Violence Against Women in 1996. CEDAW defines what constitutes discrimination against women and sets up an international standard from which states can protect women's rights nationally. On similar grounds, the Inter-American Convention focuses on the elimination of violence against women. Rather than abide by these norms that protect women's rights, from 1996 to 2001 with the forced sterilization of indigenous women, Fujimori's government violated multiple norms embedded in both conventions. From CEDAW, the state violated Article 2 section (d) on the right of women to not be discriminated; Article 10 section (h) of CEDAW, on rights of women for access to "specific educational information to help ensure the health and well-being of families" which included information on family planning; and Article 12 on providing equal access to healthcare, including family planning (UN Women 2017). As victims of forced sterilization testify, government officials who administered the family planning program did not provide women with any information about the surgery and the effects it would have in the future and specifically targeted women for sterilization.[10] Additionally, by coercing the sterilization of uninformed women such as Luisa Pinedo Rango, the state violated provisions laid out in the Inter-American Convention. These included Article 2 section (b) on women's rights to protection from violence in health facilities and Article 9 which urges states to adopt measures to protect women from being subjugated to violence (OAS 2017).

Aside from women's rights violations, the Peruvian state also violated other international agreements on indigenous peoples, above all on indigenous women's rights, even though the country has been proactive in the ratification of agreements. In 1993 Peru ratified the ILO's Convention 169, which guarantees the rights and freedoms of indigenous peoples without "hindrance or discrimination" (ILO 2017). Peru also voted in favor of adopting the United Nations Declaration on the Rights of Indigenous Peoples. The Declaration provides recognition for indigenous peoples as equivalent to all other peoples, including specific rights for indigenous women and children to enjoy protection from discrimination and all forms of violence. Finally, Peru ratified the American Convention on the Rights of Indigenous Peoples in 2016, which urges states to adopt measures to "eradicate all forms of violence and discrimination, particularly against indigenous women" (Indian Law 2017).

Despite the multiple normative markers from international agreements that point to the need of protecting not only indigenous people's rights, as a vulnerable population within a state, but more specifically women of indigenous descent, Fujimori's government continued on with its policy on family planning. Although some of these international agreements were passed after the period of 1996–2001, the legal norms of protection for women and indigenous peoples from CEDAW, the Inter-American Convention on the Prevention, Punishment, and Eradication of Violence Against Women, and the ILO Convention 169 were effective during Fujimori's administration, when forced sterilization was also being implemented. Moreover, even after the Inter-American Commission of Human Rights recommended the Peruvian state to investigate and provide reparations for María Mamérita Mestanza's case in 2003, the state failed to recognize death caused by forced sterilization as a violation of various international obligations.

Currently, the only major advancement in accordance with the Inter-American Commission and the respective international agreements that Peru ratified is on victims' reparations. In 2016, President Pedro Pablo Kuczynski's administration (2016–2021) established the Registry for Victims of Forced Sterilization. As of June 9, 2017, there were a total of 5933 registered victims with 89 separate complaints filed against the state.[11] Nonetheless, regardless of the progress in reparations, impunity is rampant as the state has yet to consider hearing, investigating, or prosecuting forced sterilization cases. This status on forced sterilization reveals the extent to which indigenous women's rights are disregarded, contested, and left aside in Peruvian politics.

Constructing the Legitimacy of Forced Sterilization Policies

Dionicia Calderón remembers the day when she was forcefully sterilized. "They took us to hospitals like animals so that we could undergo surgery."[12] This grotesque description of Dionicia's human rights violations was one of 2074 cases that were shelved by the Public Prosecutor's Office in 2016. Public Prosecutor Marcelita Gutiérrez ruled that cases against former President Alberto Fujimori and three different health ministers lacked grounds to constitute a crime against humanity or to be considered for mediated authorship (RPP 2016). To fully understand where this viewpoint, which contradicts Peru's international obligations toward human rights, stems from, it is important to understand how the PSRPF developed.

One of the first intersections of analysis on forced sterilization involves the overlapping layers of violation of indigenous rights on the basis of ethnicity and socio-economic class. Ethnicity in Peru is a fluid concept defined largely by the legacy of colonial government institutions that framed this category of identity. As conquistadors and colonizers of Peru, the Spanish ruled with the idea of ethnic superiority. Adopting a policy of cultural depreciation and ethnic subordination toward the indigenous people, anything or anyone related to the indigenous culture was regarded as inferior to that of European heritage. Nonetheless, given the demographic imbalance between the majority indigenous population and the

Spanish, the colonial government and the later republican constitutions throughout the nineteenth century understood that there was a necessity to create a middle ground for an ethnic identity that would unify the state and facilitate governance. Hence, starting from the colonial period, the state framed the ethnic identity of Peru based on *mestizaje* (Portocarrero 2013). *Mestizaje* carried multiple meanings related to the biological or cultural mixture that diluted the differences between divergent groups of individuals (Portocarrero 2013, p. 190), and one that created a hybrid concept, an identity that could continue being indigenous (De la Cadena 2006, pp. 50–56). From the biological narrative, *mestizo* was *mestizaje*'s product, the result of often "coercive" Spanish and indigenous union (Madrid 2012, p. 118), one that was seen as being capable of potentially bridging differences between the indigenous peoples and *criollos* (those of Spanish descent born in Peru). This ethnic identity represented the nationalist project of many Latin American colonial states toward whitening or coming closer to the European heritage through interracial marriage (Callirgos 1993). It was assumed that the process of whitening the predominant indigenous identity would help improve Peru's racial composition and solve the ills of society (Flores Galindo 1988, p. 276). Implicit in this idea was the association of class stratification with ethnic identity, particularly of whiteness with higher economic classes. At the time, indigenous peoples comprised the largest ethnic group, belonged to lower classes of society, resided in the rural highland areas, and looked to Cuzco, the ancient heart of the Inca Empire, to represent their national identity. Spaniards who immigrated or were born in Peru "dominated the upper class, congregated in urban coastal areas, and looked to Lima and sometimes to Spain for their identity" (Carranza Ko 2017, p. 74). Such visions of ethnicity and geographic identifications resulted in a form of stratified interethnic relations, which were mirrored in governance. The Andean region linked with the indigenous population was seen as retrograde, while the coastal city areas (including Lima) were associated with "progress" (De la Cadena 2000, p. 45). Such ideas were present even after the first Constitution of Peru in 1822 established equality of all citizens before the law, indigenous peoples from Andean and Amazon areas were referred to as "semi-human" or as "un-civilized natives" in legislations (Kania 2016, p. 13).

The colonial social class structure and association with ethnic identity continues to today. Individuals who "self-identify as mestizo" take "advantage of their cultural/ethnic whiter characteristics" and see themselves as a product of racial improvement (Paredes 2015, p. 135). The *mestizo* identity allows individuals to reject their indigenous roots and have access to social upward mobility. These ideas by default relegate the person of indigenous descent to a marginalized category of class in society. According to 2016 government statistics, the highest levels of poverty were recorded in Andean rural areas and in the Amazonian region, at 47.8 and 39.3 percent (INEI 2017). Both regions, which included the Amazons, Ayacucho, Cajamarca, Cuzco, Huánuco, Junín, Loreto, Madre de Dios, Pasco, San Martín, and Ucayali represent areas with the largest indigenous populations in Peru. These indicators of high levels of poverty in areas with large indigenous populations add weight to the social perception of indigenous groups and their close relationship with lower economic class status. Such findings are not new, as older studies from 2005 already pointed out the disparity of economic status among classes, with 63 percent of indigenous households living under the poverty line, compared to the 42 percent who were poor and of non-indigenous descent (Trivelli 2005, p. 17). These views suggest the maintenance of colonial class structure in Peru today.

These intersecting views on ethnic identity and class were very much present during the internal armed conflict when the state "allowed the murder of so many indigenous people."[13] Indigenous populations were seen as a dispensable group, who were persecuted by the state and also by guerilla movements such as *Sendero Luminoso* (Degregori 1999). Such perceptions of indigenous people as a poor and vulnerable group also influenced the development of the PSRPF (1996–2001). At the base of PSRPF's campaign was the "association between reproduction and poverty" as a problem linked with poor indigenous populations that needed remedy (Del Aguila 2006, p. 111). The family planning program thus was selectively applied to the people who were identified as the ones who produced poverty in society. The *Defensoría del Pueblo*'s (Human Rights Ombudsman's Office) reports on voluntary surgical sterilization describe how 38.5 percent of the cases on the irregular administration of PSRPF were found in the departments of Ayacucho and Huancavelica, areas with the highest poverty indicators in Peru (Defensoría del Pueblo 2000, p. 15). Other reported complaints were registered in the more impoverished Andean and Amazonian areas, along with farming communities near provincial capitals, such as Huandar in Cuzco, Puerto Mayo in Ayacucho, Raquia in Ancash, Jatumpata in Huancavelica, San Lorenzo in Loreto, and Jibito in Sullana. The areas of administration demonstrate how the program which sterilized 272,028 people of predominantly indigenous descent was "applied to the *campesinos* of the Andean rural world and not to the women in the coastal areas, and even in the Andean world it was in the rural and not urban areas."[14]

Discussing class dynamics further, CVR's President Lerner describes how PSRPF and forced sterilization cases were directed at "people who were not socio-economically appreciated," in part to "get rid of those who did not produce."[15] This observation accentuated the intersection of indigenous peoples as those who were targeted, as a non-productive group in society who were perceived as increasing poverty, and who were not at an equal footing to that of non-indigenous Peruvians. PSRPF was, therefore, a "policy of instrumental and subordinated treatment of the indigenous population" (Kania 2016, p. 18). Critics associate such views also with the omission of forced sterilization in the 2003 Final Report of the CVR. While the Commission did their work to exemplify the structural inequality of the majority of the victims of conflict, the exclusion of forced sterilization in the Final Report helped perpetuate the "racial, class divide in Peruvian society" by allowing urban residents to remain "emotionally distant" from the human rights violations in rural areas (Getgen 2009, p. 21).

In essence, the family planning program and the subsequent practices of forcefully sterilizing indigenous women reflect "racist attitudes" of the state toward the "indigenous part of Peruvian population" (Kania 2016, p. 18). The interactions between Ministry of Health officials and victims of forced sterilization exemplified this discrimination against indigenous peoples. As Dionicia Calderón describes, "When we went to the health post to complain (about the pain), the nurses would say...that we were hypocrites...and that it didn't hurt at all, and saying those things they threw us out."[16] The disregard for Dionicia and other indigenous women's complaints reflects an attitude of disdain toward the indigenous population. As one human rights expert notes, "what would have happened if the sterilized women were from Miraflores?"[17] The juxtaposition of a different outcome to this particular case, had the victims been from the wealthy neighborhood of Miraflores in Lima vis-à-vis the rural communities, affirms that the condition of the victim as a poor indigenous woman from a rural area mattered in the possibility of seeking accountability.

These views of ethnicity and class-based discrimination were also embedded in the resolutions issued by the Public Prosecutor's Office to deny the cases of forced sterilization in 2016. Rather than question why consent forms and medical records were missing, the Public Prosecutor explained that given the absence of the medical documents, there was insufficient proof that forced sterilization had occurred (Ministerio Público 2016). Moreover, it rejected the possibility that indigenous women were forced to undergo tubal ligation, arguing that the women ought to have asked for a Spanish translator if they could not understand the consent form (Ministerio Público 2016). Hence, the responsibility of the crime fell on the victims whose mother tongue was not Spanish. Feminist activists assert that these resolutions demonstrated a chauvinistic, class-based, and racist undertone that denied the state's responsibility for the crime.[18]

Gender Inequality and Forced Sterilization

Beyond class and ethnic identity, another category of intersection was also embedded in the forced sterilization case: gender discrimination. Gender inequality in Peru is incorporated in the discrimination of ethnicity and class, specifically as it relates to women. As De la Cadena explains (1992), in terms of a power spectrum, a *mestiza* woman can exercise control over a male of indigenous descent but not over those who are *mestizo*. On the other hand, a *mestizo* has power over indigenous men and women, and *mestiza* women (De la Cadena 1992). Thus women, particularly those of indigenous origin are at the lowest ladder of class hierarchy. These views on indigenous women are even more prevalent within rural farming indigenous communities. Families with daughters take on a subordinate position, as after marriage, married women are expected to live with the husband's family and contribute to his family fortune (De la Cadena 1992).

The deep roots of gender discrimination and inequality became more definitive with the internal armed conflict. Academics who reflect on sexual violence during this period have noted how such human rights violations served to reproduce hierarchical power differences in society. Rather than blame the perpetrator for having violated a women's rights, society framed the victim as the culprit. The fault was on the indigenous woman who was seen as promiscuous by "nature" and inevitably seduced men to commit their acts (Boesten 2016, p. 105). Extending such gendered hierarchies of discrimination to forced sterilization, decisions on sterilization were regarded as belonging to men, because women were not considered capable of exercising their rights on their reproductive organs, and even more so, if she was of indigenous descent.[19]

Gender discrimination was built in the PSRPF. Sex-based discrimination was rampant with the implementation of the PSRPF, which human rights experts argue was in fact an unnecessary program in Peru.[20] The large land mass and scattered levels of high and low population density throughout the state provided no reasoning for concerns over issues of overpopulation. This observation questions the reason why the program was implemented in the first place and why it was overwhelmingly directed at indigenous women from rural areas and toward poor women living in the margins of cities. Ultimately, as human rights experts suggest, the PSRPF demonstrated the state's incapacity to protect fundamental human rights of rural indigenous women, who made up the largest portion of the victim group.[21]

The program was originally designed to "provide surgical intervention to men and women" (Del Aguila 2006, p. 114). However, when it was implemented, information about other family planning options were absent and women were not given the freedom to make their choices. Although vasectomy was more economical and posed a lower health risk, the program dedicated more efforts to push for female tubal ligation (Defensoría del Pueblo 2002). Ministerial Resolution No. 089-98-SA/DM from March 10, 1998, redacts the program's objectives, which included the distribution of family planning methods to no less than 50 percent of the women in fertile age and their partners (Defensoría del Pueblo 2000, p. 79). The specific reference to "fertile" women as the recipients of the family planning policy coincided with the PSRPF's push for tubal ligation in comparison to vasectomy. The same Resolution also made reference to adolescent family planning objectives, noting the necessity for the state to be involved in preventing adolescent pregnancy. As men were not the ones bearing the child, this information applied only to adolescent females, who were also the target group for tubal ligation. As a result, 90 percent of the victims of forced sterilization were women and only 10 percent were men.[22]

Elements of patriarchal culture within indigenous communities also made the health practices of the PSRPF more skewed against indigenous women. Although not all, some men of indigenous descent feared the "*peligro de su virilidad*" (danger to virility) that vasectomy could bring and preferred for indigenous women to receive the treatment.[23] For reasons related to virility, there were also a few cases of forced sterilization without the woman's consent but with the male partner's authorization that was still carried out by health officials (CLADEM 1999, p. 41). The

Defensoría del Pueblo documents at least five cases from 1998 when the husband or male partner authorized the forced sterilization of women (2000, p. 32). The condition men faced along with their partners in decision-making was under a great amount of pressure from health officials, who used threats of incarceration or offered reduction of hospital debt in exchange for the sterilization (CLADEM 1999, p. 42). Notwithstanding the context of intimidation indigenous men faced in deciding the fate of the women, such cases of conjugal authorization from male partners represented the rejection of the woman's right to her own reproductive organs and reinforced the status of indigenous women as a subaltern group in society. Additionally, it was a sex-based discrimination against the woman's choice both from the health officials and male partners who were complicit in determining what they believed was the right choice for her. The Peruvian state and society's disregard for poor indigenous people in rural areas and women of indigenous descent helped justify the complicity of healthcare personnel involved in forced sterilization.

Conclusion

The forced sterilization of indigenous women from the latter part of the internal armed conflict period is a case that serves as an indicator as to where indigenous people's rights stand in Peru today. Understood from the lens of intersecting and overlapping layers of human rights violations, this was a case that exemplified the ways through which indigenous people's rights, women's rights, and even low-economic class rights are violated and contested. From a baseless claim of overpopulation, economic development, and population control, Alberto Fujimori's government sterilized 272,028 individuals. Of the total sterilizations, the majority of the victims who were forcefully sterilized were indigenous women of rural background, who resided in the poorest regions of Peru. The characteristics of the victims, understood from the intersection of ethnicity and class identity, revealed how the family planning program discriminately targeted people of indigenous descent who were considered to be the problem factor for economic development. Hence from this perspective, a program that controlled this particular group's reproduction or increase in population size could help the economy stabilize and grow. Forced sterilization embodied "a problem, if you will, of ethnic discrimination"[24] that existed against indigenous peoples from the colonial era. And, it was a policy that could easily and quickly help the state in the "fight against poverty" (Ewin 2014, p. 62). These views helped shape the ways through which instead of increasing education of contraceptive methods, indigenous people of poor economic classes were rounded up like animals, as victims' testimonies noted, and were put through this human rights violation.

Moreover, from the lens of women's rights violations, forced sterilization violated women's reproductive rights and their right not to be discriminated. The sterilization program selectively prioritized the application of tubal ligation, resulting in disproportionate numbers of female sterilization. Threats, intimidation, coercion, and at times complicit agreement with the male partners were used to subject the women to surgical procedures. Such acts were possible due to Peruvian society's sex-based discrimination against women, which was ingrained in colonial society and in elements of indigenous people's cultures. Thus, indigenous women were positioned at a weak position vis-à-vis that of men, in the lowest category of hierarchy of decision-making.

At the end of the public forum on forced sterilization that took place on June 9, 2017, Dionicia Calderón pleaded to the audience, "We Peruvian women have suffered...as indigenous and campesina women, we need justice."[25] Nearly two decades have passed since the PSRPF was implemented. The process of seeking accountability has confronted numerous bureaucratic obstacles, despite the call for justice from indigenous non-governmental organizations and continued pressure exerted on the Inter-American Commission on Human Rights. As of this writing, the Public Prosecutor's Office has yet to deliberate on the possibility of re-opening the 2074 cases that were shelved aside on grounds of insufficient information and non-crimes against humanity decision. The injustice that continues with this case is a clear marker of how arduous is the road for Peru's indigenous people's rights to be enforced, despite how decades of advocacy and grass-roots initiatives. The general uproar and sustained manifested popular indignation toward President Kuczynski's presidential pardon for Fujimori's condemnation in human rights violation right before Christmas 2017 may provide a turning point that will support Peru's indigenous population and women's claim for justice.

Notes

1. Author's interview with Ana María Vidal, Executive Secretary of the *Coordinadora Nacional de Derechos Humanos*, June 1, 2017. The *Coordinadora Nacional de Derechos Humanos* was an organization that nationally coordinated the agenda and work of 81 local organizations related to human rights and managed cooperation with international supporters. The *Coordinadora* acted as the spokesperson for the human rights movement since 1984, focusing on themes of innocent prisoners and recuperating democracy.
2. Peru's Truth and Reconciliation Commission's truth-seeking process began in 2001 and ended in 2003 with the publication of the Final Report of the Commission.
3. The mandate of the Truth and Reconciliation Commission covered all forms of violations of fundamental rights including acts perpetrated by state and armed groups from 1980 to 2000. From its work, the Commission determined that the immediate and fundamental cause of conflict was initiated from *Sendero Luminoso* that had declared a popular war against the Peruvian state. The conflict and resulting human rights violations were one that involved the state, the subversive forces (such as *Sendero Luminoso*), and civilians who were caught in the middle. From this perspective, forced sterilization practices fell outside the markers of the internal armed conflict, as they did not involve a conflict between the state, the subversive forces, and the civilian casualties.
4. According to human rights experts, while forced sterilization occurred during the internal armed conflict, it fell outside the political systems that defined this period, with violent confrontations between leftist groups advancing their revolutionary goals and the state instituting a militarist response. Author's interview with Dr. Francisco Soberón, President of the *Asociación Pro Derechos Humanos*, and Carmela Chávez, Sociologist—SUNEDU, May 24 and 26, 2017.
5. The number of victims reflects the corrections made to the *Defensoría del Pueblo*'s report (Defensoría del Pueblo 2015, 51).
6. Author's interview with Edith Carranza Caballero, former nurse at the San Juan de Dios Hospital, June 4, 2017.
7. Testimony, Luisa Pinedo Rango, ONAMIAP Public Forum on Esterilizaciones Forzadas, June 9, 2017.
8. Author's interview with Dr. Salomón Lerner Fébres, President of the Truth and Reconciliation Commission of Peru, May 31, 2017.
9. Testimony, Dionicia Calderón Arellano, ONAMIAP Public Forum on Esterilizaciones Forzadas, June 9, 2017.

10. Testimony, Luisa Pinedo Rango and Dionicia Calderón Arellano, June 9, 2017.
11. Statement, Sandra Enríquez Castro, ONAMIAP Public Forum on Esterilizaciones Forzadas, June 9, 2017.
12. Testimony, Dionicia Calderón Arellano, June 9, 2017.
13. Indigenous identity in the Andes has at times been synonymously used with the term "*campesino(a)*" (peasant), which emerged after the 1969 Agrarian Reform that replaced the identification of indigenous communities in the Andean region with the "peasant community" (Kania 2016, p. 15).
14. Author's interview with Dr. Francisco Soberón, May 24, 2017.
15. Author's interview with Dr. Salomón Lerner, May 31, 2017.
16. Testimony, Dionicia Calderón Arellano, June 9, 2017.
17. Author's interview with Dr. Rocio Santistéban, former Executive Secretary of the Coordinadora Nacional de Derechos Humanos, May 30, 2017.
18. Author's interview with María Ysabel Cedano, Director of DEMUS, June 28, 2017.
19. Author's interview with Ana María Vidal, June 1, 2017.
20. Ibid.
21. Author's interview with Carmela Chávez, May 26, 2017.
22. Author's interview with Ana María Vidal, June 1, 2017.
23. Author's interview with Dr. Salomón Lerner, May 31, 2017.
24. Ibid.
25. Testimony, Dionicia Calderón Arellano, June 9, 2017.

References

Amnesty International. 2017. *Amnesty International Report 2016/17: The State of the World's Human Rights*. London: Amnesty International Ltd..

APRODEH. 2008. *Rompiendo el silencio: Informe de las organizaciones de derechos humanos sobre violencia sexual contra la mujer durante el conflicto armado interno presentado ante la Comisión Interamericana de Derechos Humanos*. Lima: APRODEH.

Boesten, Jelke. 2016. *Violencia sexual en la guerra y en la paz: genero, poder y posconflicto en el Perú*. Lima: Biblioteca Nacional del Perú.

Bond, Johanna E. 2003. International Intersectionality: A Theoretical and Pragmatic Exploration of Women's International Human Rights Violations. *Emory Law Journal* 52: 71–186.

Bueno-Hansen, Pascha. 2015. *Feminist and Human Rights Struggles in Peru*. Champaign: University of Illinois Press.

Callirgos, Juan Carlos. 1993. *El racismo: la cuestión del otro (y de uno)*. Lima: DESCO.

Carranza Ko, Ñusta. 2017. Comparing the Effects of Chinese and Japanese Migration Experiences on Peruvian National Identity. *Journal of Chinese Overseas* 13: 70–93.

Cassese, Antonio. 1999. Are Human Rights Truly Universal? In *The Politics of Human Rights*, ed. Belgrade Circle, 149–166. New York: Verso.

CLADEM. 1999. *Nada personal: Reporte de derechos humanos sobre la aplicación de la anticoncepción quirúrgica en el Perú 1996–1998*. Lima: Comité de América Latina y El Caribe Para la Defensa de los Derechos de la Mujer.

El Comercio. 2016. PPK: Esterilizaciones fueron un crimen contra la humanidad. *El Comercio*, October 3. https://elcomercio.pe/politica/elecciones/ppk-esterilizaciones-crimen-humanidad-393502.

Comisión de la Verdad y Reconciliación. 2003. Final Report. *Comisión de la Verdad y Reconciliación*. http://www.cverdad.org.pe/ingles/ifinal/index.php.

Corte Interamericana de Derechos Humanos. 2003. Informe No. 71/03. *Corte Interamericana de Derechos Humanos*. https://www.cidh.oas.org/annualrep/2003sp/Peru.12191.htm.

Crenshaw, Kimberle. 1991. Mapping the Margins: Intersectionality, Identity Politics, and Violence against Women of Color. *Stanford Law Review* 43 (6): 1241–1299.

De la Cadena, Marisol. 1992. Las mujeres son más indias: Etnicidad y género en una comunidad del Cuzco. *Revista Isis Internacional-Ediciones de las Mujeres* 16: 25–46.

———. 2000. *Indigenous Mestizos: The Politics of Race and Culture in Cuzco, Peru, 1919–1991*. Durham: Duke University Press.

———. 2006. ¿Son los mestizos híbridos? Las políticas conceptuales de las identidades andinas. *Universitas Humanística* 61 (61): 51–84.

Defensoría del Pueblo. 2000. *La aplicación de la anticoncepción quirúrgica y los derechos reproductivos II: Casos investigados por La Defensoría del Pueblo*. Lima: Defensoría del Pueblo.

———. 2002. *La aplicación de la anticoncepción quirúrgica y los derechos reproductivos III: Casos Investigados por la Defensoría del Pueblo*. Lima: Defensoría del Pueblo.

———. 2015. *Decimonoveno Informe Anual de la Defensoría del Pueblo*. Lima: Defensoría del Pueblo.

Degregori, Carlos Iván. 1999. Reaping the Whirlwind: the Rondas Campesinas and the Defeat of Sendero Luminoso in Ayacucho. In *Societies of Fear: The Legacy of Civil War, Violence and Terror in Latin America*, ed. K. Koonings and D. Kruijt, 63–87. London/New York: Zed Books.

Del Aguila, Ernesto Vasquez. 2006. Invisible Women: Forced Sterilization, Reproductive Rights, and Structural Inequalities in Peru of Fujimori and Toledo. *Estudos e Pesquisas em Psicología UERJ, RJ* 6 (1): 109–124.

Ewig, Christina. 2014. La economía política de esterilización forzada en el Perú. In *Memorias del caso peruano de esterilización forzada*, ed. Alejandra Ballón, 47–72. Lima: Biblioteca Nacional del Perú.

Flores Galindo, Alberto. 1988. *Buscando un Inca*. Lima: Editorial Horizonte.

Fried, Susana. 2002. Guidelines to Integrating the Outcomes of the WCAR into Women's Human Rights Organizing. In *Women at the Intersection: Indivisible Rights, Identities, and Oppressions*, ed. Rita Raj, 86–100. New Brunswick: Center for Women's Global Leadership-Rutgers, The State University of New Jersey.

Getgen, Jocelyn E. 2009. Untold Truths: The Exclusion of Enforced Sterilizations from the Peruvian Truth Commission's Final Report. *Boston College Third World Law Journal* 29 (1): 1–34.

Hayner, Priscilla B. 2001. *Unspeakable Truths: Confronting State Terror and Atrocity*. New York: Routledge.

ICC. 2002. Rome Statute of the International Criminal Court. *ICC*. https://www.icc-cpi.int/nr/rdonlyres/ea9aeff7-5752-4f84-be94-0a655eb30e16/0/rome_statute_english.pdf.

ILO. 2017. Indigenous and Tribal Peoples Convention, 1989 (No. 169). *ILO*. http://www.ilo.org/dyn/normlex/en/f?p=NORMLEXPUB:12100:0::NO::P12100_ILO_CODE:C169.

Indian Law. 2017. American Declaration on the Rights of Indigenous Peoples. *Indian Law*. http://indianlaw.org/sites/default/files/ADRIP%201-17-17.pdf.

INEI. 2017. En el Perú 264 mil personas dejaron de ser pobres entre los años 2015 y 2016. *INEI*. https://www.inei.gob.pe/prensa/noticias/en-el-peru-264-mil-personas-dejaron-de-ser-pobres-entre-los-anos-2015-y-2016-9710/.

Kania, Marta. 2016. The Rights of Indigenous Peoples in Peru: From Socio-Political Marginalization to the Modern Principles of Multiculturalism. *Ad Americam* 17: 11–32.

Kravetz, Daniela. 2017. Promoting Domestic Accountability for Conflict-Related Sexual Violence: The Cases of Guatemala, Peru, and Colombia. *American University International Law Review* 32 (3): 707–762.

La República. 2016. Denuncia de esterilizaciones forzadas fue archivada por la fiscalía. *La República*, July 27. http://larepublica.pe/sociedad/789156-denuncia-de-esterilizaciones-forzadas-fue-archivada-por-la-fiscalia.

———. 2017a. Comisión Interamericana de DDHH solicita información a Perú sobre caso Madre Mia. *La República*, May 26. http://larepublica.pe/impresa/politica/879554-comision-interamericana-de-ddhh-solicita-informacion-peru-sobre-caso-madre-mia.

———. 2017b. Fiscalía archiva definitivamente las 77 denuncias por esterilizaciones forzadas. *La República*, December 7. http://larepublica.pe/

politica/828674-fiscalia-archiva-definitivamente-las-77-denuncias-por-esterilizaciones-forzadas.
Lerner, Salomón Febres. 2004. *La rebelión de la memoria: selección de discursos 2001–2003*. Lima: Centro de Estudios y Publicaciones.
Madrid, Raúl. 2012. *The Rise of Ethnic Politics in Latin America*. Cambridge: Cambridge University Press.
Mantilla Falcón, Julissa. 2016. El caso de las esterilizaciones forzadas en el Perú como una violación de los derechos humanos. *Ius et Veritas* 23: 10–20.
Ministerio Público. 2016. *Resolución Fiscal No. 16*. Lima: Ministerio Público Fiscalía de la Nación.
MINUS. 2017. *Registro de Víctimas de Esterilizaciones Forzadas-REVIESFO. MINUS*. https://www.minjus.gob.pe/defensapublica/interna.php?comando=1036.
Mogollón, Maria Esther. 2008. Forced Sterilization and Access to Justice in Peru. *Women's Health Journal* 1: 40–42.
OAS. 2017. Inter-American Convention on the Prevention, Punishment and Eradication of Violence Against Women Convention of Belem do Para. *OAS*. http://www.oas.org/juridico/english/treaties/a-61.html.
Paredes, Cristian L. 2015. Race and Ethnicity in Peru. In *The International Handbook of the Demography of Race and Ethnicity*, ed. Rogelio Sáenz, David G. Embrick, and Néstor P. Rodríguez, 129–150. New York: Springer.
Portocarrero, Gonzalo. 2013. La utopía del blanqueamiento y la lucha por el mestizaje. In *Hegemonía cultural y políticas de la diferencia*, CLACSO, 165–200. Buenos Aires: CLACSO.
Roberts, Kenneth, and Mark Peceny. 1997. Human Rights and the United States Policy Toward Peru. In *The Peruvian Labyrinth: Polity, Society, Economy*, ed. Maxwell A. Cameron, Philip Mauceri, and Cynthia McClintock, 213–217. University Park: Pennsylvania State University.
RPP. 2016. Fiscalía archivó caso de esterilizaciones forzadas. *RPP*, July 27. http://rpp.pe/peru/actualidad/fiscalia-archivo-caso-de-esterilizaciones-forzadas-noticia-982885.
Transfer Commission of the Truth and Reconciliation Commission of Peru. 2014. *Hatun Willakuy: Abbreviated Version of the Final Report of the Truth and Reconciliation Commission*. Lima: Transfer Commission of the Truth and Reconciliation Commission of Peru.
Tribunal Constitucional. 1993. Constitución política del Perú de 1993. *Tribunal Constitucional*. http://www.tc.gob.pe/constitucion.pdf.
Trivelli, Carolina. 2005. *Los hogares indígenas y la pobreza en el Perú. Una mirada a partir de la información cuantitativa*. Lima: Instituto de Estudios Peruanos.
UN Women. 2017. Convention on the Elimination of All Forms of Discrimination against Women. *UN Women*. http://www.un.org/womenwatch/daw/cedaw/text/econvention.htm.

CHAPTER 9

Politicization of Rights-Based Development and Marginalization of Human Rights from Below: The Case of Maternal Health Rights in India

Surma Das

Introduction

Every year nearly 300,000 women die annually from *preventable* complications arising from pregnancy and childbirth, 99 percent of which occur in developing countries. This is a conservative estimate and excludes estimates of maternal morbidity (UNFPA 2014). The recognition of the severity of the problem led to the issue being featured prominently in the Millennium Development Goals (MDGs) introduced in 2000, where states committed to reducing such deaths by three quarters by the end of 2015 (AbouZahr 2003). Insufficient progress on the issue during the previous three decades was attributed to the worth assigned to women's lives

This study was made possible by an IDRC Doctoral Research Award.

S. Das (✉)
Political Science Department, University of Alberta, Edmonton, AB, Canada
e-mail: Surma@ualberta.ca

G. Blouin-Genest et al. (eds.), *Human Rights as Battlefields*,
Human Rights Interventions,
https://doi.org/10.1007/978-3-319-91770-2_9

in many societies, poor conditions of health systems, and lack of political commitment to improving women's health, thus underscoring its political rather than "medical nature" (Maclean 2010, p. 10). Thus, some scholars proposed framing the issues as a social justice/human rights one to tackle the failure of traditional public health approaches to adequately address the issue. A human rights-based approach (HRBA),[1] scholars argued, can strategically accommodate the multifaceted gender discrimination, health disparities, and multidimensional poverty that collectively contribute to preventable maternal deaths and can communicate the political and moral urgency of the situation to help create the necessary political commitment and resources deserving of the issue (Cook and Dickens 2001; Yamin and Maine 1999). However, the lack of empirical evidence makes it difficult to assess the dynamics of such framing and its implications for social mobilization surrounding maternal health/death. This is noteworthy because there are scholarly debates about which rights should human right to maternal health advance—the right to healthcare (especially, emergency obstetric care), the right to reproductive self-determination, or both—which stem from competing normative views about the source and nature of the policy problem and disagreements over appropriate policy solutions (Cook and Dickens 2001; Yamin and Maine 1999; Gruskin et al. 2008). Additionally, debates over the discursive power of framing women's rights as human rights to improve development outcomes also cast a shadow on the normative optimism surrounding the potential of human rights to advance maternal health outcomes (Molyneux and Razavi 2003; Cornwall and Molyneux 2006; Cornwall et al. 2007).

This chapter contributes to these debates. It examines the dynamics of framing maternal health/death as a human rights issue and the implications for social mobilization surrounding the issue in the case of India, the second-largest[2] contributor to maternal deaths globally. The analysis reveals three insights that characterize the dynamics of the framing process, which include (1) the challenge of using a universal equality-based (homogenizing and essentializing) framework to an issue originating in multiple social and political inequities, (2) the proliferation of human rights-based frames competing for both political (and donor) attention and resources, and (3) the discursive intricacy of integrating human rights with "maternal" health/death, which is a fundamentally contested issue terrain. Collectively, these factors complicate the politics of framing maternal health/death as a human rights issue in India and adversely affect social mobilization surrounding it.

The chapter proceeds by outlining the relevant theoretical debates in the next section, which is followed by a brief description of the conceptual approach of the study. The fourth section provides an overview of politics of framing maternal health in India. The empirical findings related to the dynamics of human rights advocacy efforts, production of diverse narratives, and struggles over appropriate human rights framing in India are discussed next. Finally, the conclusion highlights the broader theoretical and practical implications of the findings.

Theoretical Debates

There are debates over the scope of women's rights to maternal health as a human right over whether policy solutions should address proximate (biomedical and health system) determinants required to manage obstetric complications and prevent untimely death or underlying (social and gendered) determinants that are linked to issues of ill health stemming from women's secondary status and limited reproductive self-determination (Sen et al. 2007; Gill Pande and Malhotra 2007). These tensions arise from historical and feminist struggles over linking gender inequality to women's health outcomes (Berer 2007). Historically, efforts to gain political support for women's health by framing it as a women's human rights issue have witnessed various challenges from political, conservative, and religious segments (globally and locally), leading to the emergence of competing frames of women's health in the policy discourse (AbouZahr 2003; Joachim 2007; Berer 2007). Conversely, the appearance of "reduction of maternal mortality" in the MDGs led some scholars to view the issue as a depoliticized (due to its emphasis on biomedical/technical interventions) remnant of the struggle to secure political commitment to the more contentious goal of women's sexual and reproductive health and rights (Eyben 2006; Fraser 2005; Sen and Mukherjee 2014). Yet, others embraced the separation of the issue from the politically and morally polarizing shadow of women's sexual and reproductive health and rights (Freedman 2003a, b; Yamin and Maine 2005). This separation, they maintain, has allowed for a re-focus on the lack of political prioritization and resources for functioning health systems in developing countries, which is key to managing obstetric complications and preventing maternal deaths (Yamin and Maine 1999; Freedman 2003a, b). Ultimately, this debate embodies struggles over the appropriate structural barriers to eliminate to improve maternal health outcomes. But it is deeply linked to tensions within feminist politics over the *maternal* and the tricky political terrains feminist health advocates must navigate to uphold the rights of pregnant and parturient women without solely reducing them to mothers.

Characteristics of the human rights framework—such as indivisibility and inter-relatedness of various human rights—have been of particular appeal to maternal health rights advocates because of their ability to draw political attention to the multidimensional nature (gender inequality, poverty, health disparities, and social inequities) of this complex problem (Cook 1998; Yamin and Maine 1999; Cook and Dickens 2001). Feminist development theorists have cautioned against the appropriation of the normative language of human rights to frame women's rights by various actors (the state, the development establishment) to pursue political agendas, which need not necessarily advance women's needs and interests (Molyneux and Razavi 2003; Cornwall and Molyneux 2006; Gideon 2006; Bradshaw 2006). Development, Elson (2002) argues, is a depoliticized project of social transformation designed to achieve better economic growth whereas advancing women's rights as human rights is a political claim that may be incompatible with status quo conceptions of economic growth. Others point to various status quo factors with dubious impact on progress of women's rights and question the potential of dominant notions of development to serve women's needs and interests. These include instrumentalization of women's rights in development (Yamin and Boulanger 2014), reduction of rights claiming to economically efficient transactions (pre-negotiated set of claims and entitlements as opposed to status quo arrived through continuously evolving political contestation) (Cornwall and Molyneux 2006), institutionalization of feminist demands by the state (Alvarez 1999; Bradshaw 2006; Tsikata 2007), and NGO-ization[3] of feminist movements (Alvarez 1999/2009). These are potentially consequential to examining the dynamics of human rights framing of maternal health/death in India.

There are also concerns over the tendency of human rights language to universalize and essentialize all women without recognizing the differences within and varied (reproductive) needs and interests among women from diverse backgrounds (Toyo 2006; Molyneux 2007; Cornwall et al. 2007). To prevent these differences from polarizing the discourse over reproductive choice and rights and constraining the advancement of a feminist agenda, some feminist scholars argue for less homogenizing framework that is attentive to women's secondary and unequal gender and inequitable social citizenship rights and status, despite constitutional and legal equality in many states (Goetz 2007; Mukhopadhyay and Singh 2007). Citizenship rights are defined as rights and obligations held by an individual by virtue of membership in a political community (Yuval-Davis 1997). They can capture differences within, such as identity-based differences (class, caste, race, ethnicity, religion, etc.), that can determine varying access to (or not) health and welfare services (Johnson 2014; Sen and Ostlin 2011). The citizenship perspective reveals the contested nature of rights actualization and contends that policies accompanying women's rights to maternal health as human rights must be able to accommodate varying and dynamic conceptions of the heterogeneity of women's needs and interests, depending on the given characteristics of specific sites of power struggles (Mukhopadhyay 2003; Goetz 2007). Such a way of framing women's rights helps to reveal (and collapse) the various structural (state, economy, society, family) barriers facing some women that prevent them from equally exercising their rights, in private and public spheres of their lives.

In light of these debates, the lack of theorization of the politics of framing women's rights to maternal health as a human right provides for an incomplete understanding of how the dynamics of the framing process unfolds and its implications for social mobilization surrounding the issue. The analysis in this chapter contributes to this important knowledge gap.

Conceptual Approach

For analysis, this chapter employs concepts from the framing literature used in the critical policy studies and social movements literature. A frame is defined as "underlying structures of belief, perception, and appreciation" that determines policy positions of actors involved in a policy discourse (Schon and Rein 1994, p. 23). Conflicts between frames held by different actors generally give rise to policy controversies, which are distinct from policy disagreements in that the issues are difficult, complex, and contentious in nature with conflicting frames (Schon and Rein 1994). For example, whether abortion should be legal including under what conditions is a case in point.

In a policy discourse characterized by such controversy, two or more frame sponsors may generally struggle to exert influence on the process of policy design. Their struggles are emblematic of competition over "social meaning of an issue domain" where the meaning communicates both what is wrong (or unacceptable and needs fixing) and how it is to be fixed (Schon and Rein 1994, p. 29). This fundamental difference cannot be sorted by simply appealing to facts and it results from a fundamentally different view on how a problematic situation can be addressed and to what end. As well, it is consequential to differences in mobilization strategies (Joachim 2007). The existence of multiple frames in a policy discourse leads diverse issue definitions and differences over possible solutions (Schon and Rein 1994; Fischer 2003). Each set of definition and solution only attends to a particular dimension of the policy problem and is unable to address the full scope of its complexities (Benford and Snow 2000).

The existence of multiple frames to explain the same problem also emerges from differences in frame sponsors' interests/agendas (Schon and Rein 1994; Joachim 2007). To be precise, interests/agendas may influence frame construction, and frames may be used to promote and preserve frame sponsors' interests/agendas. But frames and interests are "logically independent" concepts that are not linked in a rigidly defined "deterministic" manner (Schon and Rein 1994, p. 29). For example, a feminist critique of human rights and development points out that women's rights groups and organizations in developing countries may adopt the language of human rights and introduce it into their program, even when they nominally subscribe to such ideas, because of donor requirements on which they rely for sustenance (Bradshaw 2006). Alvarez (2009), however, has shown that women's rights advocates—while remaining dependent on donor aid—have grown to be more sophisticated (and organized as professionals) in their strategizing to secure a seat on the official policymaking table. Their frames or policy positions and framing strategies may be deliberately designed to resonate with policymakers (without completely succumbing to policymakers' positions). By being at the policy table they are able to incrementally pressure the government into making more transformative change.

The frames of frame sponsors who choose to work with policymakers to create incremental change may be in competition with those seeking transformative change and wishing to challenge state officials. Maintaining a singular frame given the constantly evolving and dynamic nature of the framing process within a master frame (e.g., women's rights as human rights) in a mobilization characterized by multiple organizations is particularly challenging because of the existence of competing narratives that aim to advance individual frame sponsor's agenda. This can dilute the key message, adversely affecting the issue under consideration (Joachim

2007). These are difficult roadblocks for women's rights advocates today—whether to work within the status quo or eliminate it (and how) entirely—as demonstrated earlier in reviewing the debates over resisting the appropriation of human rights "speak" by the state and/or the international aid/development establishment (Cornwall and Molyneux 2006).

The Indian Context

As the second-largest contributor to preventable maternal deaths globally, India is considered an outlier among low-middle income countries, including many of its neighbors in the region (WHO 2015, pp. 74–78). Until the late 1990s, maternal mortality was largely a relegated issue because the historic policy focus was on family planning for purposes of population stabilization (Shiffman 2007). However, this changed in the early 2000s as the issue concurrently became a global health and MDG priority and the rise to power of a new central government committed to improving health (Shiffman 2007). Nevertheless, the emergent political prioritization of maternal mortality reduction remains deeply intertwined with the historic politics of family planning, which complicates the introduction of the language of human rights to the discourse of maternal health in India.

The first wave of Indian Women's Health Movement (henceforth, the Movement) was formed in response to coercive population control policies (such as forced sterilization) enforced by the state, especially on women, starting in the late 1970s. It advocated for reproductive freedoms as fundamental human rights and also took particular issue with the narrow spotlight on reproductive dimensions of women's lives (Mukherjee 2002). The thrust on family planning continued until the 1990s to the point where women seeking pregnancy and post-abortion care were "arm-twisted into accepting methods like IUDs, pills or sterilization depending on the number of children and surviving sons by health workers, whose career and promotions depended on the number of 'cases they could mobilize for family planning" (Mukherjee 2002, n.p.). To complicate matters further, the Indian state also framed its aggressive family planning efforts in the language of reproductive choice/freedom (from poverty, underdevelopment, household scarcity) (Narayanan 2011). The Movement was, therefore, faced with a tricky discursive terrain surrounding the framing of reproductive freedoms as fundamental human rights (see also Mukherjee 2002; John 2012).

Simultaneously, the increased focus on vertically designed family planning interventions came at the cost of a wider and horizontal focus on maintaining the quality of primary healthcare, resulting in an overall decline in quality of healthcare available to women (Rao 2008). A functioning primary healthcare system is considered critical to not only prevent maternal deaths but also address obstetric complications (Yamin and Maine 1999; Maine and Rosenfield 1999). The deliberate state neglect of the public health system in post-independence era has remained a major obstacle to improving maternal health outcomes in India. In other words, the provision of certain reproductive choices (guaranteed by the state) has come at the cost of realization of broader human right to healthcare (see Qadeer 2008; Rao 2008).

The efforts of the Movement during the 1990s benefited from the strides made by feminists (including enthusiastic Indian participation) at the International Conference on Population and Development (ICPD) in Cairo[4] (in 1994) and the Beijing Summit[5] (in 1995). The resultant domestic policy shift promoted gender sensitive and ethical approaches to population stabilization, although it retained measures to *incentivize* adoption of family planning interventions. This new policy paradigm created in 1997/1998—Reproductive and Child Health Phase I (more expansive than family planning)—also featured the first-ever appearance of an extensive range of systematic maternal health interventions. This was an outcome of successfully tying maternal mortality reduction to broader women's health, social status, and underdevelopment issues at Cairo and Beijing (Narayanan 2011).

The focus on maternal mortality, however, was considered "epidemiologically misplaced" by some segments of the Indian women's health movement. For example, at a colloquium (held in 2001) supported by UNFPA in New Delhi, some women's health advocates argued "deaths due to reproduction, *high as this is*, accounted for *merely* 2.4 percent of deaths among females in the country" (Jain and Rao 2001, p. 1301; emphasis added). The issue of epidemiological insignificance has been partly linked to a tendency to avoid a focus on reproductive dimensions of women's lives, a historic pre-occupation of the state (see John 2012, p. 556). Imrana Qadeer, a noted Indian population health scholar, has criticized feminist activism for reproductive choice/rights, which she maintains is often co-opted by the state and met with narrow, biomedical, technically packaged reproductive health policy interventions without attending to any major health system reform (2008, p. 382). But others argued that the widening policy focus (from family planning to reproductive health, including maternal healthcare interventions) drew attention to "enabling conditions" and highlighted issues of "social rights" that would offer women opportunities to make genuine reproductive choices (Sundari Ravindran 1993; Sen et al. 1994 as quoted in John 2012, p. 556). From this perspective, the focus on maternal mortality reduction is welcome since it examines the preventable and untimely nature of these deaths that require political attention. Mary John (2012) has hypothesized that these tensions over framing between different segments of the Movement are symbolic of "new divisions and differences"[6] within (556). Thus, it is likely that these differences have grown more pronounced in the aftermath of creation of the MDGs since maternal mortality reduction (framed exclusively in biomedical and technical terms) replaced reproductive health and rights and shifted donor priorities creating a struggle over resources. Introducing human rights to the discourse of maternal health, therefore, might have led to struggles over political attention and resources between different advocacy groups.

An additional and relevant issue concerns the "kind" of women who most often experience maternal health adversities in India. Based on an extensive review of 65 empirical studies conducted between 1995 and 2012 of maternal and reproductive health disparities in India, Sanneving and colleagues have found that social status—particularly, caste,[7] tribal (or *Adivasi*), and religious affiliations—is a significant structural determinant of maternal health outcomes in addition to class and gender (2013). Another study commissioned by UNFPA India in 16 districts of 6 states in central and northern India demonstrated that 61 percent of women dying in childbirth were "Untouchables" or *Dalits* (2009, p. 6). Put simply, poor and socially marginalized women are most likely to be affected by maternal mortality suggesting that the issue is ultimately a matter of social justice. It reveals complex and differentiated notions of citizenship experienced by pregnant and parturient women. But the claim that women's rights are human rights tends to universalize and, thus, homogenize and invisibilize different notions of womanhood and women's experiences of childbearing. This is significant given that historically feminist mobilizations in India have been accused of ignoring/under-representing the needs and interests of women from marginalized segments of the society (Manorama 2008). Andharia and Batliwala maintain that the "agenda for [the] women's movement at the national level is still framed by middle-class women's perspectives" (2008, p. 12). Manorama (2008) reminds that *Dalit* women are "thrice marginalized" (gender-class-caste) and "the downtrodden among the downtrodden" and as such their concerns may fail to interest feminist advocates because they are seen to dilute (and therefore distract) women's common concerns by raising specific concerns of *Dalit* women (p. 445). The politics of maternal mortality as experienced by poor and marginalized women is likely distinct from that experienced (if at all) by their elite counterparts (who may also be skeptical of focusing on *maternal* mortality). Therefore, it is likely that the claim of women's right to maternal health as a human right will be viewed cynically by those who doubt the political attention maternal mortality has received globally and locally.

A final issue concerns the design of the Indian maternal health policy (i.e., Janani Suraksha Yojana or JSY) launched by the Central Government in 2005, which generates many concerns on the "rights" front. The JSY has been a conditional cash transfer program offered to below-poverty-line women in both public and accredited private healthcare facilities. It promised them "benefit of cash assistance with institutional care during delivery, preceded with antenatal care and immediate post-partum care" (MoHFW 2006, n.p.). But it focused on the "supply side" of the healthcare system promising to ensure availability of emergency obstetric care, strengthening first referral units, provision of frontline health workforce and emergency medical transportation (Vora et al. 2009), which was insensitive to systemic issues of inequities in access and quality. For instance, practices of systemic abuse of poor and vulnerable women, particularly *Dalits*, *Adivasis*, and sometimes Muslims, by care providers in labor rooms and demand of user fees despite JSY being a fully subsidized entitlement were widespread (Gopichandran and Chetlapalli 2012). Such denial of essential maternal healthcare is considered a major human right injustice in the literature (Yamin and Maine 1999; Cook and Dickens 2001). Additionally, cash assistance in the High Performing States[8] was limited to two births per mother during the delivery/immediately after, provided she was able to present proof of eligibility in keeping with the state's population stabilization agenda (Sri and Khanna 2012). The tricky juxtaposition of provision of maternal healthcare entitlement with limitations on reproductive freedom provides ample impetus for human rights advocates working on maternal health and reproductive rights to mobilize against the state. The dynamics of such mobilization, especially how the two groups of advocates coordinate their efforts (if at all), remains to be seen.

Empirical Findings: Human Rights Advocacy for Maternal Health in India

This section outlines two distinct narratives that emerged during key informant interviews in response to queries about the origin and dynamics of maternal health and human rights advocacy efforts in India. The interviews were conducted between 2012 and 2013 and included 30 research participants. Furthermore, 19 of these were maternal health and human rights advocates (or Advocates) working in civil society organizations (CSOs), human rights coalitions and alliances in 16 different states with widely varying incidence of maternal mortality, 3 former feminist activists, 2 health activists, and 6 scholars specializing in human rights and women's health/population health. The analysis of the responses examined the oral histories offered by participants about the origin of maternal health and human rights advocacy in India. They are significant because a comparison of two distinct emergent narratives reveals various tensions that have shaped the dynamics of framing maternal health/death as a human rights issue in India. These tensions are symbolic of lack of solidarity between human rights advocates working on maternal health and reproductive health and right, which is counterproductive to reforming the state and advancing the feminist health agenda.

A Global, Neoliberal, Donor-Led Project?

According to 16 participants (5 Advocates, 8 scholars, 2 retired feminist activists, and 1 health activist), human rights advocacy for maternal health in India was driven primarily by inclusion of the issue as an MDG, which directly influenced donor priorities and indirectly affected the agenda of Indian NGOs working on maternal health. On probing further, eight scholars and three health activists maintained that human rights advocacy for maternal health was a convenient marriage between globally established development norms and human rights-based development norms. They categorized it as neoliberal cooptation of women's rights as human rights agenda pointing to the exclusion of the more controversial sexual and reproductive health and rights from the MDGs. Their attitude resonated with feminist scholars who cautioned against instrumentalization of maternal health as a women's issue and were skeptical of the "add human rights and stir" approach that they argued was characteristic of neoliberal economic development (Yamin and Boulanger 2014).

A retired feminist activist and two Advocates observed that "human rights", "rights-based work", and "accountability work" had become popular "buzzwords" in the development discourse and were being used by some maternal health CSOs to justify their work (gain legitimacy and sound credible) without fully reflecting on them. One human rights scholar noted that human rights constituted the "social justice face of neoliberalism". Three other scholars used some combination of "social justice" and "neoliberalism" to attribute to donors and local CSOs that had supposedly appropriated a more radical and emancipatory agenda of broader gender, health, and social justice that could genuinely help poor and marginalized women. They attributed this to the growing incidence of NGO-ization of social movements in post-(economic) liberalization India. They maintained that feminist and development CSOs were increasingly taking on "development work" funded by donors, which indirectly forced them to subscribe to the views of the donor and "take on whatever projects" the donors viewed as important. Another participant argued that "the social sector has a tendency to sound good" further implying the phenomenon of establishing legitimacy. Their arguments speak to the established analyses in the literature, linking the use of human rights language by donors to support a good governance agenda that is deeply entangled in the politics of neoliberal reforms which sometimes harm the realization of women's rights and social rights (Cornwall and Molyneux 2006; Gideon 2006). Similarly, the allegations that CSOs may take on development projects framed in the language of human rights to sound legitimate and well-meaning is not unfounded either (Bradshaw 2006; Hames 2006).

Few references to the significance of "class" and "caste" in trying to understand maternal mortality were also made pointing to the tendency of human rights to essentialize issues as purely women's concerns. This was relevant because maternal mortality particularly affected poor and socially marginalized women, however, there was no explicit indication (or appreciation) of how class, caste, and gender were deeply intertwined as determinants of poor maternal health outcomes. One participant noted:

> for neoliberalism to grow, it is very important that is should have a face of justice and social security and [the human] rights movement gives that face and we forget that actually it is class and caste that is struggling, that we need to focus on.

This indicated an implicit cognizance among few participants of drawbacks of the human rights framework, but this was overshadowed by concern and an outright rejection of neoliberalism.

Many Advocates, however, were extremely cognizant of the politics of reliance on donor aid for CSOs. One participant made recurring mentions of the issue of survival struggles and reliance on funds, pointing to the ways NGO-ization of women's movements in India and reliance on donor aid had led to the endorsement of HRBAs that had gained much popularity within the international development community. This suggested the delicate balancing act facing some Advocates in furthering their grassroots agenda while also securing strategic and financial support for their sustenance. Some feminist scholars have underscored the juggling act facing feminist CSOs in poorer countries who gain access to resources by endorsing donor agenda while maintaining their grassroots commitment to advance women's human rights (Alvarez 2009; Harcourt 2013).

The explicit verbal acknowledgment and reflection by 13 Advocates of the realities of feminist development praxis—NGO-ization, donor-led agenda setting, politics of HRBAs/accountability work—made it simplistic to characterize the origin of human rights advocacy for maternal health as a purely globally driven phenomenon. The inclusion of maternal mortality reduction in the MDGs and subsequent donor attention it received might well have shed spotlight on it and generated a political space for a new discourse. But there were also various local factors, which many Advocates argued, required a measured response because of the social injustices they revealed in relation to maternal health politics in India. This alternative explanation is discussed next.

A "Glocal" Origin?

In alternative explanation, three participants reiterated that maternal mortality had failed to gain attention from the first wave of the Movement. A focus on motherhood—only one dimension of women's lives—was equated with being co-opted by the state. Two participants, an Advocate and a human rights scholar, also reminded that the relegation of maternal mortality was due to the lack of empathy among some feminist activists/practitioners toward women dying in childbirth. The Advocate observed, "The feminist movement depends so much on experience and maternal death is not an experience for women who were part of the feminist movement then (first wave of the Movement)." The human rights scholar who participated in the first wave of the Movement made a similar observation:

> Because for people like me and the kind of socio-economic background we come from, there's very little chance of us dying from pregnancy. I take it for granted that it is not the issue. But if I had a maid, she might [consider it an issue].

It is difficult to ignore the ways class privilege (and also caste) may have worked to construct an issue as deserving (or not) of political attention and a spot on the feminist collective agenda. For example, one participant, a scholar/activist, remembered instances during the early 1990s when her efforts to raise awareness about maternal mortality were dismissed by some "senior scholars" who pointed to the insignificant proportion of women who died from childbirth (relative to other causes of female mortality). The participant recalled emphasizing:

> Maternal mortality is symptomatic of various other gender inequalities and health sector problems over and above the fact that it is the death of a woman who has a life in front of her.

This characterization reminded of select accusations that the policy focus on maternal mortality was "epidemiologically misplaced" (Jain and Rao 2001, p. 1301). The participant further noted:

> It was seen as a minor issue and entangled in the politics of family planning. So demographers and public health people had more interest in the issue than feminists, human right activists and leftist groups.

A former member of the People's Health Movement (PHM) in India corroborated the above sentiment confirming that the issue drew interest from public health specialists because it was seen to be a result of failure of the health system. In any case, it raises the caution feminist scholars call for in taking for granted female solidarity pointing to complex notion of womanhood and differences within (Cornwall et al. 2007).

Four Advocates, two health activists, and two scholars further explained that the domestic policy shifts caused as a result of the strides made at ICPD in Cairo and Beijing Summit also led to a loss of momentum of the first wave of the Movement. They noted that newer challenges (sex-selective abortion, appearance of assisted reproductive technologies, and surrogacy) had begun to emerge due to "institutionalization of gender" by the government, growing economic liberalization, and particularly the growth of the unregulated private healthcare sector; but no well-organized feminist collectives with a clearly articulated message had been formed as a response (especially in the first half of the 2000s). Hence, between the late 1990s and 2005 when the Indian government created the JSY, the domestic civil society discourse on women's health lacked a focused agenda.

Nevertheless, four participants noted that there were additional changes occurring in the global aid landscape, particularly the rise of private donors—prominent in global health sector, especially reproductive health—which also influenced the emergence of human rights advocacy for maternal health in India. Two scholars explained that such donors were not inhibited by religious and conservative actors constraining bilateral donors and more willing to experiment and support innovative, including "radical work on gender" (read, rights-based/accountability). Such donors (Ford and MacArthur Foundations) were particularly prominent in India and their growing contributions supplemented the declining influence of bilateral donors in India. For instance, both Ford and MacArthur were major supporters of maternal health CSOs (and related human rights coalitions) in India including their human rights and social accountability work. Their support along with the continued spotlight on human rights in the development discourse during the 2000s further cemented provision of resources necessary for emergence of human rights advocacy for maternal health in India.

However, possibly the strongest mobilizing force that solidified the birth of the human rights advocacy for maternal health in India—on top of convergence of all other factors—was the creation of the JSY by the Indian government. Several Advocates observed that this precipitated as a result of the prime minister's attendance of the MDG+5 review in New York in 2005, where he learned about the achievements made by Bangladesh on maternal mortality and the status of India as one of two (the other being Pakistan) worst performers in the subcontinent. This offered the necessary political opportunity for the Advocates to officially engage with the state. Greater impetus for collectivization ensued as civil society consultations took place on drafts of the policy, the initial versions of which raised rights concerns due to their explicit references to the need to push family planning measures on future policy beneficiaries. One participant characterized the situation as tricky for the Advocates, who were enthusiastic about the political attention and could not reject it despite their deep concern with the various rights violations that arose as a result of the specific policy design (as discussed earlier). This gave rise to a new social justice struggle to correct the wrongs created as a result of this political opportunity which targeted the fundamental freedoms of the poorest and most disempowered maternal citizens, burdening them with the national (and political) project of population control disguised as promotion of a development program to offer a safer childbirth experience.

In sum, three major empirical insights stem from the two competing narratives outlined so far.

- First, a source of tension between reproductive health and rights activists and maternal health advocates existed because maternal mortality was considered an epidemiologically insignificant issue and the inclusion of the issue in the Reproductive and Child Health Phase I policy and programming (in 1997) was equated with further government focus on maternal dimensions of women's lives (beyond family planning). Effectively, access to quality and affordable maternal healthcare entitlements (or the lack of it) was seen as a relatively insignificant and biomedical/technical issue in comparison to violation of reproductive rights through state-sponsored coercive family planning measures.
- Second, the existing tension among advocates in India was further intensified following the inclusion of the issue in the Millennium Development Agenda in 2000. The global and donor prioritization of maternal health (followed by the same in India) shifted the spotlight away from reproductive health and rights issues, relegating the latter to the margins.
- Third, those unsupportive of maternal health/death gaining political attention assumed that the origin of the human rights advocacy surrounding the issue was primarily driven by foreign (donor/INGO) efforts (given the ongoing popularity of human rights rhetoric in the global aid and development discourse). They dismissed the possibility that such efforts might have been local and were symbolic of Indian maternal health advocates trying to strategically leverage the window of opportunity made available by global (in 2000) and domestic (in 2005) prioritization of the issue. This was due to their fears over appropriation of the language of human rights by the donor/INGO community.

Conclusion

The findings reported above point to the growing complexities of framing women's rights as human rights in relation to maternal health (theoretically speaking). First, the findings reveal the limitations of the human rights framework, especially its universalizing nature, to address a social problem that is rooted in the collective historical marginalization of women from a particular social segment (and also deprivation of other social rights, such as the right to health). Specifically, the tendency of human rights to essentialize all women's experiences in the struggle for gender equality overlooks the inequities (both gender and social) that result in adverse maternal health outcomes for some women. Effectively, the struggle for reproductive rights, which is central to the advancement of gender equality and women's right (in India and elsewhere), sidelines more immediate needs (maternal healthcare) of some women. This is not to suggest that these women will not benefit from strides made by feminists on the reproductive rights front. But such strides may still not address their essential maternal healthcare needs.

A second learning concerns the uneasy relationship between the politics of maternal health/death and family planning in the Indian context and its implications for formulating a human rights advocacy agenda. The struggle surrounding each of these issues are seen as mutually exclusive by some Indian feminist practitioners, but the status quo Indian maternal health policy design reflects a different reality. As a result, the discourses on right to maternal health and reproductive rights are intertwined, although it certainly reveals the *inequities* facing some women even in exercising their reproductive rights in order to access their citizenship entitlement to maternal healthcare. The goal, therefore, shall be to identify ways to formulate an inclusive human rights advocacy agenda that is sensitive to the different reproductive needs and interests of different groups of Indian women rooted in hierarchy of citizenship privileges.

Finally, the skepticism some feminist practitioners have regarding the politicization of human rights in development discourse runs the risk of outright dismissal of grassroots human rights claims, rather than a more nuanced engagement with the notion of human rights. However, their skepticism cannot be sidelined for their concerns are valid. The struggle, therefore, is finding the right balance between skepticism and careful and continued engagement. It is important to recognize the tactical challenges feminist activists in developing countries face—confronting the top-down, global-to-local push of rights-based development by donors while also advancing bottom-up human rights claims articulated by the poor and marginalized they (claim to) represent.

Concurrently, it may be wiser to move away from dismissing a focus on maternal health/death as exclusively anti-feminist for that is a simplistic and an "older" approach, which does not address the gender-based discrimination and human rights injustices women face as mothers. It is important to identify ways to address injustices experienced by women as mothers while resisting political focus on exclusively maternal dimensions of women's lives. This is hardly an easy task, but one that is reflective of the complexities of feminist politics in the contemporary era in India and beyond. For example, recent developments in the United States have reignited the war on women's reproductive rights, particularly access to legal abortion, yet struggles for access to basic healthcare (including maternal healthcare) especially for poor and marginalized women of color is ongoing. The United States is the only developed country with a rising rate of maternal mortality, the incidence of which is unusually high among African American women (Johnson 2014). The emergence of movements such as "Black Mamas Matter" which aims to advance "the human right to safe and respectful maternal healthcare" is encouraging, but it remains to be seen how such emergent struggles will coexist/confront the very morally and politically charged struggle for reproductive rights, including as human rights (Black Mamas Matter Alliance 2017).

It is noteworthy that the achievement of both "maternal mortality reduction" and universal access to sexual and reproductive health and reproductive rights feature on the Sustainable Development Agenda, the new global development paradigm, established in 2015. However, the former has been associated with Goal 3: Good Health and Well-Being and the latter with Goal 5: Gender Equality (United Nations 2015). The retention of maternal mortality reduction as a priority focus on the global development agenda is a result of the momentum generated by transnational advocacy networks on the issue, framed as a social justice issue, between 2000 and 2015 (Smith and Shiffman 2016). Simultaneously, the global activism for sexual and reproductive health and rights has regrouped since 2000—partly in response to exclusion of the issue framed as a right from the MDGs and partly in response to aggressive global spread of conservative and religious fundamentalism that oppose advancements of women's reproductive rights on ground of protecting the family (see March 2017 special issue on "Fundamentalisms" in *Gender and*

Development). There is hardly any research on the interactions (or lack thereof) between these two global collectives, yet both rely on the human rights framework to advance their agenda that aim to ultimately advance women's health and well-being.

Notes

1. HRBAs to development promote the principles of inclusion and non-discrimination, participation and empowerment, holding duty bearers accountable to fulfilling their obligations and to progressive realization of rights (Gauri and Gloppen 2012). They help create political and social benchmarks "both for testing decisions within development and for evaluating them" (Archer 2009, p. 21) and emphasize the multidimensional nature of development issues and the universal right to development for all (Hickey and Mitlin 2009).
2. At the time of initiating field research in 2012, India was the largest contributor to such deaths globally. At the time of drafting this chapter in 2017, it ranked second only to Nigeria.
3. NGO-ization is a phenomenon of gradual institutionalization of social movements into professional CSOs specializing in niche issues at the core of such movement (see Alvarez 1999).
4. At Cairo, women's health advocates were able to generate consensus among participants (including states) on investing in women and girls as a whole, including their health, by pointing to the ways overall improvement in status of women was connected to corresponding fertility decline in many industrialized countries. This constituted a watershed moment in the global women's health movement because the right to sexual and reproductive health came to be framed as a fundamental human right. This included recognition of "reproductive rights" and ethical approaches to family planning (as opposed to coercive population control policies that disproportionately targeted women) (AbouZahr 2003). Additionally, the ICPD in Cairo emphasized the goal of reduction of maternal deaths by 2000 as part of improving women's overall health (Fraser 2005).
5. The Beijing Declaration and Platform for Action adopted at the Fourth World Conference on Women in 1995 is symbolic of global commitment to achieve equality, development, and peace for women worldwide.
6. This is notwithstanding other complications created in framing reproductive health and choice/rights in relation to heightened incidence of sex-selective abortion and surrogacy (keeping abortion legal while criminalizing sex-selection and keeping surrogacy legal while avoiding exploitation of poor women, respectively) which are also linked to aggressive liberalization and privatization of the healthcare provision.

7. Caste is a form of social stratification largely based on hereditarily transmitted professions (the priests, the warriors, the business, and the laborers). Those outside the caste system are called "Untouchables" or *Dalits*. They are generally the most marginalized and stigmatized, politically, socially, and economically.
8. Eight states in India with high fertility and high child marriage rates and the poorest social development indicators.

References

AbouZahr, C. 2003. Safe Motherhood: A Brief History of the Global Movement 1947–2002. *British Medical Bulletin* 67: 13–25.

Alvarez, S.E. 1999. Advocating Feminism: The Latin American Feminist NGO Boom. *International Feminist Journal of Politics* 1 (2): 181–209.

———. 2009. Beyond NGO-ization? Reflections from Latin America. *Development* 52 (2): 175–184.

Andharia, J., and S. Batliwala. 2008. *The Dalit Women's Movement in India: Dalit Mahila Samiti*. Toronto: Association of Women's Rights in Development.

Archer, R. 2009. Linking Rights and Development: Some Critical Challenges. In *Rights-Based Approaches to Development: Exploring the Potential and Pitfalls*, ed. S. Hickey and D. Mitlin, vol. 21. Sterling: Kumarian Press.

Benford, R.D., and D.A. Snow. 2000. Framing Processes and Social Movements: An Overview and Assessment. *Annual Review of Sociology* 26 (1): 611–639.

Berer, M. 2007. Maternal Mortality and Morbidity: Is Pregnancy Getting Safer for Women? *Reproductive Health Matters* 15 (30): 6–16.

Black Mamas Matter Alliance. 2017. *Mission: Advancing the Human Right to Safe and Respectful Maternal Health Care*. Black Mamas Matter. July 3. http://blackmamasmatter.org/.

Bradshaw, S. 2006. Is the Rights Focus the Right Focus? Nicaraguan Responses to the Rights Agenda. *Third World Quarterly* 27 (7): 1329–1341.

Cook, R. 1998. Advancing Safe Motherhood Through Human Rights. *Planned Parenthood Challenges/International Planned Parenthood Federation* (1): 3–5. Retrieved from http://www.ncbi.nlm.nih.gov/pubmed/12293656.

Cook, R.J., and B. Dickens. 2001. Human Rights to Safe Motherhood. *International Journal of Gynaecology and Obstetrics* 76 (2): 225–231.

Cornwall, A., and M. Molyneux. 2006. The Politics of Rights—Dilemmas for Feminist Praxis: An Introduction. *Third World Quarterly* 27 (7): 1175–1191.

Cornwall, A., E. Harrison, and A. Whitehead. 2007. *Feminisms in Development: Contradictions, Contestations and Challenges*, 262. New York: Zed Books http://sro.sussex.ac.uk/10152/.

Elson, D. 2002. Gender Justice, Human Rights, and Neo-liberal Economic Policies. In *Gender Justice, Development, and Rights*, ed. M. Molyneux and S. Razavi. Oxford: Oxford University Press.

Eyben, Rosalind. 2006. The Road not Taken: International Aid's Choice of Copenhagen Over Beijing. *Third World Quarterly* 27 (4): 595–608.

Fischer, F. 2003. *Reframing Public Policy: Discursive Politics and Deliberative Practices*. Oxford: Oxford University Press.

Fraser, A. 2005. Approaches to Reducing Maternal Mortality: Oxfam and the MDGs. *Gender and Development* 13 (1): 36–43.

Freedman, L. 2003a. "Strategic Advocacy and Maternal Mortality" Moving Targets and the Millennium Development Goals. *Gender and Development* 11 (1): 97–108.

Freedman, L.P. 2003b. Human Rights, Constructive Accountability and Maternal Mortality in the Dominican Republic: A commentary. *International Journal of Gynaecology and Obstetrics* 82: 111–114.

Gauri, V., and S. Gloppen. 2012. Human Rights-based Approaches to Development: Concepts, Evidence, and Policy. *Polity* 44 (4): 485–503.

Gideon, J. 2006. Accessing Economic and Social Rights Under Neoliberalism: Gender and Rights in Chile. *Third World Quarterly* 27 (7): 1269–1283.

Gill, K., R. Pande, and A. Malhotra. 2007. Women Deliver for Development. *The Lancet* 370: 1347–1357. Retrieved from http://www.icrw.org/docs/1794-B-background-paper-V1.pdf.

Goetz, A.M. 2007. Gender Justice, Citizenship and Entitlements: Core Concepts, Central Debates and New Directions for Research. In *Gender, Citizenship and Development*, ed. M. Mukhopadhyay and N. Singh, 15. New Delhi: Zubaan and International Development Research Centre.

Gopichandran, V., and S.K. Chetlapalli. 2012. Conditional Cash Transfer to Promote Institutional Deliveries in India: Toward a Sustainable Ethical Model to Achieve MDG 5A. *Public Health Ethics* 5 (2): 173–180.

Gruskin, S., J. Cuttingham, A. Martin Hilber, E. Kismodi, O. Lincetto, and M.J. Roseman. 2008. Using Human Rights to Improve Maternal and Neonatal Health: History, Connections and a Proposed Practical Approach. *Bulletin of the World Health Organization* 86 (8): 589–593. https://doi.org/10.2471/BLT.07.050500.

Hames, M. 2006. Rights and Realities: Limits to Women's Rights and Citizenship After 10 Years of Democracy in South Africa. *Third World Quarterly* 27 (7): 1313–1327.

Harcourt, Wendy. 2013. Transnational Feminist Engagement with 2010+ Activisms. *Development and Change* 44 (3): 621–637.

Hickey, S., and D. Mitlin. 2009. The Potential and Pitfalls of Rights-Based Approaches to Development. In *Rights-Based Approaches to Development:*

Exploring the Potential and Pitfalls, ed. S. Hickey and D. Mitlin, 209. Sterling: Kumarian Press.

Jain, D., and M. Rao. 2001. National Population Policy 2000: Re-examining Critical Issues. *Economic and Political Weekly* 36 (16): 1299–1302.

Joachim, J.A. 2007. *Agenda Setting, the UN, and NGOs: Gender Violence and Reproductive Rights.* Washington, DC: Georgetown University Press.

John, Mary. 2012. Feminism, Poverty, and the Emergent Social Order. In *Handbook of Gender*, ed. Raka Ray, vol. 539. New Delhi: Oxford University Press.

Johnson, C. 2014. *Maternal Transition: A North-South Politics of Pregnancy and Childbirth.* London: Routledge.

Maclean, Gaynor D. 2010. An Historical Overview of the First Two Decades of Striving Towards Safe Motherhood. *Sexual & Reproductive Healthcare* 1 (1): 7–14.

Maine, Deborah, and A. Rosenfield. 1999. The Safe Motherhood Initiative: Why Has It Stalled? *American Journal of Public Health* 89 (4): 480–482.

Manorama, R. 2008. Dalit Women: Downtrodden Among the Downtrodden. In *Women's Studies in India: A Reader*, ed. M.E. John, 445. New Delhi: Penguin India.

MoHFW. 2006. Janani Suraksha Yojana: Guidelines for Implementation. *Ministry of Health and Family Welfare.* New Delhi. http://www.ilo.org/dyn/travail/docs/683/Janani Suraksha Yojana Guidelines/Ministry of Healthand Family Welfare. pdf.

Molyneux, M. 2007. The Chimera of Success: Gender ennui and the Changed International Policy Environment. In *Feminisms in Development: Contradictions, Contestations, and Challenges*, ed. A. Cornwall, E. Harrison, and A. Whitehead, 227. London: Zed Books.

Molyneux, M., and S. Razavi. 2003. Introduction. In *Gender Justice, Development and Rights*, ed. M. Molyneux and S. Razavi, 1. Oxford: Oxford University Press.

Mukherjee, V. N. 2002. Gender Matters. *Seminar, 511.* http://www.india-seminar.com/2002/511/511 vanita nayak mukherjee.htm

Mukhopadhyay, Maitrayee. 2010. Creating Citizens Who Demand Just Governance: Gender and Development in the Twenty-First Century. *Gender and Development* 11 (3): 45–56.

Mukhopadhyay, M., and N. Singh. 2007. *Gender Justice, Citizenship and Development.* New Delhi: Zubaan and International Development Research Centre.

Narayanan, H. 2011. Women's Health, Population Control and Collective Action. *Economic and Political Weekly* xlvi (8): 39–48.

Qadeer, I. 2008. Reproductive Health: A Public Health Perspective. In *Women's Studies in India: A Reader*, ed. M.E. John, 381. New Delhi: Penguin India.

Rao, M. 2008. Two-child Norm and Population Policy. In *Women's Studies in India: A Reader*, ed. M.E. John, 297. New Delhi: Penguin India.

Sanneving, L., N. Trygg, D. Saxena, D. Mavalankar, and S. Thomsen. 2013. Inequity in India: The Case of Maternal and Reproductive Health. *Global Health Action*. https://doi.org/10.3402/gha.v6i0.19145.

Schon, D.A., and M. Rein. 1994. *Frame Reflection: Toward the Resolution of Intractable Policy Controversies*. New York: Basic Book/HarperCollins Publishers.

Sen, G., and A. Mukherjee. 2014. No Empowerment Without Rights, No Rights Without Politics: Gender-Equality, MDGs and the Post-2015 Development Agenda. *Journal of Human Development and Capabilities* 15 (2–3): 188–202.

Sen, G., and P. Ostlin. 2011. Gender Inequity in Health. In *Improving Equity in Health by Addressing Social Determinants*, ed. T.C. on S.D. of H.K. Networks, J.H. Lee, & R. Sadana, 59. Geneva: World Health Organization.

Sen, G., Östlin, P., and George, A. 2007. *Unequal, Unfair, Ineffective and Inefficient Gender Inequity in Health: Why It Exists and How We Can Change it Final Report to the WHO Commission on Social Determinants of Health*. http://www.who.int/social_determinants/publications/womenandgender/en/.

Shiffman, J. 2007. Generating Political Priority for Maternal Mortality Reduction in 5 Developing Countries. *American Journal of Public Health* 97 (5): 796–803.

Smith, S.L., and J. Shiffman. 2016. Setting the Global Health Agenda: The Influence of Advocates and Ideas on Political Priority for Maternal and Newborn Survival. *Social Science & Medicine* 166: 86–93.

Sri, B. S., and R. Khanna 2012. *Maternal Health Policy in India: From Institutional Deliveries to Safe Deliveries, A Position Paper*. Vadodara. www.commonhealth.in

Sundari Ravindran, T.K. 1993. Women and the Politics of Population and Development in India. *Reproductive Health Matters* 1 (1): 26–38.

Toyo, N. 2006. Revisiting Equality as a Right: The Minimum Age of Marriage Clause in the Nigerian Child Rights Act, 2003. *Third World Quarterly* 27 (7): 1299–1312.

Tsikata, D. 2007. Announcing a New Dawn Prematurely? Human Rights Feminists and the Rights-Based Approaches to Development. In *Feminisms in Development: Contradictions, Contestations, and Challenges*, ed. A. Cornwall, E. Harrison, and A. Whitehead, vol. 214. London: Zed Books.

UNFPA. 2014. *Trends in Maternal Mortality: 1990 to 2013 Estimates by WHO, UNICEF, UNFPA, the World Bank and the United Nations Population Division*. http://www.unfpa.org/public/home/publications/pid/17448.

UNFPA India. 2009. *Concurrent Assessment of JSY in Select States*. http://india.unfpa.org/en/publications/concurrent-assessment-jananisuraksha-yojana-jsy-selected-states.

United Nations. 2015. Sustainable Development Goals. *Sustainable Development Knowledge Platform*. https://sustainabledevelopment.un.org/sdgs.

Vora, K.S., D.V. Mavalankar K.V. Ramani, M. Upadhyaya, B. Sharma, S. Iyengar, and K. Iyengar. 2009. Maternal Health Situation in India: A Case Study. *Journal of Health, Population, and Nutrition* 27 (2): 184–201.

WHO. 2015. *Trends in Maternal Mortality: 1990–2015: Estimates by WHO, UNICEF, UNFPA, World Bank Group and the United National Population Division*. https://data.unicef.org/resources/trends-maternal-mortality-1990-2015/.

Yamin, A.E., and D. Maine. 1999. Maternal Mortality as a Human Rights Issue: Measuring Compliance with International Treaty Obligations. *Human Rights Quarterly* 21 (3): 563–607.

———. "Maternal Mortality as a Human Rights Issue: Measuring Compliance with International Treaty Obligations". In Perspectives on Health and Human Rights, S. Gruskin, M. A. Grodin, G. J. Annas, & S. P. Marks, 427. New York: Routledge, 2005.

Yamin, A.E., and Boulanger, V.M. (2014). *Why Global Goals and Indicators Matter: The Experience of Sexual and Reproductive Health and Rights in the Millennium Development Goals*. https://doi.org/10.1080/19452829.2014.896322.

Yuval-Davis, N. 1997. Women, Citizenship and Difference. *Feminist Review* 57: 4–27.

PART III

Social Contestation and the Broadening of Human Rights' Meanings

CHAPTER 10

Indigenous Peoples in Chile: Contesting Violence, Building New Meanings for Rights and Democracy

Marie-Christine Doran

Re-appropriation of International Law: The Case of Chile in the Recent Latin American Context

In many Latin American countries, indigenous people and Afro-descendants are the most strongly affected by structural violence, racism, and poverty as well as by conflicts—especially in Colombia—and the

I would like to thank the Social Sciences and Humanities Research Council of Canada for its support for the fieldwork and collection of material used in this chapter. With the kind permission of Routledge, some interview extracts and data from this material, which were also included in part in an article published in French in 2017 ("Convention 169 et conceptions des droits et du politique dans les communautés autochtones au Chili : luttes pour la légitimité et conflits pour les ressources naturelles") in the *Canadian Journal of Development Studies*, 38(2): 216–233, will be used in this chapter, although analyzed in a different light.

M.-C. Doran (✉)
School of Political Studies, University of Ottawa, Ottawa, ON, Canada
e-mail: Marie-Christine.Doran@uottawa.ca

G. Blouin-Genest et al. (eds.), *Human Rights as Battlefields*, Human Rights Interventions,
https://doi.org/10.1007/978-3-319-91770-2_10

anti-popular authoritarian regimes (Marques-Pereira and Garibay) which plagued the continent throughout the 1980s and also during the authoritarian period of the Fujimori regime in Peru, as Ñusta Carranzo-Ko demonstrates in her analysis of policies of forced sterilization of indigenous women in Peru in Chap. 8 of this book.

Chile, today considered to be a model of stability of its democratic institutions, is no exception. The ravages perpetrated by the dictatorship (1973–1989) had specific impacts on indigenous peoples in Chile. In addition to numerous crimes against humanity, which remain protected by the amnesty law[1] the authoritarian legacy of the military regime specifically affects the Mapuche peoples (Samaniego 2003; Mella Seguel 2007, p. 64), notably because it deregulated private logging (Akhtar 2013) in the vast ancestral lands which had previously been recognized and redistributed to Mapuche communities during the Salvador Allende government's agrarian reform (reversed by the dictatorship in 1973), literally leaving these communities with neither home nor means of subsistence. As a consequence, poverty indicators of the Chilean indigenous communities are extreme: at least twice as high as they are for the rest of the population, according to data between 2003 and 2011 (*Informe de Desarollo Social* 2012).

Often viewed as a model of institutional stability since the return to democracy in 1990 (Navia 2010), Chile is nevertheless one of five Latin American countries in which the criminalization of collective action mostly targets rights defenders (FIDH 2012, pp. 258–265).

In particular, the anti-terrorist law (Law 18.314), inherited from the Augusto Pinochet dictatorship, is still today 99% of the time applied to indigenous people (Doran 2017a, b), accused of undermining the social peace and threatening national (economic) interests, particularly in regions where natural resource management is portrayed as giving rise to violent conflict. The anti-terrorist law was strengthened in 1997 by the Eduardo Frei's government, much after the end of the dictatorship. Still in force in Chile, this law allows individuals to be criminalized for "inciting violence" or "terrorist intention." Then are arrested and judged by military courts involving anonymous witnesses and judges. Military court provisions and sentences of up to 30 years of imprisonment are often applied. Many Mapuche indigenous leaders and activists, very proactive in the defense of the environment and ancestral lands against megaprojects, are currently serving sentences of this kind. In 2010, after large-scale mobilizations for justice for Mapuche political prisoners, new legal provisions ensured that individuals accused of "threatening national interests" were judged by civilian courts, but under provisions that can sometimes lead to even more severe sentencing.[2]

Many authors, such as Akhtar (2013), report on the barriers created by the fact that the laws on indigenous peoples date from the dictatorship and legislative measures put in place by democratic governments since transition have not changed the authoritarian and discriminatory spirit of these laws:

> The fundamental rights of the Mapuche can only be respected when there is acknowledgment of the international covenants and the Declaration of the Rights of Indigenous Peoples. This will surmount the barriers that have been imposed by the Chilean state, the most obvious being the retention of the anti-terrorist and national security law that was enacted by the martial law government. (Akhtar 2013, p. 576)

As this extract seems to indicate, there is no doubt of the importance of recourse to international law, alongside strong national mobilizations for indigenous rights, whether in Chile—where, as numerous works have shown, this is often the only possible avenue in a country with legislation closed on indigenous issues (Contesse 2011; Nesti 2002; Cuadra Montoya 2016)—or in the whole of Latin America. Thanks to an extraordinary resilience and will to assert their differences in a huge movement of Indian awakening (Le Bot 2009) pushing many Andean countries toward plural democracies (Gros 2001; Verdo and Vidal 2012), the indigenous peoples and Afro-descendants of the continent are now viewed as central actors in the implementation of international law in Latin America. Many rich case studies show the importance and utility of international human rights law in indigenous mobilizations and the significant gains—not only for their rights but for democratic rights in general (Bellier 2012; Gros 2001; Dixon 2008)—it allows in societies in which indigenous peoples and Afro-descendants are mobilized. In particular, both Gros and Dixon underscore the fact that, where appropriation of international law is of primary importance, this process is mainly bottom up.

In keeping with the literature on this subject in Latin America, numerous authors have examined the re-appropriation of human rights by indigenous peoples in Chile. According to Samaniego (2003), as well as Carruthers and Rodriguez (2009), various examples of re-appropriation of the idea of human rights strongly affect, in particular, the demands of

Mapuche indigenous peoples who refuse to leave their lands which have been conceded by the government for different megaprojects involving multinational companies. Their exposure to the impact of environmental conflicts on human rights (Aylwin and Silva 2015) is one of the most notable contributions of indigenous re-appropriations of human rights. The reorientation of collective Mapuche actions around demands referencing human rights and justice allowed them to reach diverse international organizations which have sent several observation missions to Chile since 2005, but also created alliances with many politicized parts of the student movement which surprised the entire world with the student and social strikes and the demand for the constituent assembly in 2011–2012. However, important struggles over meaning arise around the notion of rights and human rights in the Chilean context and show the issues of "disputes" over the definition of the term "rights."

While recognizing the central importance of the appropriation and mobilization of international law and notably international human rights law in defending indigenous causes in Chile and elsewhere, our analysis, based on research results and data collected between 2012 and 2017 in Chile,[3] suggests another hypothesis. In fact, like other recent work on conflicts of meaning between indigenous conceptions and government conceptions of rights (Bauer 2016), our research shows that the representations of rights and politics in indigenous Chile challenge the narrow institutional definition of rights (Barrera-Hernandez 2005), including some advances made through a recourse to international law, such as joining and implementing International Labor Organization (ILO) Convention 169 on indigenous people's right to consultation within the Chilean legislative framework. In this way, the conceptions of rights used by indigenous people in their mobilizations enter into a struggle over meaning (Laclau and Mouffe 1985), not only with the very cautious use of the term "rights" by diverse Chilean governments since the return to democracy—coupled with ferocious repression and constant criminalization of indigenous mobilizations—but also with some legal provisions. Enabled by the advances from international law, these notably include indigenous people's right to consultation: the notion of territory and political representation inscribed in the provisions of Convention 169 are in this way re-interpreted within the indigenous political imaginary (Doran 2016, pp. 286–289) in Chile.

Thus, an analysis of the recent mobilizations for their rights by indigenous populations in Chile, as well as interview material collected with

Mapuche community members (in the south of the country) and Diaguitas-Huascoaltinos and Atacameños (in the north) reveal indigenous conceptions of politics and rights which go beyond a pure application and re-appropriation of international law. In fact, as we will see in this chapter, these demands, while deeply rooted in a relationship with territory, do not command a property relationship, not even a collective one. Without claiming that access to territory is not important, there appears to be a greater emphasis on a universe of representation in which this question is more broadly situated in a conception requiring equality and justice among humans and with nature, affecting political organization and having an impact on demands for rights and even on the application of certain legal advances allowed by international law, such as Convention 169. The will of the indigenous peoples to actively participate in (re)defining the terms of Convention 169 prevents governments in power from using it in order to simply legitimize contested mining projects. In this way, the "strategic" use of international law, whether by the Chilean government or indigenous communities, is far surpassed by proposals for new articulations between rights and politics proposed by indigenous political imaginaries in Chile, as in many other countries as Svampa (2011) also analyzes with the notion of the "eco-territorial turn of struggles."

This even leads to practices of land-sharing (demanded or achieved) with non-indigenous people, on the basis of the creation of a political subjectivization around a common condition of the imperative of justice (Doran 2016) for the defense of nature as a very broad and polysemic notion developed as a central element of the grassroots project for a constituent assembly in Chile, under discussion since 2012, and which includes a strong indigenous representation, unprecedented in Chile and which will also be examined in this chapter.

Challenging the Closed Legislative Framework and Renewed Context of Violence Against Indigenous Peoples Mobilizing for Rights

As Haughney (2012) contends, in Chile, one of the main legacies of the dictatorship (1973–1989) still circulating in institutions, is the "neoliberal" definition of rights. Our own analysis of Chilean presidential discourse on rights between 1990 and 2016 (Doran 2016) confirms this predominance of a narrow definition of rights and a strong desire to control its meaning, despite the presence in Chile of a government body responsible for indigenous development, the National Corporation of Indigenous Development (CONADI), since 1991. Thus, we can see in presidential speeches since the democratic transition, a great reserve toward the notion of rights (Doran 2016) and in particular the rights of indigenous populations, for example, the following extract of a presidential speech to the nation by President Ricardo Lagos in 2000:

> Thus, the policy which I am committed to developing in relation to the original peoples is a policy which must be born in the depths of Chile's soul. ***Not to do justice towards them***, much as this must also be done, ***but really*** to understand that preserving their culture is what allows us to ***maintain greater wealth as a nation***. For this, our desire for recognition and reparations towards these peoples ***must not be confused with*** infinite concessions to ***small groups who disturb the public order or attack the rule of law***. (President Ricardo Lagos 2000, p. 17, our emphasis[4])

This desire to control the meaning of rights is consistent with Haughney's theses (2012) showing that the Chilean government empties indigenous rights of their liberatory/emancipatory content, enabling a rhetoric of rights and legal reforms entirely compatible with a neoliberal definition of democracy and participation. Haughney goes so far as to describe an "authoritarianization" of rights (Haughney 2012, p. 214) within the Chilean democratic framework and in legal reforms implemented during successive governments of the Coalition of Parties for Democracy, the center-left coalition which has held power for most presidential terms since the return to democracy.

Generally, the literature on indigenous rights in Chile notes significant barriers to the adoption of a legal framework which would allow the fundamental rights of indigenous people to be respected. Moreover, the reservations about the very notion of rights, illustrated in the extract cited above, is part of a dominant narrative in which social mobilizations and conflicts are viewed as having led to the Pinochet dictatorship. This explains, according to Moulián (1993), Chile's "low-intensity democracy"; by Avilés' definition, which also applies to Colombia (Avilés 2006) and Peru (Avilés and Rey Rosas 2017), this means an institutionally strong democracy which nevertheless tolerates an active fight, including violence, against social mobilizations. Exhaustive studies of the various governments' responses since the transition (Aylwin 2008, p. 271) point in the same direction and show the many ambiguities in governmental discourse and policies, in addition to a growing criminalization of indigenous demands, especially Mapuches (Aylwin 2008, p. 259).

In this context that many have qualified as "post-dictatorship" instead of democracy (Vera Gajardo 2008), indigenous struggles—particularly Mapuche struggles—like all social conflicts in Chile are viewed by mainstream media and part of Chilean society as violent because of the pervasiveness of low-intensity democracy, which sees dissensus and social conflict as the main enemies. The repression of groups deemed conflictual is "justified" in this way, and in spheres far beyond governmental discourse, as a study by Segovia Lacoste (2015) shows: the terms used in the media to characterize Mapuche demonstrations and collective actions—such as "strategic retreat" and "armed confrontation"—are borrowed from military vocabulary. These discursive practices, which construct an "indigenous threat," make it easier to legitimize the criminalization of indigenous demands and help exclude these communities from public space (Doran 2015, p. 226 and following), and in the process also narrowing democratic space.

The degree of violence of the Chilean state against indigenous peoples, in particular the Mapuche communities in the south of the country, has been met with outrage by international institutions for many years. Arrests and prolonged arbitrary detention, torture, military occupation of indigenous villages, forced disappearances at the hands of police forces, and targeted assassinations of indigenous leaders, all common practices during the dictatorship bit still currently happening (Parra 2016). They are the lamentable consequences of the perpetuation, even intensification, of structural violence directed against these communities.

The closed attitude and violence of all Chilean governments toward the rise of the Mapuche movement saw no exception during the Bachelet government, though the latter was otherwise recognized for its progress on women's rights. This government's first term was marked by increased indigenous mobilizations and joint recourse to international law by various cases (see Baleizao et al. 2014) at the Inter-American Court of Human Rights (IACHR). In the north of Chile, the resistance and mobilization of Aymara, Diaguita, and Huascoaltina communities intensified around very mediatized cases such as Barrick Gold mining company's plans to melt the millennial glaciers of Pascua Lama to reach minerals at the heart of the Andes, which would affect access to water for many communities in the region. The communities decided to take legal action against the Chilean government and in the end obtained a moratorium on the Barrick Gold project, for non-compliance with environmental criteria in force in Chile. In the south, major mobilizations against diverse megaprojects affecting the environment (BBC News World 2014) and a new strategy of recuperation and "productive occupation" of lands stolen from Mapuche communities during the dictatorship provoked unprecedented repression. The indigenous mobilizations of this period appeal to human rights and justice as essential components of democracy (Samaniego 2003; Carruthers and Rodriguez 2009), and highlight the impact of environmental conflict on human rights (Aylwin and Silva 2015).

The number of cases against the Chilean state at the IACHR multiplied after 2005 and several cases were able to clearly establish the political persecution of indigenous peoples by the Chilean state, as well as serious violations of individual civil and political rights. Iconic cases such as those of Segundo Aniceto Norin Catriman (12.576), Juan Patricio Marileo Saravia (12.611), Victor Ancalaf Llaupe and others (12.612) versus the government of Chile[5] brought national and international attention and encouraged a better social reception—and greater cultural sensitivity—of indigenous mobilizations, which had continued without respite in parallel to the legal cases. These cases show that the use of international law by indigenous peoples can help legitimize their demands for human rights in adverse contexts like Chile (González-Parra and Simon 2014).

The unprecedented social support for the major hunger strikes by Mapuche political prisoners in 2010 confirmed this openness by new sectors of the public—notably environmental defenders, students' associations, unions, political parties, and land occupation movements dedicated to housing to the plight of indigenous peoples. Our previous work on the *political imaginary of shared suffering* in the poorer sectors in Chile (Doran 2010, 2016) also shows how identification with collective suffering connected to (political or economic) oppression is a hegemonic feature of *poblaciones* and *campamentos* (slums and shanty towns) dwellers. It allows them to embrace other segments of the public in this "we suffer," which constitutes the bedrock of collective action (especially land occupation) for the poorer classes, fighting the social shame of poverty in the Chile of the "Pacific jaguars" (Angelcos and Doran 2014). The hunger strike by Mapuche political prisoners made a very emotional appeal which was important in bringing to light their suffering and tempering the accusations of violence with which Chilean society and media usually greet their actions.

The lack of openness on the part of the Bachelet government, which had almost systemically refused dialogue in 2008 and 2009 and supported the use of the anti-terrorist law, with unprecedented levels of repression in democracy, confirmed the damning judgments of the Chilean state by the IAHRC. In August 2009, the death of the young Mapuche activist Jaime Facundo Mendoza Collío, tortured by the police, became the symbol of oppression of an entire people, following the deaths of other Mapuche youth, some of whom were killed under torture, strongly condemned by various organizations such as the UN Committee Against Torture (UNCAT).[6]

This tragic incident sparked intensified protest as of 2010, under the first Sebastián Piñera government, whose party claimed the authoritarian legacy of Pinochet. Under Piñera's right-wing government, the Mapuches entered a new phase of mobilization using hunger strikes as a complementary strategy to the legal processes.[7] They condemned the criminalization of their mobilizations and demands and required that they be tried under civil processes rather than military courts as provided by anti-terrorist law. Their protest movement, which stirred public opinion both in Chile and internationally, highlighted the authoritarian provisions of anti-terrorist law which were systematically used against Mapuches mobilized around rights defense and land/environmental protection, protesting forestry and hydro-electric companies. According to a report of the Ethics Commission against Torture,[8] active since 2003 to denounce the conditions of Chilean political prisoners during the dictatorship and the democracy, there were 106 Mapuches imprisoned for political reasons in June 2010, almost doubled over 2009.

The Mapuches' liquid hunger strike, which lasted 82 days, was castigated by the Piñera government as an "act of violence against the Chilean nation" (Passmore 2014). It ended on 1 October 2010 after an agreement with the government that the anti-terrorist provisions (Ley No. 18.314) would no longer be systematically used and that the accused would be tried exclusively in civilian courts, a change that failed to prevent further human rights violations however. This long and arduous hunger strike, centered on a critique of the Chilean legal and political system and a general claim for justice, allowed Mapuche organizations and their supporters to highlight in a striking way all the authoritarian aspects of the Chilean legal system and its criminalization of collective action, despite reforms over the years.

In this context, it is noteworthy that our interviews material shows that political conflict has great legitimacy as a *means of accessing rights.* While these strategies—legal and social mobilization—are often contrasted, we observe in Chile that indigenous respondents saw them as complementary, as the diversity of their repertoire of collective action also demonstrates. This unified vision of collective action succeeded in affirming the importance, to the same degree, of both legal and protest strategies. In this way, indigenous communities are overcoming the divide between "street protest" and legal means and contributing to the understanding that human rights can be "fought for" both individually and collectively. The message from indigenous people to Chilean society, where many politicians still consider the "violence of the streets" to be equivalent to that of the "barracks" (see Doran 2016, pp. 92–93), is thus very clear. In addition to the vast new acceptance of social conflict and demonstrations that became obvious in the extraordinary mass demonstrations of the student strikes and their social repercussions (Peñafiel 2012), there was another clear sign of the greater acceptability of Mapuche-led social conflict (Cuadra Montoya 2016) in the famous Chilean street murals. These murals, a powerful tool of resistance during the dictatorship which re-emerged as of 2005 (Doran 2016, pp. 276–277), began to include paintings of numerous imprisoned Mapuche political and spiritual leaders—*Machis*. These powerful images, completely new to the emancipatory symbols usually chosen for the Chilean murals, signal an important change in the social acceptance of indigenous struggles in Chilean society. Mobilizing/connecting with/resonating with/inspiring poor and middle-class neighborhood alike, these indigenous struggles for human rights have become a symbol for a general cry for justice in Chile.

In this way, it is remarkable all indigenous respondents asserted the legitimacy of social conflict, as we can see in the following extracts in which protest (conflictual mobilization or *protesta* in Spanish) and conflict are seen as the necessary conditions for attaining and having rights respected:

> We know that ***protest*** (*protesta*) is the basis for which are flouted or directly violated.

Again,

> I think that, in the absence of something better, ***protest*** is what exists and ***right***, as they say, is ***the right to question***, the right ***to rebel***.

This strong legitimacy of social conflict, directly associated by the respondents with the advancement of rights, also enters into dialogism with neoliberal versions of rights driven by international financial institutions and is very influential according to several writers (Barrera-Hernandez 2005). These versions maintain that respect for rights must be conditional on achieving political stability and economic growth, implying a heavy bias against social conflicts, seen as responsible for instability. This conceptualization is very similar to that of the Chilean government, as previously seen in President Lagos' speech. It is in this context that Convention 169, long demanded by indigenous peoples and all human rights defenders in Chile, is being implemented. While previous governments also used repression and criminalization—it can be recalled that the anti-terrorist law was strengthened by the democratic government of Eduardo Frei in 1997—the repressive dynamic unleashed under Bachelet's government provoked greater national and international reaction (Perez 2009). At the end of her first term in December 2009, the then very popular president was bitterly reproached for her tolerance of the anti-terrorism law. Michelle Bachelet then ratified Convention 169 on behalf of Chile. It entered into force in Chilean law on 15 September 2009, just before the presidential elections in December which gave the victory to the first right-wing alliance government elected since the 1990 transition. Convention 169 stipulated that indigenous and tribal peoples must be consulted on political processes and development affecting them, particularly in regards to plans to develop and exploit land and natural resources but more generally about participation in public life.

Political Imaginaries and Transformations of Key Concepts in the Horizon of Rights by Indigenous Peoples

As we saw above, until Convention 169 was ratified by Bachelet's government, and then implemented by the Piñera government in 2010, mobilizations and legal recourses undertaken by indigenous peoples allowed the construction of a certain legitimacy not only for indigenous rights defense but for rights in general. This is also seen in many other cases analyzed in

Latin America (Dixon 2008). However, this significant contribution of indigenous struggles to the expansion of rights in Chile was to enter a new phase with the struggles over meaning developing around the important breakthrough—from the perspective of international law—represented by innovations introduced by Convention 169 and the right of indigenous peoples to consultation in "good faith."

In the context of very tense relations between indigenous peoples and governments in Chile, many observers feared a strategic use—to gain international credibility—rather than effective consultation. Moreover, these fears were heightened by the fact that the implementation of the Convention coincided with the entry into power of the government of the right-wing "Alliance for Chile," proud heir to the neoliberal model and the authoritarian past (Walder 2010). The Piñera government did indeed put its stamp on the process by quickly introducing, via Supreme Decree 66/2013,[9] a new, very restrictive, legal framework for consultations with indigenous peoples and tribes, despite warnings by the Supreme Court in 2012,[10] and numerous criticisms of the resulting restrictions on consultation. Moreover, an inventory of consultations carried out during this period shows that the Piñera government assiduously avoided applying the Convention in cases of projects with environmental impacts, applying it only to creating cultural centers and road repair (Doran 2017a, p. 223) This circumvention of the goals of the Convention was made very clear when the main environmental conflict in Chile, the very mediatized mining project of Pascua Lama (Berger 2014), did not give rise to any consultation.[11] Sharp criticisms of this lack of consultation were swept aside by the government, which discredited them in a racist branding of indigenous opponents as being "backward" and "having no interest in a progressive and cautious process of evolution."[12]

Michelle Bachelet's second government, elected again for a new four-year term in December 2014, planned to transform the conditions for applying Convention 169, in addition to creating three new institutions dedicated to indigenous questions: a Ministry of Indigenous Affairs, a Council of Indigenous Peoples, and an Agenda for the Development of Indigenous Peoples. While these plans seem to indicate a salutary change of attitude in relation to charges of backwardness, the discourse around the Convention and these new community relations and institutions carefully avoided all allusion to the notion of rights, as we can see here:

> We will begin consultations now, quickly, as required by Convention 169, so that all these bills ***bring the point of view and perspective*** of ***our first peoples.*** The Agenda of Indigenous Development will be established through a participatory process ***with*** indigenous peoples so that it is ***coherent with their needs*** and on the basis of diagnoses which ***we will establish jointly***. (Bachelet 2014, p. 30)

In addition to the remarkable absence of the term "rights" in discussing a Convention which is precisely about rights, we can observe in this extract an emphatic attempt to control the idea that indigenous peoples can be subjects of autonomous rights. They are not "the" indigenous peoples but "ours"; the participatory process is "with" them and not for them; the process aims at coherence with "needs" and not rights; and the needs are to be defined "jointly" with the government.[13]

In fact, despite repeated demands and mobilizations by indigenous peoples (Correa 2014), neither Supreme Decree 66 limiting the process of consultation (Romero 2014) nor Supreme Decree 40 governing the process of environmental impact assessment were ever revised in Chile. In fact, while access to water is a vital issue for the communities, particularly those of *Norte Grande* and the mythical desert of Atacama, the communities were not consulted in 2015 but rather "informed" of a major reform of the Water Code.[14] Struggles over the meaning of the terms "consultation" and "indigenous rights" are very evident in the interviews as these extracts show:

> When they respect our customs, our beliefs, our traditions, then we could begin to say, "ah yes! 'when they consult us'" ...when they consult us, but not in their way, rather as we want to be consulted, with our own ways of being.

And again,

> I think that indigenous rights, as long as Chile does not recognize that there are ***peoples*** who were there before, that there are peoples who have different customs, traditions, ways of being, that we need ***distinct laws*** in which we can be recognized for our beliefs, ***for our way of discussing and deliberating***, there can't be no well-founded rights.

As the Water code example demonstrates, it seems that the governmental vision of including the "point of view" and the "joint definition of the needs" of indigenous peoples does not allow for the inclusion of access to water or the right to a clean environment. It also does not provide for an end to serious human rights violations, threats and imprisonment of indigenous leaders on the basis of suspicion, the forced disappearances, the military occupation of Mapuche villages.

As established in the first chapter of this book, the theoretical perspective of discursive hegemonic relations developed by Ernesto Laclau and Chantal Mouffe (1985) and Laclau (2000) enables us to understand that society and politics are deeply constituted by struggles over meaning. This perspective sheds light on the fact that there are "deep power relations at play in the process of constitution and subversion of meaning and that we might seize them and analyze them to see effective social and political change" (Doran 2016, p. 45). In this case, using Laclau and Mouffe's terminology, we can see that terms such as "consultation" and "rights" are "antagonisms" directly contesting the hegemonic definition of "nodal points"[15] that are crucial for hegemonic discursive formations. These antagonisms may be transformed and translated into discursive chains that will make many voices converge and achieve counter-hegemonic meaning, thus contesting and sometimes transforming the shared meaning of a particular signifier. This particular possibility seems to be at play in some of the current indigenous struggles for rights in Chile.

In fact, the evacuation of rights from government discourse and initiatives is deeply contested at various levels by communities who continue to mobilize and turn to international bodies for recourse. Interviews with indigenous rights defenders reveal conceptions which deepen and transform the notion of rights. We can observe this in the first place by measuring the extent to which communities using the notion of ***human rights*** and intrinsically linking it to that of the *political rights* of mobilized indigenous populations shows the importance of indigenous people as ***political subjects of rights***. We can see this in the following extracts:

> Really, indigenous movements are fighting above all for dignity, for recognition, and to be ***recognized as subjects*** capable of naming themselves, of ***making their own decisions. A subject is intelligent.***

Again,

> In Chile there are many and continual ***attacks on*** **human rights**. The first […] is the ***Chilean political system which excludes citizens*** from ***their basic human rights such as*** **participation** ***in decision-making***.

It is difficult to imagine a greater difference than between these conceptions of the "intelligent" political subject and political exclusion defined as an "attack on human rights" of the indigenous respondents and the government's logic. It is moreover remarkable that these conceptions intersect with Kriegel's analysis of the incompleteness of universal rights, which in her view lack the dimension of political convocation. As we discussed in Chap. 2, Kriegel (1986, p. 291) contends that the current Universal Declaration of Rights (1948) relies on an "intangible basis" because the right to political participation is not in any way guaranteed, leading to a superficial application of rights because stakeholders cannot contest political decisions on the basis of their rights. This is precisely what indigenous communities are pointing out in their current struggles.

Yet the political role of rights also opens the door to the articulation of a *new universe of meaning*, as can be seen in this extract:

> [a] right where we can have lands, where we can develop freely, where there is respect, where they don't keep watching us even as they steal all the water, here, in the North, without knowing that it is with water ***that we, the peoples***, live ***with the earth***, that ***more water means more life. We gain nothing in being masters of the whole desert if there is no water***, it is like having a body emptied of its blood. Everything is connected: ***the earth is connected to its water to give life, so as long as there is no respect for that***...

This eloquent example of representations of rights and politics intrinsically links the necessity of respecting the "earth connected to its water" "to give life" and rejects exclusive ownership of the land (in this case the desert) and of the water, so central to extractive projects (Bauer 2016). Far beyond the logic of simple territorial gains ("we gain nothing in being masters of the desert"), we see the deployment of a conception which profoundly questions the legal mechanisms around the conception of property necessary to extractive development. The relationship to space and land here is not strictly based on identity nor based on territorial ownership, even collective. Without denying that access to land is not important, greater emphasis seems to be placed on a universe of representations in which the question of land is situated more broadly in a conception of the need for equality and justice between humans and nature (environment or *Wallmapu*).

Other profoundly innovative political conceptions emerge from our interview material. Many indigenous respondents emphasized, for example, the importance of understanding politics as a relationship intrinsically centered on respect for the environment. The Mapuche conception of *Admapu*, an important aspect of their cosmology, was highlighted by respondents who referred to it as a relationship between rights and political organization which *necessarily* changes according to the influence of the land (territory) on which the community is established, and according to an ever-renewed alliance with aspects of surrounding nature. The elective, reversible, and consensual nature of political representation and leadership[16] in the Mapuche world—a characteristic enabling indigenous populations to resist in turn the Inca empire, the Spanish conquest, and finally the land grabs south of the Bio-Bio river up until 1865, as the extraordinary work of the historian José Bengoa (1987) shows—takes on a new meaning here.

The Indigenous Peoples' Enduring Quest to Be Recognized as *Political Subjects of Rights*

Yet, numerous representatives of indigenous communities—especially Mapuche—are still political prisoners, imprisoned for "terrorist intentions." Recent legal suits brought by indigenous people against the Chilean state show the degree to which the issue of rights as access to the status of *political subject* is at the heart of the political persecution of these communities and constitutes the main reason state violence against them is perpetuated. In this context, important recent judgments such as the IACHR Catrimán decision[17] are landmarks establishing the "systematic" (Baleizao et al. 2014) obstruction of the political rights of indigenous people through the application of anti-terrorist law to Mapuche collective action. The ground-breaking Catrimán judgment states that Chilean anti-terrorist legislation violates "many civil and political rights" including freedom of expression, which is inseparable from the right to the dissemination of opinion and freedom of thought. The IACHR also found that the political rights of the Mapuche peoples, notably the right to representation, had been violated by the anti-terrorist law because Mapuche leaders were silenced; either by arrest for actions with a suspected terrorist intent or because fear of repression thwarted them in their duties to defend their community's collective interests (Baleizao et al. 2014, pp. 4–6). The profoundly anti-democratic nature of the anti-terrorist law and its pervasive effects on indigenous political representation was thus affirmed clearly from a legal perspective. Interestingly, recent mobilizations by indigenous communities have also started emphasizing violations of the communities' religious rights through imprisonment of their religious and political leaders, such as the recent case of *Machi* Francisca Linconao (Mapuche World Press 2018). The *Machis* are traditional female religious leaders in Mapuche communities and their imprisonment cause great distress and disorganization of the community's spiritual well-being. This testifies to the constant re-appropriation and re-interpretation of rights by the indigenous communities, and to the vitality and dynamism of deeply rooted conceptions of human rights.

On this note, it is revealing that indigenous respondents consider criminalization by the state as arising from a confrontation between different conceptions of rights, showing a consciousness of struggles over meaning and the legitimacy of using this key concept of democracy as is shown here is a young Mapuche Law student's analysis:

> The fact is, the state concedes or recognizes certain individual rights but when it comes to exercising them the individual faces many limitations: the same thing does not happen for recognition of economic rights as for rights which have an impact on individual freedoms, or even rights which could have repercussions on collective issues, such as the right to the environment. (…) When these individuals demand to exercise these rights which they cannot exercise freely because of the state, the state responds by criminalizing them. Why? Because the exercise of these rights somehow contradicts the values of the economic system, so the response from the state, which has all the repressive apparatus to carry out the criminalization, is obvious.

An unprecedented and spectacular step in political mobilization is underway in indigenous communities in Chile. Indigenous rights defense is now converging with the need for profound transformation of the entire institutional system which came out of the democratic transition, and with the demand for a constituent assembly, advocated by diverse social and political sectors in Chile and articulated around the demand for justice (Doran 2016, p. 275 and following) and for "the right to have rights." Only one month after the hunger strikes were resolved, far from being content with what they had won with such difficulty in 2010, Mapuche organizations gathered in an assembly on the sacred mountain of Cerro Ñielol, in Temuco (a border town symbolically marking the entrance to Mapuche lands in the south of Chile). There they formally decided to join the mobilization demanding a constituent assembly. Characterized in the media as a "decision of great historical transcendence," this unhoped-for entry of the Mapuche peoples into the movement for a constituent assembly marks their will to be full political actors in this process of transformation, alongside sectors of Chilean society struggling against injustice, an important theme of the Cierro Ñielol Declaration, as well as further on in Indigenous mobilizations. The Mapuche leaders, thus,

> [m]ake an appeal to conscious Chilean people to create an alliance between the two societies with the goal of reformulating the Chilean constitution through a constituent assembly. This act can change the situation of injustice, racism, poverty and pettiness that our two societies live in this state which now calls itself Chile, because the current dominant system promotes social inequality.[18]

Conclusion: Indigenous Proposals on Human Rights: Confronting the Limits of Chilean Democracy

The constant introduction of new megaprojects without good faith consultation in Chile continues to provoke waves of mobilization, land occupations, hunger strikes, but also the creation of political parties aiming to recover Mapuche sovereignty over their lands—and a growing desire by many organizations and mobilized sectors to actively take part in politics, in order to participate in democratic renewal.[19] Along with other indigenous nations of Chile, the Mapuches' desire to actively participate in politics is also a remarkable novelty: long distrustful of political parties, having often been manipulated for electoral purposes by right and left, Mapuche organizations are including their demands and protests in Chile's big cities at various events where they offer their support and thus take part in many mobilizations from diverse social sectors. The *Mapuche Pact for Self-Determination,* suggesting an alternative path of dialogue for consultation of development projects, has also been launched. It proposes mechanisms to consult indigenous populations which are better able to meet the conceptions of the communities. This testifies to a clear desire to constitute themselves as political interlocutors according to the modalities of their forms of representation and participation (Enlace Mapuche Internacional 2018).

The ground-breaking Cerro Ñielol Declaration, emanating from traditional Mapuche authorities with a political representativity most recognized by all Mapuches in Chile, and appealing to all oppressed Chileans in an unprecedented move toward political alliance for democratic expansion, was followed by several other deliberative councils or *Futatrawun*. The positions adopted clearly demonstrated, to all the critics of alleged Mapuche "violence" and "terrorist intention," the absurdity of such accusations in the face of the manifest desire of indigenous peoples to be agents of transformation of laws and political norms alongside other Chilean democratic forces. The deeply innovative conceptions of rights and politics, at the heart of the perseverance and democratic will of the indigenous peoples, despite the constant persecution they suffer, will likely continue to contribute new articulations of meaning open to constant transformation of relations between politics and nature, which the world needs, in Chile and elsewhere.

As this chapter, based on research results and data, suggests, indigenous conceptions of rights and democracy directly contribute to a wider social acceptance of human rights struggles in Chile. Because the indigenous demands and struggles for rights are clearly conceived in terms of democratic expansion, they directly confronted the coherence of Chile's institutions and also actively contributed to the social understanding of human rights in the country. They share new meanings, making them available to other community-based and grassroots demands for justice and democracy and thus contributing significantly to the democratic renewal currently underway in Chile. In the end, these new meanings paradoxically bring us back to the fundamental idea of universal human rights as a utopia or to the utopic vision of universal human rights. As a young Mapuche law student very clearly expressed it,

> Our struggles and values have always been the same as the ones inscribed in the traditions of fundamental rights and liberties: justice and equality.

Notes

1. The decree on amnesty covers all crimes committed (assassinations, kidnappings, torture) during the period of the dictatorship from March 1973 to March 1978. Before 1998, Chilean courts refused to hold trials and automatically applied the amnesty, eliminating all possibility of guilty verdicts at least symbolically important.
2. Interviews by the author with four lawyers specializing in cases involving anti-terrorist law Temuco, Chile, December 2014.
3. The fieldwork material used in this article is based on 20 open interviews with Indigenous respondents defining themselves as "rights defenders" between 2012 and 2017, throughout Chile. Some indigenous rights defenders were grassroots activists, some were leaders, and others were lawyers or law students. In order to guarantee the security of the participants in a very tense context, neither specific places, indigenous communities, or even pseudonyms have been associated with the extracts cited in this chapter. An additional material of ten interviews with human rights lawyers involved in national and international trials involving indigenous causes will also be used throughout the chapter but will be cited in a distinct way when used.
4. In order to facilitate the interpretation of the extracts cited here, we will use bold for the parts of the analyzed extracts we want to highlight to the reader, both for government speeches and indigenous rights defenders. To avoid weighing down the text, this system of highlighting will not be mentioned explicitly after each extract analyzed.
5. Inter-American Commission on Human Rights, *Report No. 176/10, Fondo Chile,* (CASOS 12.576, 12.611 Y 12.612, SEGUNDO ANICETO NORIN CATRIMAN, JUAN PATRICIO MARILEO SARAVIA, VICTOR ANCALAF LLAUPE Y OTROS), 5 de noviembre de 2010.
6. See "Por el derecho a la vida de la nación mapuche en Chile. Comunicado de Prensa – 13 de agosto, 2009," Enlace Mapuche internacional/noticias. http://www.mapuche-nation.org/espanol/html/noticias/cmdo-403.htm.
7. http://www.observatorio.cl/node/181.
8. http://www.lanacion.cl/mapuches-en-huelga-de-hambre-para-exigir-garantias-judiciales/noticias/2010-07-12/211838.html.
9. For a detailed exposé, see Diario Constitucional 2014 as well as the *Informe anual sobre derechos humanos en Chile 2012*, 169–174.
10. See, for example, the following judgments by the Supreme Court of Chile: (Corte Suprema, Sentencia de 30/03/2012, Rol N° 11.040-2011), Parque Eólico Chiloé (Corte Suprema, Sentencia de 22/03/2012, Rol N°

10.090-2011) and El Morro (Corte Suprema, Sentencia de 27/04/2012, Rol N° 2211-2012).

11. Interviews by the author with lawyers defending the indigenous party to impose a moratorium on the Pascua Lama project (January 2015).
12. Speech by the Minister of Bruno Baranda, cited in Areyuna 2013.
13. In discourse analysis, the enunciative taboo constitutes a mechanism which reveals the enunciator's discursive marks of fear of the danger of potential subversion of the terms by competing meanings in circulation in other discourses and thus preferring not to use the term at all, at the risk of losing credibility with listeners. In this instance, the presence of an enunciative taboo testifies to the fact that the presidential discourse fears that other discourses using the notion of rights transform the meaning.
14. Soy Arica.cl, "En Arica CONADI informó a comunidades y organizaciones sobre la Reforma al Código de Aguas" http://www.conadi.gob.cl/index.php/2-noticias/1524-en-arica-conadi-informo-acomunidades-y-organizaciones-sobre-la-reforma-al-codigo-de-aguas.
15. Nodal points are important and visible sites of power relations where the subversion and transformation of previous hegemonic meaning can be seen at play (Laclau and Mouffe 1985).
16. Similar conceptions of political powers could be found in the Iroquois Confederation in Canada and the USA. For a detailed analysis of the democratic mechanisms existing among the Iroquois political organizations, see Iris Marion Young, "Hybrid Democracy: Iroquois Federalism and the Postcolonial Project," in D. Ivison, P. Patton, and W. Sanders (Eds.), *Political Theory and the Rights of Indigenous Peoples*, Cambridge\New York: Cambridge University Press, 2000: 237–258.
17. See in particular Comisión Interamericana de Derechos Humanos, Informe No. 176/10, CASOS 12.576, 12.611 Y 12.612 Segundo Aniceto Norin Catriman, Juan Patricio Marileo Saravia, Victor Ancalaf Llaupe y Otros, FONDO CHILE·5 de noviembre de 2010. https://www.oas.org/es/.../corte/12.576FondoEsp.doc.
18. "La Asamblea Constituyente de los pueblos de Chile ya es demanda Mapuche," *El Ciudadano*, http://www.elciudadano.cl/2010/12/14/30063/la-asamblea-constituyente-de-los-pueblos-de-chile-es-ya-demanda-mapuche/.
19. A summary of Mapuche collective and political actions since 2008 can be found on this website: http://www.mapuche.info/news/anews00.html.

References

Akhtar, Zia. 2013. Mapuche Land Claims: Environmental Protest, Legal Discrimination and Customary Rights. *International Journal on Minority and Group Rights* 20 (4): 551–576.

Angelcos, Nicolas, and Marie-Christine Doran. 2014. L'expérience participative des pobladores au Chili : entre résistance aux modes de gestion de la pauvreté et nouvelles formes de politisation. *Lien social et politiques* 3 (71): 159–178.

Areyuna, Hector. 2013. Comunidades indígena acusan vulnerabilidad de procesos consulta. *Diario Uchile*. http://radio.uchile.cl/2013/12/17/acusan-de-sobre-reglamentacion-y-vulnerabilidad-en-procesos-de-consulta/. Consulted 13 Sept 2017.

Avilés, William. 2006. Paramilitarism and Colombia's Low-Intensity Democracy. *Journal of Latin American Studies* 38 (part 2): 379–408.

Avilés, William, and Yolima Rey Rosas. 2017. Low-Intensity Democracy and Peru's Neoliberal State. The Case of the Humala Administration. *Latin American Perspective* 44 (5): 162–182.

Aylwin, José. 2008. Las recomendaciones del informe del Relator Especial de la ONU para los derechos indígenas sobre Chile y la respuesta del Estado y de otros actores interpelados. In *Globalización, Derechos humanos y Pueblos Indígenas*, ed. José Aylwin and Álvaro Bello, 246–271. Temuco: Observatorio de derechos de los Pueblos indígenas.

Aylwin, José, and Hernando Silva. 2015. *Los impactos de las empresas en los Derechos humanos del Pueblo Mapuche en Chile*. Temuco: Observatorio Ciudadano & Grupo International de Trabajo sobre Asuntos Indígenas WGIA.

Bachelet, Michelle. 2014. Mensaje Presidencial, 21 de Mayo. http://www.bcn.cl/historiapolitica/mensajes_presidenciales.

Baleizao, Jennifer, Jean-Jacques Hible, and Florence Leonzi. 2014. La Cour interaméricaine des droits de l'Homme remet en cause l'application de la loi antiterrori.ste chilienne aux communautés autochtones. *La Revue des droits de l'homme* [En ligne]. https://doi.org/10.4000/revdh.875. URL: http://revdh.revues.org/875. Consulted 5 Mar 2017.

Barrera-Hernandez, Lila. 2005. Indigenous Peoples, Human Rights and Natural Resource Development : Chile's Mapuche Peoples and the Right to Water. *Annual Survey of International & Comparative Law* 11 (1): 1–28.

Bauer, Kelly. 2016. Land Versus Territory: Evaluating Indigenous Land Policy for the Mapuche in Chile. *Journal of Agrarian Change* 16 (4): 627–645.

BBC News World. 2014. Chile Rejects Huge Hydro-Electric Project in Patagonia. *BBC*. http://www.bbc.com/news/world-latin-america-27788286. Consulted 10 June 2017.

Bellier, Irène. 2012. Les peuples autochtones aux Nations Unies : un nouvel acteur dans la fabrique des normes internationales. *Critique internationale, Presses de Sciences Po (P.F.N.S.P.)* 1 (54): 61–80.

Bengoa, José. 1987. *Historia del pueblo mapuche*. Santiago: LOM.

Berger, Lucio Cuenca. 2014. Pascua Lama La insólita desfachatez de un proyecto agónico. *El Desconcierto.cl*. http://www.eldesconcierto.cl/2014/06/05/pascua-lama-la-insolita-desfachatez-de-un-proyecto-agonico/. Consulted 5 June 2017.

Carruthers, David, and Patricia Rodriguez. 2009. Mapuche Protest, Environmental Conflict and Social Movement Linkage in Chile. *Third World Quarterly* 30 (4): 743–760.

Contesse, Jorge. 2011. Indigenous Peoples in Chile : The Quest to Become a Constitutional Entity. *Studies in Law, Politics, and Society* 55: 19–41.

Correa, Paula. 2014. Entre críticas incumplimientos avanza la Consulta Indígena a lo largo del país. *Diario Uchile*. http://radio.uchile.cl/2014/09/21/entre-criticas-e-incumplimientos-avanza-la-consulta-indigena-a-lo-largo-del-pais/. Consulted 21 Sept 2017.

Cuadra Montoya, Ximena. 2016. La revendication autochtone contre le projet hydro-électrique Neltume au Chili: Un regard décolonial sur les antagonismes sociaux. *Cahiers du CIÉRA* 13: 60–78.

Dixon, Kwame. 2008. Transnational Black Social Movements in Latin America. In *Latin American Social Movements in the Twenty-First Century*, ed. R. Stahler-Sholk, H.E. Vanden, and G.D. Kuecker, 181–195. Boulder/New York: Rowman and Littlefield Publishers.

Doran, Marie-Christine. 2010. Les effets politiques des luttes contre l'impunité au Chili: de la revitalisation de l'action collective à la démocratisation. *Revue internationale de Politique comparée* 17 (2): 103–126.

———. 2015. La criminalisation de l'action collective dans la crise actuelle des droits humains en Amérique latine. *Revue Québécoise de droit international*, Hors-série, L'État de droit en Amérique latine: 221–246.

———. 2016. *Le réveil démocratique du Chili: une histoire politique de l'exigence de justice: de la transition à l'Assemblée constituante (1990–2016)*. Paris: Karthala.

———. 2017a. Convention 169 et conceptions des droits et du politique dans les communautés autochtones au Chili : luttes pour la légitimité et conflits pour les ressources naturelles. *Canadian Journal of Development Studies* 38 (2): 216–233.

———. 2017b. The Hidden Face of Violence in Latin America: Assessing the Criminalization of Protest in Comparative Perspective. *Latin American Perspectives* 44 (5): 183–206.

Enlace Mapuche Internacional. *Pacto Mapuche por la Autodeterminación*. https://www.mapuche-nation.org/espanol/html/documentos/doc-116.html. Consulted 1 Apr 2018.

FIDH. 2012. (Fédération internationale des ligues des droits de l'Homme) et OMCT (Organisation mondiale contre la torture) - Observatoire pour la protection des défenseurs des droits de l'homme (2011) Rapport annuel 2011 - L'obstination du témoignage. http://www.fidh.org/IMG/pdf/obs_2011_fr-complet-2.pdf.

González-Parra, Claudio, and Jeanne Simon. 2014. International Norms and National Indigenous Politics: Mapuche Demands for Territory in Chile. *Nationalism and Ethnic Politics* 20 (1): 79–98.

Gros, Christian. 2001. Métissage et identité. La mosaïque des populations et les nouvelles demandes ethniques. *Pouvoirs* 3 (98): 147–159.

Haughney, Diane. 2012. Defending Territory, Demanding Participation: Mapuche Struggles in Chile. *Latin American Perspectives* 39 (4): 201–217.

Kriegel, Blandine. 1986. *Les chemins de l'État*. Paris: Calmann-Lévy.

Laclau, Ernesto. 2000. *La guerre des identités, Grammaire de l'émancipation*. Paris: La Découverte/M.A.U.S.S.

Laclau, Ernesto, and Chantal Mouffe. 1985. *Hegemony and Socialist Strategy, Towards a Radical Democratic Politics*. London: Verso.

Le Bot, Yvon. 2009. *La grande révolte indienne*. Paris: Robert Laffont.

Mapuche World Press. *La guérisseuse Mapuche Francisca Linconao Huircapan et le pouvoir judiciaire chilien*. https://mapuchenl.wordpress.com/2016/11/02/machi-linconao-un-cas-exemplaire/. Consulted 1 April 2018.

Mella Seguel, Eduardo. 2007. *Los Mapuche ante la justicia. La criminalización de la protesta indígena en Chile*. Santiago de Chile: Ediciones LOM.

Ministerio de Desarollo Social. 2012. *Informe de politica social 2012*. Santiago: Ministerio de Desarollo Social. http://www.ministeriodesarrollosocial.gob.cl/ipos-2012/media/ipos_2012_pp_12-29.pdf.

Moulian, Tomás. 1993. Démocratie de consensus ou démocratie de conflit? *Problèmes d'Amérique latine* 11: 17–25.

Navia, Patricio. 2010. Living in Actually Existing Democracies: Democracy to the Extent Possible in Chile. *Latin American Research Review* 45 (Special Issue): 298–328.

Nesti, Lorenzo. 2002. The Mapuche–Pehuenche and the Ralco Dam on the Biobío River : The Challenge of Protecting Indigenous Land Rights. *International Journal on Minority and Group Rights* 9 (1): 1–40.

Observatoire pour la protection des défenseurs des droits de l'homme, Fédération internationale des ligues des droits de l'Homme (FIDH), Organisation mondiale contre la torture (OMCT). 2011. *Rapport annuel 2011 – L'obstination du témoignage*. http://www.fidh.org/IMG/pdf/obs_2011_fr-complet-2.pdf.

Parra, Julio César. Comunero víctima de emboscada policial en Tirúa: 'Nos querían matar'. *El Desconcierto.cl*. http://www.eldesconcierto.cl/2016/12/27/comunero-victima-de-emboscada-policial-en-tirua-nos-querian-matar/. Consulted 27 Dec 2016.

Passmore, Leith. 2014. Force-Feeding and Mapuche Autonomy : Performing Collective Rights in Individual Prison Cells in Chile. *Journal of Latin American Cultural Studies* 23 (1): 1–16.

Peñafiel, Ricardo. 2012. Le printemps chilien. Dépassement des 'demandes' et radicalisation de l'action collective contestataire. *Lien social et politiques* 68: 121–140.

Perez, Benito. 2009. Le drame mapuche, l'échec de Michelle Bachelet, Le courrier, December 2009.

Romero, Maria Cristina. 2014. Gobierno anuncia revisión de decretos 66 y 40 relacionados con pueblos indígenas. *Emol.* http://www.emol.com/noticias/nacional/2014/11/05/688489/gobierno-anunciarevision-de-decretos-66-y-40.html. Consulted 5 Nov 2017.

Samaniego, Augusto. 2003. Identidad, territorio y existencia de la nación mapuche ¿Derechos políticos autonómicos?. *Revista Atenea*, Universidad de Concepción: 131–145.

Segovia Lacoste, Pablo. 2015. Nommer le 'conflit mapuche' dans la presse chilienne. In *Le discours politique identitaire dans les média*, ed. Arnaud Richard, 139–165. Paris: L'Harmattan.

SoyArica. 2015. Dirigentes de Arica molestos al no ser consultados por la reforma al Código de Agua. *SoyArica.* http://www.soychile.cl/Arica/Sociedad/2015/05/30/325427/Dirigentes-de-Aricamolestos-al-no-ser-consultados-por-la-reforma-al-Codigo-de-Agua.aspx. Consulted 30 May 2017.

Svampa, Maristella. 2011. Néo-'développementisme' extractiviste, gouvernements et mouvements sociaux en Amérique latine. *Problèmes d'Amérique latine* 81 (3): 101–127.

Vera Gajardo, Antonieta. 2008. Les discours de genre dans la campagne présidentielle de Michelle Bachelet : une critique féministe. *Raisons politiques* 31 (3): 81–103.

Verdo, Geneviève, and Dominique Vidal. 2012. L'ethnicité en Amérique latine : un approfondissement du répertoire démocratique? *Critique internationale/Presses de Sciences Po (P.F.N.S.P.)* 4 (57): 9–22.

Walder, Paul. 2010. El sueño neoliberal de Piñera: la privatización del Estado. *Punto Final* 707: 16–29, avril. http://www.puntofinal.cl/707/privatizacion.php. Consulted 14 Dec 2017.

Young, Iris Marion. 2000. Hybrid Democracy: Iroquois Federalism and the Postcolonial Project. In *Political Theory and the Rights of Indigenous Peoples*, ed. D. Ivison, P. Patton, and W. Sanders, 237–258. Cambridge\New York: Cambridge University Press.

CHAPTER 11

Improving HIV/AIDS Drugs Access: A Genealogy of the Human Right to Health from Below

Gabriel Blouin-Genest and Mikey Erb

Introduction: Human Rights, Battlefields, and In/Visibility

Aiko Akemi[1] is a financial advisor for a major Japanese tech company in Tokyo. Having never felt to be a "man", Aiko seeks to be recognized as transgender by the government, for which a procedure exists in Japan. However, to do it, Aiko not only needs to be diagnosed a "Gender Identity Disorder", which translates his/her feelings into a disease, but he/she must also prove that he/she "permanently lack[s] functioning gonads", which might need intrusive surgical operations. This corresponds to forced sterilization and is recognized as such by international organizations, including the WHO and the UN, but not by her own government.

The opinions and views expressed in this chapter are the author's alone and are not intended to reflect GAO's institutional views.

G. Blouin-Genest (✉) • M. Erb
Department of Political Science, Virginia Tech, Blacksburg, VA, USA
e-mail: gblouin@vt.edu; mikeye7@vt.edu

G. Blouin-Genest et al. (eds.), *Human Rights as Battlefields*,
Human Rights Interventions,
https://doi.org/10.1007/978-3-319-91770-2_11

Corinne Cointreau[2] lives in Fos-sur-Mer, South of France. Fos-sur-Mer is the home of the biggest industrial center in France and one of the most important one in Europe. Chemical industries, metallurgic groups, energy facilities, and a major port are never far out of sight in this city beautifully positioned on the Mediterranean Sea. Corinne, although in her early 50s, already had five cancers, thyroidal problems, cardiovascular diseases as well recurrent hormonal disorder. The rate for these diseases is three to five times higher in this area than in the rest of France. French authorities have for long negated any "environmental" causes for these problems.

Aiko and Corinne have in common that their human right to health has been, at some point and for different reasons, violated. They are, as such, invisibilized. The human right to health represents one of the most contested—and violated—of all the human rights recognized by international law. It is also the product of complex relationships between different types of actors—local, national, and international—and has encountered multiple difficulties in its recognition and implementation since the end of the Second World War (Mann 1998).

The main objective of this chapter is to understand how the language and practice of human rights have been used to produce, translate, modify, and/or contest the reality of the human right to health as originally defined by international actors, documents, or practices (in particular the Universal Declaration of Human Rights (UDHR) and the following "general comments"). To do so, we use HIV/AIDS, and in particular the question of access to essential drugs and medicines, as our main case study. We seek in this perspective to underline the key "battlefields" or struggles (Blouin-Genest and Paquerot 2016a, b—see Chap. 2 for the theoretical framework used here) that have punctuated the improvement of HIV/AIDS drugs access—as a human right to health—since the late 1990s. HIV/AIDS is a particularly fruitful case study, as it has been subject to both strong battles to frame it as a human right issue *and* at the same time has always been "the face of our failure to protect human rights", as reminded by Navi Pillay, former UN High Commissioner for Human Rights.

In short, this chapter shows that the human right to health, rather than being imposed from above by international actors, organizations or practices, emerged from below, especially through the work of civil society, community groups, and activists involved "battlefields". More than being just a legally recognized instrument inscribed in international regulations, the human right to health is also a contested object shaped by struggles, debates, and contestation from below. This is especially true when it comes to the access of essential drugs and medicines for HIV/AIDS, as this issue rapidly became one of the central battlefields for the emergence and materialization of the human right to health in the 1990s.

As underlined by Blouin-Genest and Paquerot (2016a), "[h]uman rights [...] establish themselves not only as a formal limit imposed upon power, but as a space for claims and contestation against this same power, simultaneously structuring the vocabulary of, and means for, actions organized in their own name – that is, in the name of human rights" (p. 137). The human right to health is a good example, as exemplified later, of how human rights emerge from below, through struggles and conflicts, rather than being imposed from above. We thus follow Blouin-Genest and Paquerot in their definition of human rights battlefields as "the social and political space through which different human rights actors become organized and mobilized in order to claim a specific understanding/practice of these rights through a logic of emancipation from their original context or objectives" (Blouin-Genest and Paquerot 2016a, p. 140).

These battlefields are not just to advocate for one solution to one problem, they are spaces to enact resistance to invisibility. As Preciado claims in *Testo Junkie*, "[t]he thousands of seropositive people who die each day on the continent of Africa are precarious bodies whose survival has not yet been capitalized as bioconsumers/producers by the Western pharmaceutical industry. For the pharmacopornographic system, these bodies are neither dead nor living [...] They are bodies excluded from the technobiopolitical regime" (Preciado 2013, p. 52). There is power in exclusion, which is underlined by Sedgwick's understanding of knowledge in the *Epistemology of the Closet*. In that book, she claims that:

> [i]nsofar as ignorance is ignorance of a knowledge – a knowledge that may itself, it goes without saying, be seen as either true or false under some other regime of truth – these ignorances, far from being pieces of the originary dark, are produced by and correspond to particular knowledges and circulate as part of particular regimes of truth. (Sedgwick 1993, p. 8)

Ignorance means invisibility, and these actions on the part of those located within regimes of power are thus actions, taken on a battlefield of human rights, to be recognized within and helped from a system that ultimately ignores their existence. In so doing, these actors mobilize the human right to health, created and defined in their own way, to gain visibility.

This in/visibility is key to the politics of human rights we argue here, which is ultimately a "politics of visuality" (Leese 2016), of being seen and recognized or not. Human right in/visibility can be retraced through the issues used to justify better practices, the populations supported, and/or how the concept of human right is articulated—or not—with other issues. This is what ultimately can or cannot be seen and thus be subjected to policies, programs, or public attention. The term "in/visibility" is preferred over other expressions, such as presence/absence (see, e.g., Callon and Law 2004) or silence/elocution. In/visibility, we suggest, implies a deliberate and active act of inclusion/exclusion fueled by ignorance; it means politics, and especially here, a politics of evidence regarding legitimized knowledge, stressing what Sedgwick termed the "violent power relations of knowledge" (Sedgwick 1993).

In order to underline this in/visibility process, we analyzed key documents produced by activists, patients, and community groups[3] involved in HIV/AIDS advocacy as well as more recent transformative moments[4] when the concept of human right to health has been invoked and rendered visible to improve or facilitate access to HIV/AIDS drugs. We conclude by an overview of the invisibilization of some aspects of the human right to health when it comes to preventative strategies using new—and categorized as non-essential—drugs, such as PrEP (pre-exposure prophylaxis).

Finding the Human Right to Health: The Contentious Politics of Health as a Human Right

The relationship between health and human rights is a complex one. This relationship goes back to the history and sociology of human rights in general and their conflicting understandings and practices. On the one hand, commonsense meanings of human rights are—at least intuitively—shared (Doise 2003): most of the people know what they generally mean. On the other hand, human rights are largely context and issue dependent and, maybe more importantly, are definitely a byproduct of western liberalism (Piotte 2007), thus creating resistance in some cultures or actors. They are at the same time overwhelmingly opposed and violated (Risse and Sikkink 1999, p. 4), including by country signatories of human rights conventions, private groups, and even international organizations.[5] Human rights are at the same time invisible and hypervisible. The human right to health faces in this regard the same complexity and contradictions.

As such, and even though there is an "inextricable connection between health and human rights" (Mann 1998, p. 143), the human right to health is fundamentally ambiguous and controversial (Dembour 2010). There is a widespread confusion regarding the meaning and implications of the human right to health (Hendriks and Toebes 1998), which is, however, also true for human rights in general (Dembour 2010). The main problem, in this case, is "the general lack of understanding about what the right to health is and what it means in practice" (Editorial, The Lancet 2008, p. 2001), which, of course, has been partially answered by recent international legal developments (more on this later). It is still, however, far from clear what exactly is at stake when the human right to health is invoked (Sen 2008, p. 2010). Individual health? Collective health? Healthcare and technologies? Access to scientific discoveries and knowledge? Echoing the General Comment 14 itself, the debate is still on regarding what exactly this human right is about and how it can be translated into practices.

The UDHR is usually presented as the first international instrument framing health as a human right. However, there is no clear and specific definition/identification of the human right to health in the UDHR, contrary to what it is usually believed. Its Article 25 states, for example, that:

> Everyone has the right to a standard of living adequate for the health and well-being of himself and of his family, including food, clothing, housing and medical care and necessary social services, and the right to security in the event of unemployment, sickness, disability, widowhood, old age or other lack of livelihood in circumstances beyond his control. (UN 1948, art. 25)

The human right to health is only indirect and implicit. The UN human right declaration also shows that health by itself is not a human right but is rather linked with other factors (e.g., so-called standard of living) or even other human rights (e.g., human right to food, clothing, or housing). In fact:

> it was not until 2000 that the UN Committee on Economic, Social and Cultural Rights adopted general comment 14, which states that in addition to access to health care, the right to health also includes underlying determinants of health, freedom from discrimination, participation, and accountability. (Editorial, The Lancet 2008, p. 2001)

The General Comment 14 takes its root in Article 12.1 of the 1966 International Covenant on Economic, Social and Cultural Rights. This article declares that "[t]he States Parties to the present Covenant recognize the right of everyone to the enjoyment of the highest attainable standard of physical and mental health" (UN 1966, art. 12.1). However, they do so without defining what health[6] is or what these highest standards of health are, which, of course, is highly problematic for a planet characterized by stark inequalities in terms of resources and living conditions. This question is partly answered by the General Comment 14 of 2000:

> [h]ealth is a fundamental human right indispensable for the exercise of other human rights. Every human being is entitled to the enjoyment of the highest attainable standard of health conducive to living a life in dignity. The realization of the right to health may be pursued through numerous, complementary approaches, such as the formulation of health policies, or the implementation of health programs developed by the World Health Organization (WHO), or the adoption of specific legal instruments. (CESCR 2000)

The WHO was also influenced by this approach since its foundation. Its constitution clearly states that "the highest attainable standard of health [is] a fundamental right of every human being" (WHO 1995), which includes, still according to the WHO, "access to timely, acceptable, and affordable healthcare of appropriate quality."[7] It "requires a set of social criteria's that is conducive to the health of all people, including the availability of health services, safe working conditions, adequate housing and nutritious foods. Achieving the right to health is closely related to that of other human rights, including the right to food, housing, work, education, non-discrimination, access to information, and participation."[8]

As all human rights, the human right to health is thus entwined with other rights or factors and is what we could describe as a systemic human right, meaning that its implementation and respect depend on other human rights and issues/factors (determinants of health, such as water, sanitation, food, environment, and education) (UNHCHR & WHO 2008). It emerges from a system of rights.[9] Key to this system is, however, civil society, activists, and community groups, which push for specific meaning and understanding of these rights, we argue in this chapter. This is largely erased and invisibilized from academic/legal debates about human rights.[10]

Being a fabulous example of contentious politics, the human right to health brings a lot of debates and struggles regarding its meaning or implementation. The human right to health has been in this perspective highly contested by many different actors (Marks 2013, p. 4). The inclusion of the human right to health itself in UN treaties and documents was in fact subject to a lot of contestation by state and non-state actors (Hendriks and Toebes 1998), far for the general perception of human rights as being "banalized" (Slaughter 2009).

According to ABIA, the Brazilian Interdisciplinary AIDS Association, there are "political and normative struggles aimed at the realization of the right to health".[11] Although the human right nature of health itself seems largely recognized, what is generally missing are the actual tools, policies, or programs needed for its implementation and respect. This might be the main struggle facing by the realization of the human right to health: "public health practitioners and policy makers assert, without much embarrassment, that saving lives does not require policy and programs to be also guided by human rights".[12] This is where community groups and activists got involved: to make this human right visible.

HIV/AIDS has been at the forefront of the battlefields and struggles of the recognition and definition of the human right to health since the beginning of the epidemic in the early 1980s. They are the actors that made it visible as a human right issue.

HIV/AIDS as a Human Right Battlefield: Emergence, Translation, and Contestation

HIV/AIDS is widely recognized as the "frontline"[13] for numerous struggles and battles. Issues, groups, and demands have been made in/visible depending on the context and the actors involved. The history of the pandemic is instructive in that matter. HIV, or human immunodeficiency virus, was discovered in 1983 by French and American scientists. However, studies show that "the first transmission of SIV to HIV in humans took place around 1920 in Kinshasa in the Democratic Republic of Congo (DR Congo). The same area is known for having the most genetic diversity in HIV strains in the world, reflecting the number of different times SIV was passed to humans. Many of the first cases of AIDS were recorded there too."[14]

A brief timeline of the response to the discovery of AIDS by western scientists is given by Luc Montagnier in "A History of HIV Discovery". He claims, for example, that:

> HIV was identified and shown to be the cause of AIDS less than 2.5 years after this disease was first identified. It took only another 2 years for blood tests to become commercially available, reducing almost to zero transmission of AIDS through blood transfusion in developed countries. In 1987, the first anti-HIV drug, AZT, which blocks HIV RT activity was introduced. With the arrival of the HIV protease inhibitors and triple drug therapy in 1995, many patients are alive today who would otherwise have died. (Montagnier 2002, pp. 1727–28)

HIV/AIDS is considered as a frontline because, after 30+ years of research and development, access to treatment is still limited and many groups affected by it are still invisible. In several countries, HIV is still among the top causes of avoidable death: "[f]or every individual who receives treatment for human immunodeficiency virus (HIV), an estimated 4 additional persons require treatment" (Cohen and Gay 2010). The UNAIDS report of 2015 HIV AIDS Targets recalls that "[a]t least 10 countries (Botswana, Cape Verde, Eritrea, Kenya, Namibia, Rwanda, South Africa, Swaziland, Zambia and Zimbabwe) reported reaching 80% or more of adults eligible for antiretroviral therapy, under the 2010 WHO guidelines. However, new WHO guidelines on HIV treatment in 2013 have since made many more people eligible for treatment" (UNAIDS 2013, p. 4). The report also underlines that:

> [t]he trends towards increased antiretroviral therapy coverage across Africa masks significant national gaps. In at least 14 countries in Africa, 80% or more of people who were estimated to be eligible for treatment under the 2013 WHO guidelines were not receiving antiretroviral therapy as of December 2012. People living with HIV in Eastern and Southern Africa are more likely to obtain treatment services than people in Western and Central Africa. The largest gap in treatment in Africa is in North Africa, where only 11% of people living with HIV currently receive antiretroviral therapy. (UNAIDS 2013, p. 4)

Some claim that the reasons that HIV is on such a rise in Northern Africa are the negative "stigma and discrimination in the region", the "cultural and religious norms disapproving and penalizing a sex between men", and a lack of adequate data on at-risk groups in the region (Gökengin et al. 2016). This is what means being invisible despite the advances in drugs, technologies, and human rights. For example, the global gap in access to antiretroviral therapy for the year 2012–2013 was 66% (UNAIDS 2013). An update to this report published in 2016 (UNAIDS 2016) shows that the trends are showing an increase in the number of people living with HIV on antiretroviral therapy. However, the Middle East/North Africa region remains at the lowest percent compared to other regions (idem).

What this brief history shows is that one of the major battles in HIV/AIDS was, and still is, access to treatment, and especially its universality. Improving universal access to drugs has been at the cornerstone of the public response to the HIV/AIDS epidemic since its outset in the 1980s. Even if it never materialized fully, universal drug access has always been the main objective. One strategy used by the different actors involved was to shape/frame the drug access as a human right issue, as concerning the human right to health. By doing so, these actors were both relying on an already existing concept and (re)defining it we argue in this chapter. By making it their own, these groups translated and contested the actual meaning and scope of the human right to health. They tried to make it visible, to fight ignorance.

There is still, however, this idea that human rights (their meaning/understanding) are imposed from above, mainly from international organizations. That was well summarized by Brazil's National AIDS Program ex-director Paulo Teixeira when arguing that:

> The biggest challenge for the future of the Brazilian National AIDS Program is the maintenance and the sustainability of the policy of free and universal access to ARVs. This is directly linked to a change in the world economic order with regard to medicines. It will depend [...] on the strengthening of international alliances that are beginning to form with the World Health Organization, the World Trade Organization, the United Nations Special Session on HIV/AIDS, and the Global Fund to Fight AIDS, Tuberculosis and Malaria. It is extremely important that these alliances are maintained and intensified to guarantee the conquests already achieved. (Quoted in Galvão 2005)

Without negating the role of international organizations and international laws, communities and activists also played a key role in the framing of HIV/AIDS as a human right, rendering it as such visible, especially through the issue of universal drug access. In fact, the Brazilian case itself[15] wasn't without its own struggles, challenges, and conflicts, even with key organizations such as the WTO or countries like the USA (Galvão 2005). However, it is community and patient groups that led these struggles, rather than the Brazilian government.

The framing of HIV/AIDS as a human right issue by civil society and community groups involved is partly due to the fact that human right violation has always been a key challenge for people living with HIV/AIDS, especially (but not only) in developing countries (Galvão 2005, p. 1111). In fact, human right violations have even been linked, in some context, with increased propagation of HIV/AIDS (Galvão 2005; Mann 1998), rendering more than urgent for these communities/groups to frame HIV/AIDS as a human right issue, to make themselves visible and subject of human rights (and not only the object of human rights—see the introductory chapter for more on this). As reminded by Rodriguez Garcia, "it became clear that a lack of respect for human rights and dignity was a major contributor to the HIV/AIDS problem" (quoted in DeGioia 2014, p. 168). Framing this issue as a human right one rapidly imposed itself as the main strategy to adopt for civil society and patient groups to gain access to treatment and care.

The language of human rights is now well diffused in international organizations or groups working on health issues.[16] One must however be careful not to read this—now dominant—use of human right language as preexisting the struggles and conflicts community groups, patients, and activists went through to render possible the language of human rights for HIV/AIDS.

The access to essential drug medicine[17] played a key role in the definition/translation of HIV/AIDS issue as a human right one. It served the purpose of being the revealer of its human right-related nature. Many different actors were involved in this—ongoing—struggle. Among them several activist groups from so-called developing countries were especially active in the definition, organization and contestation of HIV/AIDS drug access as a human right issue through their direct involvement in several clashes with public authorities, international organizations[18] and private corporations (mainly pharmaceutical industries). They played a critical role in shaping access, for example, to tritherapy[19] as a human right issue.

According to ABIA, "the HIV response was a community response before it was framed in legal human rights terms".[20] It was not a top-down approach imposed by other actors or international law documents. The human right to health, especially when it comes to drug access, didn't emerge from international legal instruments. It came from below; it was made visible by community-based actions. Community/patient groups and activist involvement rapidly became the main vehicle for improving HIV/AIDS drug access framed as a human right issue: "[c]ivil society's role expands far beyond advocacy. Its technical expertise has been integral to removing barriers to medicines access, driving and shaping research agendas, and creating momentum for policy and programmatic changes at the national and global levels."[21]

The struggles to facilitate HIV/AIDS drug access were multidimensional. As mentioned by the Treatment Action Group (TAG), "[t]his fight was won in courtrooms and in the streets", thus involving both legal and activist-based tools/strategies (TAG 2010, p. 3). Women's groups were especially important at the early stage of the epidemic.[22] Their fights were later recuperated by some international organizations to justify their own actions. For example, it is now clear that "[w]ithout civil society's work, the Global Fund to Fight AIDS, Tuberculosis and Malaria (GFATM) would not have been established".[23]

HIV/AIDS and human right were merged progressively through different phases (from Galvão 2005; Gruskin et al. 1996). It started with human right groups and activists opposing officials and governments regarding unjust and/or unsafe measures (mandatory testing, obligatory HIV/AIDS status divulgation, quarantine, etc.). It was followed by the responses by health officials and governments regarding treatments infringing human rights (based on efficiency issues; the fact that they did work). Activists and community groups then argued that human right violations and vulnerabilities play a central role in the progression of the epidemic. Treatment and universal drug access then became the cornerstone of HIV/AIDS activists (through the concept of "essential medicines", among others).

Interestingly, it is today the access of HIV/AIDS drug that is predominantly understood as a human right issue (or alternatively, the lack of, as a human right violation). This is what is visible when it comes to the human right to health and HIV/AIDS. As an example, the resolution 2001/33 of the UN High Commissioner for Human Rights states that the:

> access to medication in the context of pandemics such as HIV/AIDS is one fundamental element for achieving progressively the full realization of the

> right of everyone to the enjoyment of the highest attainable standard of physical and mental health. (UNHCHR, 2006)

Not having access to HIV/AIDS drugs interfere in the realization of multiple other human rights, including (The Right to Health Fact Sheet no. 31[24]; Cohen and Ezer 2013):

1. Right to non-discrimination and equality
2. Right to life (and life of dignity)
3. The right to the highest standard of health
4. The right to enjoy the benefits of scientific progress and its applications (patents)
5. The right of women (and children)
6. Freedom from torture and cruel, inhuman, and degrading treatment (prison)

Interestingly, this framing of HIV/AIDS as a human right issue (especially the universal access to drugs) doesn't mention directly the human right to health.[25] It also comes at a price. Some suggested, for example, that framing HIV/AIDS as a human rights issue was somewhat unwise, or at least that it brings some problems with it. Shiba Phurailatpan, from the Asian Pacific Network of People Living with HIV/AIDS (ANP+), summarized well that point: "[i]s this a trap that we ourselves have created? We have strongly called for human rights frame in order to improve the public health response and now we get technological-based public health interventions that may gloss over rights."[26] Things, issues, or populations might have been invisibilized through the "internationalization" of HIV/AIDS as a human right issue.

The inclusion of the concept of "essential medicine" in debates and struggles for the realization of the human right to health in some sense diverted, we argue here, the attention from human right per se to technical/technological matters, which are not in the first place the human right to health (they are although very important, it is necessary to stress, but they come with potentially unintended consequences). In particular, the concept of "essential medicine" suggests that there are different "levels" of health and that only some "essential" parts of health are subject to human rights (not necessarily health itself). The concept of essential medicine raises pressing questions: What means essential? For whom? Decided by whom? In particular, essential medicines are deeply embedded with the concept of "profitable medicine", which has been largely described for its negative impacts on the realization of the human right to health (see, e.g., Attaran 2004). Health, as a systemic object, cannot be divided between essential and non-essential factors. There is no hierarchy between the elements forming health. There is no part that is more important, and thus subject to human rights, than others.

Even though we recognize that the concept of "essential medicine" played a key role in a better access to antiretroviral drugs in the early stage of the epidemic, it represents today a form of limit to the realization of the human right to health as it confines the debate to technical/technological matters. It invisibilizes issues or groups. Another problem is that it comes from the pharmaceutical industry/private actor's discourses, which are recuperated by international actors and ultimately limits the application of the human right to health. In short, we see the colonization of the human right to health (practices/discourses) by profitable medicine, stressing as such the paradoxical process of human right from below (and limiting the potential of the human right to health).

As an example, the current understanding of the human right to health cannot be used to argue in favor of the accessibility of PrEP drugs (see next section), which has been largely shown to help prevent new HIV/AIDS cases for some specific populations or groups, which appear to be invisibilized by the current practices legitimized under the human right to health.

Essential Medicine and the Human Right to Health: PrEP as a (Counter) Example

PrEP is a drug that reduces the risk of HIV infection. Its main objective is to lower the risk of HIV transmission for people categorized as being at "very high risk".[27] This includes usually injection drug user or his/her partner, the sexual partner of an HIV-positive individual, women trying to get pregnant from an HIV-positive partner, as well as "gay or bisexual man who has had anal sex without using a condom or been diagnosed with an STD in the past 6 months, or heterosexual man or woman who does not regularly use condoms during sex with partners of unknown HIV status who are at substantial risk of HIV infection".[28] This treatment is subject to several controversies (see, e.g., Cairns et al. 2016; Cohen et al. 2012 or Zalewski et al. 2009), the most important one probably being the prohibitive cost of this preventative treatment. The drug costs "between $8,000 and $14,000 per year", not including the cost of "four medical check-ups annually and possible lab tests", which can be very expensive without health insurance.[29] Side effects of Truvada, a brand of PrEP, include among others "worsening of hepatitis B infection, kidney problems (including kidney failure), too much lactic acid in your blood, severe liver problems, and bone problems".[30] Increased Sexually Transmitted Infections (STI) has also been documented as a potential indirect side effect of PrEP.[31]

The Center for Disease Control (CDC) published two reports about best practices for PrEP, on for Men who have Sex with Men (MSM) and one for heterosexual individuals (CDC 2012). The study guidelines have much in common, but the fact that they were published separately reflects the differences in threat of infection between the two communities. In the MSM guidelines, the CDC explains that "[o]n November 23, 2010, investigators for the Pre-Exposure Prophylaxis Initiative (iPrEX) study announced results from a multinational, randomized, double-blind, placebo-controlled, phase III clinical trial of daily oral antiretrovirals [...] to prevent acquisition of HIV infection among uninfected but exposed MSM" (Smith et al. 2011, p. 65).

This study was done on MSM in a variety of countries, one of which was South Africa. It gives a chart of best practices: "[b]efore initiating PrEP, beginning PrEP medication regimen, follow-up while PrEP medication is being taken, and on discontinuing PrEP". This chart is very similar to a chart that was added to the heterosexual guidelines. The heterosexual guidelines report that "[d]aily oral TDF/FTC use in two studies has been shown to be safe in reducing the risk for sexual HIV acquisition by heterosexual women and men when consistently used" (Smith et al. 2011, p. 65). A third study conducted by the CDC found results that were in conflict with these conclusions. However, the guidelines maintain that PrEP is safe and effective at reducing HIV infection in heterosexual individuals (Smith et al. 2011, p. 65).

Because of this success in preventing AIDS transmission, many have tried to gain access to PrEP using human rights language and framing. However, and as a well-documented example, PrEP access in South Africa has been limited despite the country's claim that health is a human right. Singh remembers, for example, that:

> Truvada, a licensed HIV treatment drug, has been found to reduce the risk of HIV infection by up to 92%. To date, the US Food and Drug Administration has licensed Truvada as an HIV pre-exposure prophylaxis (PrEP) agent, and the US Centers for Disease Control and the World Health Organization have published comprehensive PrEP clinical guidelines. Notwithstanding these factors, South Africa's drug regulatory authority is yet to license Truvada as a PrEP agent and the government is yet to commit to PrEP adoption. Seen in this context, the right to health has failed to ensure that PrEP trial participants in South Africa enjoy post-trial access to PrEP. (Singh 2015, p. 59)

In this case, PrEP was not considered to be an "essential medicine" and therefore not part of the human right to health narratives and rationales. What this example shows is that there is a fundamental flaw in invoking the human right to health through the concept of essential medicine, even though promoted by activists and community groups. The main problem being that some groups (e.g., MSM) or issues (PrEP access in this case) are invisibilized, largely because of ignorance.

When it comes to HIV/AIDS, there are cycles of advocacy for treatment and resources that don't revolve around the right to health itself but rather around a specific treatment. The advocacy around PrEP is not one that spans all AIDS treatment, gender-specific health issues, diseases caused by the environment, and any other issue that would be considered a part of the right to health umbrella. Instead, the advocacy for access to PrEP, access to Tritherapy, and many other healthcare issues are focused on specific pharmaceutical products rather than the right as a whole, what we called previously health as a systematic right.

This slows down the development of human rights to health frameworks because access to any in-demand drug becomes a fight. The cycles of need for drugs, drug creation, drug overpricing, advocacy for drug inclusion in essential medicine, and eventually, if ever, acceptance of that drug as essential benefits the pharmaceutical companies at the expense of the sick and dying.

This isn't to say that advocacy and activism work in these places is flawed, but rather to highlight pharmaceutical industries benefit from creating demand based on restricting the human right to health to individual battles as opposed to wholesale human rights enforcement. In this way, pharmaceutical companies benefit from maintaining ignorance to the possibilities of the human right to health.

There is power in ignorance as Sedgwick claimed, and the human right to health appears to be a noteworthy example through the case of PrEP access.

Conclusion: The Colonization of the Human Right to Health

On the one side, and as documented previously, community/patient groups and activists were key to the development and reformulation of the human right to health. On the other side, the concept of essential medicine seemed to have colonized contemporary practices of the human right to health, limiting as such what some groups can achieve or obtain in terms of the realization of the human right to health. Although beneficial, groups and issues are also invisibilized by contemporary human right practices linked to health.

Under no circumstance should this observation be used to criticize actions by community/patient groups and activists for a better access to HIV/AIDS treatment and drugs. These actors took on the human right to health as a vehicle not only to promote and strengthen the access to HIV/AIDS drugs but also to organize their social and political actions through specific battlefields/struggles, thus underlining key aspects of the human right to health. They also produced key documents/analysis to strengthen the access to HIV/AIDS drugs as a human right issue.

Conversely, these actions and practices in return shaped the materialization and reality of the human right to health in general. The human right to health, through the example of HIV/AIDS universal drug access, thus represents an interesting case of what actors make of human rights, of how human rights are produced from below through conflicts and struggles.

In particular, it shows that the human right to health, through the example of HIV/AIDS drug access, is a constantly changing object resulting from struggles, oppositions, debates, and so on. This human right framing also includes, however, counter perspectives (such as the concept of essential medicine, as underlined in the analysis above), which limits the direct realization of the human right to health.

This shows that the human right to health is a multipolar object shaped by different forces, constantly readapting and readjusting to the specific context from which it emerges. This reminds us of the importance of the different cycles of advocacy underlined previously. In this perspective, there is a pressing need to problematize the concept of essential medicine when it comes to the human right to health.

This colonization of human right language by profitable medicine appears, in the current scientific context, to limit the realization of the human right to health for particularly sensitive groups, which are clearly made invisible. If human rights apply to everyone without discrimination, there is no reason why one of its key conceptual elements de facto excludes some groups. This is a matter of gaining visibility in current human right struggles. The fight against invisibility is an ongoing one, and the battlefields on which it is fought take on a cyclical nature of ignorance, fight, limited recognition and ignorance. Human right is a changing object. Practices should adapt to this characteristic of human rights, not the reverse.

Notes

1. Name changed. Story inspired freely from Kanae Doi and Kyle Knight, "Japan Forces Sterilization on Transgender People", Human Right Watch, published on 29 November 2017, accessed on 13 December 2017, https://www.hrw.org/news/2017/11/29/japan-forces-sterilization-transgender-people.
2. Name changed. Story inspired freely from Géraldine Hallot, "Pourquoi tant de maladies rares à Fos-sur-Mer?", France Culture, published on 17 November 2017, accessed on 13 December 2017, https://www.franceculture.fr/environnement/pourquoi-tant-de-maladies-rares-a-fos-sur-mer.
3. These documents are CEHURD: Intellectual property and HR, a guide for journalists; TAG: Activist Strategies for Increasing Access to HCV Treatment in Low- and Middle-Income Countries; TAG historical report; I-MAK: The critical role of civil society in shaping the market for antiretroviral therapy; Harvard FXB: Center for health and human right: 2017 resource guide; BMA and the Commonwealth Medical Trust The right to health: a toolkit for health professionals; MSF document; Thai Network of People with HIV/AIDS—Thai example—community participation.
4. Which are counterfeit versus generic drugs; drug patents/prices the case of inventiveness; trip flexibilities, IPR; denial of medical care; Colombian court: life of dignity.
5. The World Bank is a good example, as it has been criticized for its responsibility in a cholera outbreak in South Africa following its recommendation to cut water access as a retaliation measure for nonpayment (Pauw 2003; Lee et al. 2011).

6. The WHO constitution defines health as “a state of complete physical, mental and social well-being and not merely the absence of disease or infirmity” (WHO 1995, p. 1).
7. WHO Media Center (no author), “Human rights and health: Fact sheet”, published in December 2017, accessed on 16 December 2017, http://www.who.int/mediacentre/factsheets/fs323/en/.
8. WHO Media Center (no author), “Human rights and health: Fact sheet”, published in December 2017, accessed on 16 December 2017, http://www.who.int/mediacentre/factsheets/fs323/en/.
9. As reminded by Navanethem Pillay, the previous UN High Commissioner for Human Rights, human rights is “an indivisible and organic whole, inseparable and interdependent, and all of equal importance” (Pillay 2008, p. 2005).
10. What we of course find with other human rights.
11. ABIA (no author), “HIV and AIDS in the mandate of the Special Rapporteur on the Right to Health: genealogies, lessons learned, challenges that remain”, ABIA—Brazilian Interdisciplinary AIDS Association, published on 10 December 2014, accessed on 2 November 2017, http://gapwatch.org/news/articles/hiv-and-aids-genealogies-lessons-learnd-and-challenges/124.
12. ABIA (no author), “HIV and AIDS in the mandate of the Special Rapporteur on the Right to Health: genealogies, lessons learned, challenges that remain”, ABIA—Brazilian Interdisciplinary AIDS Association, published on 10 December 2014, accessed on 2 November 2017, http://gapwatch.org/news/articles/hiv-and-aids-genealogies-lessons-learnd-and-challenges/124.
13. ABIA (no author), “HIV and AIDS in the mandate of the Special Rapporteur on the Right to Health: genealogies, lessons learned, challenges that remain”, ABIA—Brazilian Interdisciplinary AIDS Association, published on 10 December 2014, accessed on 2 November 2017, http://gapwatch.org/news/articles/hiv-and-aids-genealogies-lessons-learnd-and-challenges/124.
14. The history of HIV in itself is not exempt of controversies: “[p]eople sometimes say that HIV started in the 1980s in the United States of America (USA), but in fact this was just when people first became aware of HIV and it was officially recognized as a new health condition. In 1981, a few cases of rare diseases were being reported among gay men in New York and California, such as Kaposi’s Sarcoma (a rare cancer) and a lung infection called PCP. No one knew why these cancers and opportunistic infections were spreading, but they concluded that there must be an infectious ‘disease’ causing them. At first the disease was called all sorts of names relating to the word ‘gay’. It wasn’t until mid-1982 that scientists realized

the 'disease' was also spreading among other populations such as hemophiliacs and heroin users. By September that year, the 'disease' was finally named AIDS." AVERT (no author), "Origin of HIV/AIDS", AVERT, published on 11 January 2017, accessed on 9 January 2018, https://www.avert.org/professionals/history-hiv-aids/origin.

15. Brazil has a free antiretroviral access policy, one of the best and most elaborated one. The Brazilian government "controls the costs of the program by encouraging local laboratories to produce ARVs, which decreases Brazil's need to import vital drugs from foreign countries" (Galvão 2005, p. 1111). They also promote and favor the use generic drugs.
16. See, for example, The Global Fund (no author), "Human Rights", Published 22 August 2017, accessed on 22 November 2017, https://www.theglobalfund.org/en/human-rights/; Susan Ariel Aaronson and Jean Pierre Chauffour, WTO, "The Wedding of Trade and Human Rights: Marriage of Convenience or Permanent Match?", no publication date, accessed on 17 November 2017, https://www.wto.org/english/res_e/publications_e/wtr11_forum_e/wtr11_15feb11_e.htm; or WHO (no author), "Health topics: Human rights", WHO, no publication date, accessed on 17 November 2017, http://www.who.int/topics/human_rights/en/.
17. For a review of this concept, see among others Hogerzeil (2004).
18. In particular, the World Trade Organization (WTO).
19. Tritherapy is a generic term that refers to any use of three methods/drugs that are used simultaneously to cure a particular illness. In the case of AIDS, it usually refers to a combination of the following drugs: D4T, 3TC, and nevirapine.
20. ABIA (no author), "HIV and AIDS in the mandate of the Special Rapporteur on the Right to Health: genealogies, lessons learned, challenges that remain", ABIA—Brazilian Interdisciplinary AIDS Association, published on 10 December 2014, accessed on 2 November 2017, http://gapwatch.org/news/articles/hiv-and-aids-genealogies-lessons-learnd-and-challenges/124.
21. HEP Coalition (no author), "The Critical Role of Civil Society in Shaping the Market for Antiretroviral Therapy and Direct-Acting Antiretrovirals", HEP Coalition, published on April 2015, accessed on 10 January 2018, http://hepcoalition.org/IMG/pdf/report_on_civil_society_april_1_2015_1-2.pdf.
22. ABIA (no author), "HIV and AIDS in the mandate of the Special Rapporteur on the Right to Health: genealogies, lessons learned, challenges that remain", ABIA—Brazilian Interdisciplinary AIDS Association, published on 10 December 2014, accessed on 2 November 2017, http://gapwatch.org/news/articles/hiv-and-aids-genealogies-lessons-learnd-

and-challenges/124. See also the documentary *We were here* (https://wewereherefilm.com/).

23. HEP Coalition (no author), "The Critical Role of Civil Society in Shaping the Market for Antiretroviral Therapy and Direct-Acting Antiretrovirals", HEP Coalition, published in April 2015, accessed on 10 January 2018, http://hepcoalition.org/IMG/pdf/report_on_civil_society_april_1_2015_1-2.pdf.
24. Available at http://www.ohchr.org/Documents/Publications/Factsheet31.pdf, accessed on 15 November 2017.
25. Although it can be argued that "the right to the highest standard of health" can be interpreted as a softer reformulation of the right to health.
26. HEP Coalition (no author), "The Critical Role of Civil Society in Shaping the Market for Antiretroviral Therapy and Direct-Acting Antiretrovirals", HEP Coalition, published on April 2015, accessed on 10 January 2018, http://hepcoalition.org/IMG/pdf/report_on_civil_society_april_1_2015_1-2.pdf.
27. CDC (no author), "PrEP", CDC, last reviewed on 23 March 2018, accessed on 12 November 2017, https://www.cdc.gov/hiv/basics/prep.html.
28. CDC (no author), "PrEP", CDC, last reviewed on 23 March 2018, accessed on 12 November 2017, https://www.cdc.gov/hiv/basics/prep.html.
29. New York Department of Health (no author), "Pre-Exposure Prophylaxis (PrEP) to Prevent HIV Infection: Questions and Answers", New York Department of Health, no publication date, accessed on 15 November 2017, https://www.health.ny.gov/publications/0265/.
30. TRUVADA (no author), "What are possible side effects of TRUVADA for PrEP™?", TRUVADA, No publication date, accessed on 15 November 2017, https://start.truvada.com/side-effects.
31. See, for example, a recent review by CATIE, a Canadian NGO targeting knowledge transfer regarding HIV and other STI: Sean R. Hosein, "U.S. simulation explores the intersection of PrEP and some sexually transmitted infections", CATIE, published on 2 October 2017, accessed on 15 November 2017, http://www.catie.ca/en/catienews/2017-10-03/us-simulation-explores-intersection-prep-and-some-sexually-transmitted-infectio.

References

Attaran, Amir. 2004. How Do Patents and Economic Policies Affect Access to Essential Medicines in Developing Countries? *Health Affairs* 23 (3): 155–166.

Blouin-Genest, Gabriel, and Sylvie Paquerot. 2016a. Environmental Human Rights as a Battlefield: A Grammar of Political Confrontation. *Journal of Human Rights and the Environment* 7 (1): 132–154.

———. 2016b. Les droits humains comme grammaire de "l'en-commun". Confrontations politiques et champ de bataille de "l'en-commun". *Sociologie S.*

Cairns, Gus P., Kane Race, and Pedro Goicochea. 2016. PrEP: Controversy, Agency and Ownership. *Journal of the International AIDS Society* 19 (7 Suppl 6): 1–3.

Callon, Michel, and John Law. 2004. Introduction: Absence—Presence, Circulation, and Encountering in Complex Space. *Environment and Planning D: Society and Space* 22: 3–11.

Centers for Disease Control and Prevention (CDC). 2012. Interim Guidance for Clinicians Considering the Use of Preexposure Prophylaxis for the Prevention of HIV Infection in Heterosexually Active Adults. *MMWR. Morbidity and Mortality Weekly Report* 61 (31): 586.

CESCR (Committee on Economic, Social and Cultural Rights). 2000. General Comment No. 14: The Right to the Highest Attainable Standard of Health (Art. 12). *Adopted at the Twenty-Second Session of the Committee on Economic, Social and Cultural Rights, on* 11. Available at http://www.refworld.org/pdfid/4538838d0.pdf.

Cohen, Jonathan, and Tamar Ezer. 2013. Human Rights in Patient Care: A Theoretical and Practical Framework. *Health and Human Rights* 15 (2): 7–19.

Cohen, Myron S., and Cynthia L. Gay. 2010. Treatment to Prevent Transmission of HIV-1. *Clinical Infectious Diseases* 50 (Suppl_3): S85–S95.

Cohen, Myron S., Kathryn E. Muessig, M. Kumi Smith, Kimberly A. Powers, and Angela D.M. Kashuba. 2012. Antiviral Agents and HIV Prevention: Controversies, Conflicts, and Consensus. *AIDS (London, England)* 26 (13): 1585.

DeGioia, John J. 2014. *Human Dignity and the Future of Global Institutions.* Washington, DC: Georgetown University Press.

Dembour, Marie-Bénédicte. 2010. What Are Human Rights? Four Schools of Thought. *Human Rights Quarterly* 32 (1): 1–20.

Doise, Willem. 2003. *Human Rights as Social Representations.* London/New York: Routledge.

Editorial (The Lancet). 2008. The Right to Health: From Rhetoric to Reality. *The Lancet* 372: 2001.

Galvão, Jane. 2005. Brazil and Access to HIV/AIDS Drugs: A Question of Human Rights and Public Health. *American Journal of Public Health* 95 (7): 1110–1116.

Gökengin, Deniz, Fardad Doroudi, Johnny Tohme, Ben Collins, and Navid Madani. 2016. HIV/AIDS: Trends in the Middle East and North Africa Region. *International Journal of Infectious Diseases* 44: 66–73.

Gruskin, Sofia, Aart Hendriks, and Katarina Tomasevski. 1996. Human Rights and Responses to HIV/AIDS. *AIDS in the World II*: 326–340.

Harvard FXB. 2017. *Health and Human Rights – Resource Guide.* Boston/New York: FXB Center for Health and Human Rights and Open Society Foundations.

Hendriks, Aart, and Brigit Toebes. 1998. Towards a Universal Definition of the Right to Health. *Medicine and Law* 17: 319.

Hogerzeil, Hans V. 2004. The Concept of Essential Medicines: Lessons for Rich Countries. *BMJ British Medical Journal* 329 (7475): 1169.

Lee, Kelley, Derek Yach, and Adam Kamradt-Scott. 2011. Globalization and Health. In *Global Public Health: Diseases, Programs, Systems and Policies*, ed. M. Merson, R. Black, and A. Mills, 3rd ed., 885–913. New York: Jones & Bartlett.

Leese, Matthias. 2016. 'Seeing Futures': Politics of Visuality and Affect. In *Algorithmic Life: Calculative Devices in the Age of Big Data*, ed. Louise Amoore and Volha Piotukh, 143–158. London: Routledge.

Mann, J. M. (1998). AIDS and Human Rights: Where Do We Go from Here?. *Health and Human Rights*, *3*(1), 143–149.

Marks, Stephen P. 2013. The Emergence and Scope of the Human Right to Health. In *Advancing the Human Right to Health*, ed. José M. Zuniga, Stephen P. Marks, and Lawrence O. Gostin, 1–24. Oxford: Oxford University Press.

Montagnier, Luc. 2002. A History of HIV Discovery. *Science* 298 (5599): 1727–1728.

Pauw, Jacques. 2003. The Politics of Underdevelopment: Metered to Death—How a Water Experiment Caused Riots and a Cholera Epidemic. *International Journal of Health Services* 33 (4): 819–830.

Pillay, Navanethem. 2008. Right to Health and the Universal Declaration of Human Rights. *The Lancet* 372 (9655): 2005–2006.

Piotte, Jean-Marc. 2007. *Les neuf clés de la modernité*. Québec Amérique.

Preciado, Paul B. 2013. *Testo Junkie: Sex, Drugs, and Biopolitics in the Pharmacopornographic Era*. New York: The Feminist Press at CUNY.

Risse, Thomas, and Kathryn Sikkink. 1999. The Socialization of International Human Rights Norms into Domestic Practices: Introduction. *Cambridge Studies in International Relations* 66: 1–38.

Sedgwick, Eve Kosofsky. 1993. Epistemology of the Closet. In *The Lesbian and Gay Studies Reader*, ed. Henry Abelove, Michèle Aina Barale, and David M. Halperin, 45. New York: Routledge.

Sen, Amartya. 2008. Why and How Is Health a Human Right. *The Lancet* 372 (9655): 2010.

Singh, J. 2015. How Bioethics Is Complementing Human Rights in Realizing Health Access for Clinical Trial Participants: The Case of Formative PrEP Access in South Africa. *Health and Human Rights* 17 (1): E58–E62.

Slaughter, Joseph. 2009. *Human Rights, Inc.: The World Novel, Narrative form, and International Law*. New York: Fordham University Press.

Smith, D., R. Grant, P. Weidle, Amy Lansky, Jonathan Mermin, and K. Fenton. 2011. Interim Guidance: Preexposure Prophylaxis for the Prevention of HIV

Infection in Men Who Have Sex with Men. *MMWR. Morbidity and Mortality Weekly Report* 60 (3): 65–68.

Treatment Action Group (TAG). 2010. *Activist Strategies for Increasing Access to HCV Treatment in Low- and Middle-Income Countries*, 31.

UN. 1948. Universal Declaration of Human Rights. *UN General Assembly.* Available at http://www.un.org/en/udhrbook/pdf/udhr_booklet_en_web.pdf.

———. 1966. International Covenant on Economic, Social and Cultural Rights. *United Nations, Treaty Series* 993(3). Available at http://www.ohchr.org/EN/ProfessionalInterest/Pages/CESCR.aspx.

UNAIDS. 2013. *Access to Antiretroviral Therapy in Africa: Status Report on Progress Towards the 2015 Targets.* Geneva: Joint United Nations Programme on HIV *AIDS*, 1–12.

———. 2016. *Global AIDS Update 2016.* Geneva: UNAIDS.

UNHCHR. 2006. *Access to Medication in the Context of Pandemics Such as HIV/AIDS Commission on Human Rights Resolution 2001/33.* Available at https://www.law.umich.edu/facultyhome/drwcasebook/Documents/Documents/UN%20Commission%20on%20Human%20Rights%20Resolution%202001-22%20Access%20to%20medication%20in%20the%20context%20of%20pandemics%20such%20as%20HIV-AIDS.pdf.

UNHCHR & WHO. 2008. *The Right to Health Fact Sheet No. 31.* Available at http://www.ohchr.org/Documents/Publications/Factsheet31.pdf.

World Health Organization (WHO). 1995. *Constitution of the World Health Organization.* Geneva: World Health Organization.

Zalewski, Bartłomiej M., Monika Jabłońska, and Tomasz Mikuła. 2009. Pre-exposure HIV Prophylaxis (PrEP)–Background and Controversies. *HIV & AIDS Review* 8 (4): 8–10.

CHAPTER 12

Internet Access as Human Right: A Dystopian Critique from the Occupied Palestinian Territory

Fabio Cristiano

Introduction

Since the outset of the Arab Spring in 2010, authorities across the region undermined political uprisings through the closure, partial or total, of internet[1] access. Whereas Tunisian activists witnessed restrictions on their political liberties through surveillance, hacking, and violent repressions, authorities implemented full shutdowns[2] in Egypt, Libya, and Syria. Similarly, censorship furthered in Bahrain and Saudi Arabia when, in response to political uprisings, authorities closed down numerous websites in combination with the arrest of several bloggers and activists. As a result, for the very first time, denial of internet access appeared to the international community as a serious violation of fundamental political freedoms. In response, internet access (and the denial thereof) came to be included into the human right discourse[3] for its instrumental role in those processes of mobilization and (attempts at) demobilization of political action. On

F. Cristiano (✉)
Department of Political Science, Lund University, Lund, Sweden
e-mail: fabio.cristiano@svet.lu.se

G. Blouin-Genest et al. (eds.), *Human Rights as Battlefields*,
Human Rights Interventions,
https://doi.org/10.1007/978-3-319-91770-2_12

the other hand, internet accessibility also developed into a political battlefield of its own (with political campaigns focusing primarily on this issue[4]). Far from being an isolated contextual issue,[5] governments' internet shutdowns have been globally on the rise in recent years, with more than 30 countries experiencing one or more shutdowns between the beginning of 2015 and the time of writing of this chapter.[6] In response to the growth of this phenomenon, and following those first tentative legislations on the topic, the United Nations Human Rights Council (UNHRC) released, in the summer of 2016, a non-binding resolution that established internet access as a human right, thus condemning governments' intentional disruption (most commonly referred as 'shutdown') as a response to political contestations (UNHRC 2016).

Incorporating internet access—the so-called right to broadband—within the human rights agenda primarily stems from the necessity of discouraging authoritarian regimes to retain online spaces and possibilities for political dissent, and participation at large (UNHRC 2016; Lucchi 2011). At the same time, the framing of internet access as a human right pertains the basic recognition that access to the internet determines and facilitates the enjoyment of political freedoms: reversely, closing access to the internet would constitute a violation of these very fundamental liberties. These proposed legislative schemes make in fact an explicit reference to Article 19 of the Universal Declaration of Human Rights, adding internet access to those rights that are considered necessary for individual self-determination and the conduct of a free life (UNGA 1948).

Many have since long criticized this approach arguing that internet access can only be considered as an enabler of other rights and not a right in its own terms (McDowell 2012; Skepys 2012). Put it differently, critics argue that defending the right to access sets forth a causal nexus between being connected online and the enjoyment of political freedoms that, in reality, does not occur automatically. In this critical spirit, while acknowledging the liberating potential that internet access might disclose, critical voices highlight 'qualities' over 'availability', thus shifting the focus from 'access' to broader 'digital rights'[7] (as convincingly argued by Vinton G. Cerf (2012), Google's vice-president). As internet technologies are nowadays the battlefields of political contestation on different grounds—net neutrality, copyright, band per capita, content censorship, infrastructure privatization, and more—these questions are thought to be inseparable from the 'right to broadband'.

In particular, these lines of critique point to those existing technical and practical facets that constitute internet access as an issue that is not only of governmental concern. As service provision occurs through complex apparatuses of governance—which include governments, infrastructural proprietorship, and service providers—content management, and digital rights more in general, should also be integrated into debates on human rights. In a context where sovereignty escapes territorial and jurisdictional borders, opening up the human rights discourse interrogates whose and what type of internet remains to be desired for enabling, and also practicing, political freedoms—thus rethinking the emancipatory potential of technology.

In fact, this dispute dusts off the underlying debate on whether technological progress in itself determines access to a freer life, in the spirit of those technological determinists that saw in technology the drive toward a utopian-free society (as theorized by sociologist McLuhan in 1967). Expanding the overall debate[8] in this direction, this chapter proposes to reflect beyond technical, legislative, and procedural aspects of internet access. Rather, through a reflection on the intrinsic determinism that characterizes both advocates and opponents of the 'right to broadband', it proposes to re-politicize the role of internet access within mainstream human right discourses. As critique primarily builds on a prescriptive and normative understanding of human rights as static apparatuses of power, this chapter ultimately proposes to rethink human rights as battlefields, rather than enablers, of political change.

In order to do so, this chapter relates to those contextual experiences and legislations that, within the context of Palestine/Israel, allow rethinking digital rights and internet access as a way to ultimately interrogate how technology and human rights intersect on deterministic grounds. For its peculiarities—that is, the Israeli military and infrastructural occupation, as well as the restrictive policies implemented by the Palestinian Authority (PA) with regards to online freedoms—this dystopian case constitutes a privileged point of observation to reflect on the relationship between technology and freedom. And, in turn, to argue that implementing human rights 'from above' might in turn detract, rather than enable, political and individual freedoms (cfr. Perugini and Gordon 2016). After this introductory section, this chapter proceeds by presenting a human rights reading of the debate on internet access and content management (with a specific focus on the conceptual duality common/right). Following, an analysis of the dystopian status quo of Palestinian internet access and digital rights precedes a conclusive section where the specificities of this context are then related to the broader debate on the essence of human rights.

Internet as a Collective Common, Internet as a Right

The main argument against the recognition of internet access as human right ultimately points to the feeble equation between accessing the internet and enjoying a freer life. Alternatively, it is argued that the enablement of political freedoms does not depend on internet access, but on how access and contents are managed, censored, or freed. Albeit opposed and different in degrees, these views share a fundamentally deterministic understanding of technology and human rights: the possibility of realizing a technology that maintains a non-social and neutral role in the mediation of human relations and freedoms. Whereas technology at all costs or freeing it up from structures of control, both views are centered on the assumption that technology, and internet more specifically, possesses the power to constitute and drive modernity alongside its inherent liberties (on this, see Joyce 2015).

This chapter is inspired instead from the understanding that technology, existing only within those human relations it produces, maintains a perennial status of 'becoming', being re-modulated through its usage, time, battles, and context (cfr. Green 2001). In line with scholarship often referred to as 'social construction of technology' (SCOT), the relationship between internet and society (and how it is debated) appears instead to relapse primarily into the understanding of technology as a political battlefield of its own, rather than as a normative and neutral enabler of freedoms. Above all, the dispute on the essence of technology primarily unfolds on the terrain of the uneasy relationship between a service (understood here in terms of 'public utility') and the freedoms it might or might not enable. Analogously, as argued by Brown (1997), normative discourses on human rights predict a cause-and-effect formula between top-down adoption and future societal change.

Concerns regarding internet access, and digital rights in general, often accompany various types of activism and political campaigning—as shown in many recent instances of political turmoil (Gezi Park in Turkey, Occupy Movement in the United States, etc.). As activists increasingly coordinate online, demanding internet access mainly appeals to the safeguard of freedom of expression, assembly, and so on. At a very basic level, then, the right to internet access tends to be framed as a question of freedoms, and access to these freedoms. Drawing a classical parallelism with the Greek *agora* (Rheingold 1994; Castells 2001), it can be argued that having access to the internet remains only an instrumental prerequisite for engaging in the battle over digital rights and political freedoms.

Comparing cyberspaces to common spaces, however, appears problematic in different ways, and beyond the question of whether they correspond to national territories or possess a physical existence (cfr. Cristiano 2018). Infrastructural ownership—public, private, or hybrid—determines the extent in which internet can be considered as a common (a space for the many, rather than for the few) and, similarly to other 'services', enjoy the status of a human right. In reality, broadband diffusion (and thus access) tends to follow profit dynamics, as much as infrastructural developments and expansion depend on Internet Service Providers' (ISPs) market interests and decisions. As such, infrastructural ownership and broadband coverage regulate access to cyberspace (the 'square') and thus compromise the extent in which political freedoms online are to be enabled collectively, and for the collectivity. In a global context of growing public-private partnerships over service delivery, governments continue to retain power over kill-switches,[9] that is, the possibility to disconnect an entire country or territory from the internet (for attacks coming from the outside). At the same time, this defense instrument often comes to be adopted to close internet access in the event of a domestic political turmoil—as in the cases of 2011 Egypt and frequent India's shutdowns on Kashmir (Human Rights Watch 2017). In this sense, as governments and service providers regulate access to the internet through infrastructural control, it seems hard to separate the 'right to broadband' from net neutrality movement's claims on the publicity of the service[10]—and from the restrictions imposed on existing alternatives (in terms of proprietorship). In these terms, opposing normative human rights agendas also calls into question the extent whether a human right can be subjected to, and dependent on, market rules.

In order to circumvent lacks of service or access blocks, the battle over free and public internet access necessarily unfolds at the infrastructural level. Besides advocating for public internet access, 'taking back the tech' strategies also focus on creating and designing independent networks[11] that offer parallel access points through, for instance, mesh-networking (Hildenbrand 2016; Petersen 2014). Based on a non-hierarchical type of connection, in this model, infrastructural nodes connect directly and dynamically, self-configuring in order to route data from and to clients. Claiming the publicity of the service, then, goes hand in hand with the understanding of both technology and human rights as non-neutral institutions, and thus always in the making from below. Moreover, the battle over internet as a common also appears to be consistent with Westra's (2011) argument in favor of prioritizing collective rights over individual ones. In fact, for its very interconnected nature, human relation to the internet escapes the framing of individualism (i.e. the individual as the ultimate recipient of rights—cfr. Peters 2016). At the very best, the individual can be situated online in a type of relational subjectivity that Castells (2007) defines as 'networked individualism'.[12]

The importance of discussing infrastructural ownership—'who owns the internet'—of course not only pertains how access to the service comes to be managed and regulated but also affects how contents are shared, controlled, and battled for. For example, while enjoying the benefits of the world's fastest connection and a broad territorial coverage, users in Beijing are obliged to communicate, access, and share data exclusively through government-approved applications (MacKinnon 2008). In other words, the sole access to cyberspace does not necessarily mean access to political freedoms: even if entirely public and accessible, squares have always served—symbolically and not—authoritarian regimes to seize and reaffirm power. Rather than through formal 'access' and entitlement, then, participation (and the rules underlying this participation), determines how rights and spaces of liberties can be defined and conquered from below (cfr. McNeilly 2015, 2017).

Whereas infrastructural control relapses into collaborative efforts between governments and ISPs, content management also involves those who 'host' these data, such as websites, servers, and applications. With information and data being channeled through fewer and fewer websites and platforms (with experts pointing at the risk of monopolies of data), government's control over content becomes gradually facilitated, and relies on the partnership with those companies that manage large quantities of data (such as main social media corporations).[13] Similarly to infrastructural proprietorship, data are ordered and managed through complex apparatuses of public-private collaborations. At the same time, despite global internet usership reaching its peak in 2017,[14] free online spaces—such as darknet and anonymous networks (I2P[15])—are increasingly deserted. Their accessibility depends on know-hows that, due to the commercialization of online spaces and users' limited degrees of computer and digital literacy (Nielsen 2016), are only accessible to few. In fact, particularly in developing countries (with lower computer and digital literacy, but at higher risks of internet closure and censorship), users tend to use one-purpose applications and websites rather than using internet technology as a multipurpose service, as it was originally designed by the World Wide Web Consortium (W3C).

Along these lines, the debate pertaining internet as a collective common—and its related proprietorship—engages ownership not only over infrastructure but also over contents (i.e. 'who owns the data', a battle, for instance, conducted through *Creative Commons*), and its management (i.e. 'who controls and polices the data'). As personal data are considered a valuable resource both for commercial uses and for political and security ones, privacy rights are challenged also in relation to individual intellectual properties[16] (and whether profit generated through their acquisition should be redistributed to users). All these content-related issues are the focus of the so-called net neutrality movement and debate. Focusing on digital rights as battlefields in their own terms, rather than being instrumental to a specific political campaign or endeavor, its proponents argue in favor of overcoming those discriminations (such as IP address, protocol, and peering) that preclude users from reaching contents, and vice versa. More specifically, net neutrality advocates make pressure on governments to recognize internet as a service of public utility for its instrumental role in the realization of political freedoms (Wu 2003).

Beside advocacy campaigns, this battle unveils through the retainment of data and, in turn, of privacy rights. As governments increasingly rely on the acquisition of online information for intelligence and security operations—such as predictive policing systems (PPS)—the battle over data protection becomes a fundamental concern to counter invasive security governance and to protect political freedoms (see Drezner 2004). PPS largely relies on monitoring online traffic and deep packet inspection, that is, filtering passing data and guiding them through an inspection point (Bendrath and Mueller 2010). Once inspected, set criteria define whether an information is allowed to pass or should be blocked and routed toward a different end, in a way that resembles offline checkpoints. Whereas this technique allows neutralizing contents that are of security concern or containing an abuse, its use in authoritarian contexts might lead to severe violations of freedom of speech, as well as of privacy rights. Of course, this depends on how the filtering is set: as a variety of parameters defines the value of a content, semantics—but also its reach and popularity—determine whether a content can get through inspection points. In order to protect data, and thus privacy rights, the battle predominantly involves gaining control on their movement through re-routing techniques (such as VPN) to bypass checkpoints.

The focus on internet access vis-à-vis broader digital rights subtends two different ways to think and theorize about the internet, but in fact signals a similar understanding of the causality that exists between technology and political freedoms. While on the one hand internet access itself is argued to bring about freedoms (i.e. as a neutral public utility), on the other hand these political freedoms are thought to be dependent on the qualities of the utility (i.e. data management).[17] At the same time, both views imply a causal nexus between human rights and freedom—in line with traditional theorizing on the topic (cfr. Bobbio 1996). In this sense, besides being of relevance for reflecting on those conditions that enable freedoms online, the inclusion of digital rights into the discourse on human rights provides relevant insights for disputing their mainstream agenda as a whole.

TANGO DOWN! Palestinian Digital Rights in a Vise

In one of his most famous writings, Edward Said (1999) states that Palestine, more than a place, resembles a displacement, a state of consciousness. As a natural stage that is blessed and cursed with heightened visibility, it forks the world into two classes: observers and performers. In recent years, this visibility progressively revealed on online platforms: besides the greater mediatization of the conflict that followed the Al-Aqsa Intifada in the early 2000s, today's so-called battle of ideas—the virtual conflict—is extensively fought online.[18]

In the last years, Israeli government's efforts into creating a pro-Israeli presence online, under the auspices of the so-called *hasbara* (Hebrew for "explaining"), have been enormous (Aouragh 2016). Mainly calling on Israeli citizens and Jewish diaspora to take arms into this virtual battle of ideas, extensive resources have been devoted into training advocates (the so-called *hasbara* trolls) in aggressive techniques of social media presence. Israeli authorities' incursions in this battle are common: State Attorney's Office Cyber Division regularly sends numerous takedown requests to Twitter and other media,[19] demanding to remove certain content or to block Israeli users from viewing it (Schaeffer Omer-Man 2016). Israel Defense Forces (IDF) made most recent war declarations on Twitter and actively engaged with advocacy campaigns in the context of what Kuntsman and Stein (2015) define as 'digital militarism'.[20] Besides this virtualization, debates and campaigning related to internet access and digital rights became recently integrated into pro-Palestinian advocacy and struggles. While this, of course, parallels other contexts—as in fact today's battle for digital rights has reached a global dimension—contextual peculiarities make the Palestinian case a unique point of observation to scrutiny how power manifests in the relationship between internet access and (the denial of) political freedoms—and thus how human rights could be hijacked or potentially re-politicized.

In a context of the permanent state of exception (see Abujidi 2009), the limitations imposed by the long-lasting Israeli occupation, as well as the recent legislations of the PA, undermine Palestinian digital rights, and the battle thereof. Israeli control over Palestinian internet pertains both its infrastructural dimension and the management and control over contents and data. In defiance of the Oslo agreements (1993), that had in view a progressive transition of service governance to the PA, Israel still retains control over internet infrastructures for the entire Palestinian territory (Tawil-Souri 2013), with a coverage that is only limited to most populated urban areas.[21] This implies that Israel holds the power to kill-switch internet access for Palestinians, as shown during the recent Israeli military operations in Gaza. Primarily, this raises the question of whether digital rights are ever attainable in a context where infrastructures are not only subjected to market rules but in fact owned and managed through a sophisticated system of security governance—that includes Israel, ISPs, and the PA.

In line with the argument relating content and service management to infrastructural control, Palestinians' online activities and contents are increasingly subjected to Israeli censorship and used to validate punishment. As the occupation moves toward robotic and unmanned forms (cfr. Tawil-Souri and Aouragh 2014), Israeli predictive policing systems culminated in the recent application of an algorithmic scanning of Palestinians' social media contents (Nashif 2017). The algorithm focuses on statuses, comments, and pictures in order to identify contents that are critical of Israeli policies or considered an 'incitement to violence'.[22] Leading to the arrest and detention of around 800 Palestinians since 2015,[23] the justification for this measure lies in the assumption that online incitement constitutes an early warning of crime, thus preluding violence. In other words, Palestinians' freedom of speech appears not to be violated through access denial (that, however, remains limited and technologically obsolete).

Rather, having access to internet at these conditions creates an additional layer of separation between Palestinians and their denied liberties.

Besides a series of Arabic words—such as martyr, freedom, Al-Aqsa mosque, and Al Quds—Palestinian human and digital rights organizations (such as 7amleh and the Palestinian Center for Human Rights) reported how the algorithmic settings also filter contents—such as poetry, journal articles, and political statements—that criticize Israeli occupation without any direct reference to violence. As shown in the emblematic detention case of poet Dareen Tatour,[24] there appears to be a direct correlation between popularity and punishment: the more users like, share, and circulate a content, the higher and severe the punishment will be. In this sense, arrest and detention precede the individual perpetration of a crime, and regard subjectivity not only in relation to individual rights, but rather focus on how individual subjectivities are networked and socialized (as in Castells' theorizing).

With the Israeli security governance of online content set out to get critical Palestinians with a fine-tooth comb of mechanic control, spaces for dissent online decrease to make the way for a battlefield where access, more than crime, might signify arrest. Moreover, this argument appears further corroborated by a 2014's report, undisclosed by 43 Israeli intelligence agents (of the most elite unit, known as 8200)—admitting the use of spying and hacking techniques to collect private users' data to blackmail them in exchange for information. Targeting particularly those considered vulnerable because of their sexual orientation, this violation of privacy rights aims at forcing victims to share security-relevant information with Israeli security apparatuses (Derfner 2014; Levy 2014). For Palestinians, in other words, having internet access—even without willfully sharing any content—de facto signifies becoming a suspect.

Along the same lines, the PA's legislation, such as the recently approved law on cybercrime,[25] further narrows and deteriorates the already limited privacy rights and political freedoms that Palestinians enjoy online because of the Israeli occupation. Several Palestinian NGOs, unions, media, and activists pointed to the controversial democratic procedure that leads to its approval. Due to the suspension of the Palestinian legislative council in 2007—because of frictions between Fatah and Hamas—the president holds reduced legislative power, limited in fact only to emergencies. Regardless of whether cybercrime should be considered an emergency for the PA (given Israel's infrastructural ownership), critics opposed the newly approved law and called on President Abbas for a more participative and transparent legislation. To this scope, the Palestinian NGO Al-Haq—engaged in the defense of human rights since 1979—has drawn the attention of the UN Special Rapporteur on the Promotion and Protection of the Right to Freedom of Opinion and Expression on the closure of freedoms associated to the new legislation (Abdeen 2018).

Besides criticizing its democratic *iter*, opponents also emphasize the closure of democratic spaces and liberties this legislation produced. First, their critical focus falls on the concepts of 'national unity' and 'social harmony' (Article 51) that, besides being very controversial in the context of Palestine, are brought up to justify restrictive measures on fundamental liberties. Far from being achieved in reality, these concepts are vaguely described in the legislation, thus allowing broad and instrumental interpretations. For example, publishing or propagating contents deemed offensive to 'national unity' or 'social harmony' might lead to a sanction from three to fifteen years of forced hard labors, in clear violation of the human right to freedom of speech. Likewise, hurting online 'public manners' (Article 16) or committing 'immoral acts' (Article 15) leads to similar detention sanctions. Additionally, these violations of human rights are contingent on public-private collaborations in the domain of content management. In fact, Article 32 calls upon ISPs and tech companies to cooperate with the PA and take down websites or contents deemed to be in contravention of the legislation's 'values'. The involvement of tech companies, and particularly of ISPs, into security governance breaches the neutrality argument set forth by digital rights' proponents.

While awareness on digital rights intensifies within Palestinian civil society, thank to work of organizations such as 7amleh, these battles mainly focus on advocacy. The imposed obsolete internet technologies available to Palestinians (cfr. Arafeh et al. 2015)—that would represent an infringement of the digital right to band per capita—seriously undermine alternative engagements (such as I2P, VPN, and mesh-networking) and the making of digital rights from below. Alongside the Israeli occupation, the PA's legislation further punishes the use of alternative ways to connect online: Article 31 outlaws accessing internet through VPNs and weakens the extent in which users can elude traffic blocks and algorithmic scanning. In turn, these governance arrangements make PA's political opponents particularly vulnerable, as in fact several journalists have been arrested, and critics' websites are constantly taken down. To counter this trend, Palestinians activists launched different online campaigns demanding social media and video sharing platforms not to violate their right to freedom of expression through the removal of contents.

Tightening the 'vise' over Palestinian digital rights through the continuous fine-tuning of jaws of censorship and control, Israeli and PA's practices and legislations inspire a reflection on those risks that are connected to thinking human rights in normative and prescriptive terms. As Palestinians have generally access to their right to broadband, the existing violations of human rights escape UNHRC's scheme. Relatedly, shielding policing measures over content management through concerns over security appears to further advance the contextual framework that Perugini and Gordon (2016) define the 'human rights to dominate'. Through the definition and setting up of normative schemes that are coherent (and lawful) with liberal human rights framework—imagining a casual correlation between technology and freedom—lawfare and policing seize Palestinian cyberspace for the practice of dissent, freedoms, and the making of human rights from below.

Conclusions

In Philip K. Dick's 1956 sci-fi novel *The Minority Report*, three mutants are able to foresee all crimes before they occur. Taking place in a future world, these 'precogs' are connected into a great machine and assist the crime division to arrest suspects before any unlawful behavior actually manifests in reality. While questioning how political control and individual autonomy intersect on security grounds, this short story foresaw how dogmatic approaches to technology can lead to a reduction of those same liberties that technology ought to enable or protect. As shown in the case of Palestine, accessing internet appears to lead to the disabling, rather than enabling, of political liberties and individual freedom. 'Who owns' the infrastructures also affects how contents are managed and disciplined, thus calling into question the de-politicization of technologies at large.

In this sense, the first critique toward the inclusion of the right to broadband can be raised. The equation between internet access and increased political freedoms appears to be consistent with liberal approaches to (internet) technology as well as to human rights. As the UNHRC (2016, p. 2) recognizes the strategic role of "advanced technology to better predict, analyze and respond to critical human rights situations", the internet would serve as a tool for advancing the human rights agenda. As pointed out by opponents of the resolution, this deterministic understanding of internet access, and technological infrastructures more in general, reflects those mainstream views on technology that assume infrastructures to be neutral and independent from political considerations. Being in their surface detached from political discourses, in fact, infrastructures are thought to enable the fruition of a service, or a human right. As shown in the context of the Israeli occupation—where access to internet for Palestinians signifies becoming a suspect—it appears problematic to detach rights to broadband from questioning infrastructural ownership and control, that is, re-establishing internet as a common in the spirit of its founders.

Secondly, the disconnect between the battle for digital rights and the inclusion of the right to broadband into the human rights agenda appears to stem from the risk that, by formalizing very low standards for how contents are managed (i.e. accessed, policed, censored, etc.) through the framing of human rights, governments might normalize the implementation of restrictive, yet lawful, measures—as shown in the context of denied Palestinian digital rights. Whereas the inclusion of digital rights into the agenda of human rights might put pressure on authoritarian regimes for guaranteeing decent standards, it might prove to be detrimental in those contexts where these battles aim higher. In this sense, choices for digital rights activists appear to be of a tactical nature and differ depending on the context. At the same time, rethinking human rights as dynamic battlefields, that is, re-politicizing them, opens up opportunities for 'taking back the tech' for all. In this spirit, it is not enough to guarantee access to internet through individual rights, but the discourse should shift its focus also on collective ones.

Besides being seen as a displacement, Palestine often comes to be seen as a 'precog' itself. Observing Palestine, and its political dynamics as a lab (see Turner 2015; Khalili 2010), we are always reminded of how humanity goes lost, but always reconfigures through productive desire and steadfastness. While issues of digital rights are common to the entire world, and interrogate the future of political freedoms and human rights, the vise of the Israeli occupation and the recent PA's legislation constitutes the Palestinian case as a unique standing point to reflect on the 'type' of internet, and technologies more in general, we have to expect and thus articulate and desire as an alternative. This begins with challenging the normative and deterministic assumption that mainstream human rights proponents have about internet technology, that is, that accessing internet makes us freer. As soon as Dick's imagined machine reports future unlawful endeavors committed by the director of the crime division, he finally starts believing that the machine is unreliable, and he's forced to resign. Approaching his successor, he whispers: "Better keep your eyes open. It might happen to you at any time" (Dick 1956, p. 14).

Notes

1. In this chapter, the word internet is used without capitalization. On the one hand, this choice reflects what has become largely the norm in European publications. On the other hand, the common noun appears more coherent with the arguments proposed throughout this piece.
2. The non-governmental organization AccessDown defines an internet shutdown as the "intentional disruption of internet or electronic communications, rendering them inaccessible or effectively unusable, for a specific population or within a location, often to exert control over the flow of information". More information and empirical studies can be found at https://www.accessnow.org/ (Last accessed on 7 January 2018).
3. Already in 2003, under the auspice of the United Nations (UN), the World Summit on the Information Society (WSIS) underlines the importance of protecting the 'information society' to guarantee freedom of expression. Only in 2011, however, the UN Special rapporteur on the promotion and protection of the right to freedom of opinion and expression recognized the importance of the internet, and access to it, as "unlike any other medium, the internet enables individuals to seek, receive and impart information of all kinds instantaneously and inexpensively across national borders" (Recommendation nr. 67).
4. Different global campaigns have a strong focus on monitoring and advocating for the 'right to internet access': such as AccessNow established in 2009 after the Iranian elections and promoting the campaign #KeepItOn (now joined by hundreds of other networks and organizations) or ONE.org that focuses on the relationship between internet access and sustainable development.
5. Among those peculiar factors that are commonly referred to as triggering the Arab Spring—authoritarian regimes and poverty (see Gelvin 2012)—the importance of social media, and internet more in general, is debated between cyberphiles and cyberskeptics. Whether facilitating and igniting protests (see Stepanova 2011), or existing only as subordinated to protests in the 'real world' (Khondker 2011), the young age of Arab populations (and thus a very high percentage of digital natives) collided with the authoritarian policies of the regimes.

6. Produced by AccessNow's Shutdown Tracker Optimization Project (STOP), this data includes "full network shutdowns, bandwidth throttling, and service-based blocking of two-way communication platforms, such as social media (for example, Twitter, WhatsApp, and Viber) or email" (https://www.accessnow.org/keepiton-shutdown-tracker/).
7. At its very beginning, the digital rights movement focused on questions related to copyright, data privacy, and its proprietorship (as internet technologies were mainly available in the West). Only in the aftermath of internet shutdowns across the globe, digital rights activists included internet access in their political platforms, whereas many international organizations prioritized accessibility over the broader range of digital rights (as their focus primarily targeted developing countries).
8. Far from being established in academic circles, this debate has mainly opposed 'technologists' (i.e. tech professionals) to international organizations. In this sense, the critique has largely focused on internet access and its essence, rather than taking issue with what constitutes a human right.
9. The term kill-switch, mainly employed in cyber-defense discourses, refers to a government's activation of a single shutoff system for the closure of internet access and traffic for its entire territory. Different countries—such as Egypt, India, Turkey, and the United Kingdom—adopted legislations entrusting the military to activate internet kill-switches in cases of threats to national security.
10. For example, in response to pressures about enforcing net neutrality, the United States' Federal Communications Commission (FCC) classified Internet Service Providers (ISPs) as 'common carriers'. In common law countries, this definition applies to carriers that, in line with specific legislations, are bound to provide services to the general public (as opposed to 'contract carriers' that do not have the same obligation). However, this distinction does not exist in civil-law systems.
11. Independent wireless communities, available across different countries, consist of computer networks that are built by users without a central control or ownership, contrarily to traditional single-entity ISPs that manage the network.
12. Of course, this debate also pertains how embodied experiences occur in the encounter between the individual and the web (cfr. Cristiano 2018).
13. According to Twitter and Facebook transparency reports, available on their websites, the respective sites remove a significant amount of content at the request of governments around the world. The reports note that the companies fulfill government requests upon finding that the post violates either their Community Standards or the requesting government's laws.

14. As of June 2017, 51% of the world's population is on internet. In 2015, the International Telecommunication Union estimated 75% would be online by the end of the year.
15. I2P consists of an anonymous overlay network, that is, 'a network within a network'. Its scope resides into the protection of data from dragnet surveillance and monitoring by third parties such as ISPs. More info at https://geti2p.net/en/about/intro.
16. Also in this case, identifying the 'individual' (and their individual data) is not a univocal process—as data are produced in relation to other dynamics of proprietorship.
17. As in fact no network can ever be fully 'secure'—in terms of data and privacy protection—many activists (especially in North America and Western Europe) decide to withdraw from the internet and coordinate only offline.
18. Palestinian Authority's (PA) online public relations have become increasingly professionalized (Craig Parsons, 2005). Palestinian political parties, armed factions, and advocacy groups have strengthened their online presence. Aligning Israeli occupation policies to apartheid South Africa, Boycott Divestment and Sanctions (BDS) campaigners mainly rely on digital platforms to advocate for an economic, academic, and cultural boycott of Israel (Barghouti 2011).
19. Evidence shows how Israel makes pressure to social media companies in order to remove contents that are critical of Israel. Moreover, *The Guardian* has leaked information regarding the inclusion of the category 'Zionists' in those that are to be protected in content management. Similarly, Facebook, solicited by the Israeli Cyber Unit, suspended several accounts of Palestinian journalists associated to large news networks.
20. In 2015, IDF also released a virtual game—*IDF Ranks*—that provides players with the opportunity of making a virtual career in the army. By commenting on online pro-Israeli news or sharing IDF's media contents, users earn points and thus virtual career advances. The so-called gamification of the conflict also encompasses full immersive and augmented reality video games (cfr. Cristiano and Distretti 2017).
21. Only in 2017, Palestinian ISPs and mobile companies provided 3G internet services in the West Bank, when Israeli authorities finally lifted a ban on the technology as a result of an agreement reached with the Palestinian Ministry of Telecommunications and Information Technology (MTIT). The ban, however, was not lifted on the Gaza Strip that still relies on 2G connectivity.
22. This only applies to Palestinians both in the territories and in Israel, whereas Israelis enjoy wide freedom of speech online (as in the emblematic case of Ayelet Shaked, Ministry of Justice, who wished a genocidal solution for Palestinians).

23. Convicted Palestinians are not informed about which online activity led to their administrative detention.
24. In October 2015, poet Dareen Tatour was arrested for posting a poem about resistance to Israel's 50-year-old military rule. She spent time in jail and has been under house arrest for over a year and a half. Civil rights groups and individuals in Israel, the Occupied Palestinian Territory (OPT), and abroad have criticized Israel's detention of Tatour and other Palestinian internet users as violations of civil and human rights.
25. The full English translation of the Presidential Decree No. 16 is available at: https://goo.gl/Dj1t1Q.

References

Abdeen, Isam. 2018. *Measures Taken by Al-Haq to Counter the Law by Decree on Cybercrimes*. Ramallah: Al-Haq – Law for Human Right.

Abujidi, Nurhan. 2009. The Palestinian States of Exception and Agamben. *Contemporary Arub Affairs* 2 (2): 272–291. https://doi.org/10.1080/17550910902857034.

Aouragh, Miriyam. 2016. Hasbara 2.0: Israel's Public Diplomacy in the Digital Age. *Middle East Critique* 25 (3): 271–297. https://doi.org/10.1080/19436149.2016.1179432.

Arafeh, Nur, Bahour, Sam, and Abdullah, Wassim. 2015. "ICT: The Shackled Engine of Palestine's Development", *Al-Shabaka Policy Brief*, 9 November, 2015. https://al-shabaka.org/briefs/ict-the-shackled-engine-of-palestines-development/

Barghouti, Omar. 2011. *Boycott, Divestment, Sanctions: The Global Struggle for Palestinian Rights*. London: Haymarket Books.

Bendrath, Ralf, and Mueller, Milton. 2010. The End of the Net as We Know It? Deep Packet Inspection and Internet Governance. *SSRN Publication*, August 5. https://doi.org/10.2139/ssrn.1653259

Bobbio, Norberto. 1996. *The Age of Rights*. New York: Wiley.

Brown, Chris. 1997. Universal Human Rights: A Critique. *The International Journal of Human Rights* 1 (2): 41–65. https://doi.org/10.1080/13642989708406666.

Castells, Manuel. 2001. *The Internet Galaxy. Reflections on the Internet, Business, and Society*. Oxford: Oxford University Press.

———. 2007. Communication, Power and Counter-power in the Network Society. *International Journal of Communication* 1: 238–266.

Cerf, Vinton. 2012. Internet Access Is Not a Human Right. *The New York Times*, January 4. http://www.nytimes.com/2012/01/05/opinion/internet-access-is-not-a-human-right.html.

Craig Parsons, Nigel. 2005. *The Politics of the Palestinian Authority: From Oslo to Al-Aqsa*. London: Taylor & Francis.

Cristiano, Fabio. 2018. Bodies of Cyberwar: Violence and Knowledge Beyond Corporeality. In *Experiences in Researching Conflict and Violence*, ed. Althea Rivas and Brendan Browne, 145–160. Bristol: Policy Press.

Cristiano, Fabio, and Emilio Distretti. 2017. Along the Lines of the Occupation: Playing at Diminished Reality in East Jerusalem. *Conflict and Society* 3 (1): 130–143. https://doi.org/10.3167/arcs.2017.030111.

Derfner, Larry. 2014. Against Spy Revelations, Israel Doth Protest Too Much". *+972mag*, September 16. https://972mag.com/against-spy-revelations-israel-doth-protest-too-much/96781.

Dick, Philip. 1956. *The Minority Report*. London: Victor Gollancz.

Drezner, Daniel. 2004. The Global Governance of the Internet: Bringing the State Back In. *Political Science Quarterly* 119 (3): 477–498. https://doi.org/10.2307/20202392.

Gelvin, James. 2012. *The Arab Spring: What Everybody Needs To Know*. New York: Oxford University Press.

Green, Lelia. 2001. *Technoculture: From Alphabet to Cybersex*. Crows Nest: Allen & Unwin.

Hildenbrand, Jerry. 2016. How Wi-Fi Mesh Networks Work. *Android Central*. October 13. https://www.androidcentral.com/how-wifi-mesh-networks-work?_ga=2.118951497.1982325821.1494489061-1333092243.1494489050.

Human Rights Watch. 2017. *India: 20 Internet Shutdowns in 2017*. https://www.hrw.org/news/2017/06/15/india-20-internet-shutdowns-2017. Accessed 10 Mar 2018.

Joyce, Daniel. 2015. Internet Freedom and Human Rights. *European Journal of International Law* 26 (2): 493–514. https://doi.org/10.1093/ejil/chv021.

Khalili, Laleh. 2010. The Location of Palestine in Global Counterinsurgencies. *International Journal of Middle East Studies* 42 (3): 413–433. https://doi.org/10.1017/S0020743810000425.

Khondker, Habibul Haque. 2011. Role of the New Media in the Arab Spring. *Globalizations* 8 (5): 675–679. https://doi.org/10.1080/14747731.2011.621287.

Kuntsman, Adi, and Rebecca Stein. 2015. *Digital Militarism: Israel's Occupation in the Social Media Age*. Palo Alto: Stanford University Press.

Levi, Elior. 2014. IDF Intelligence Soldiers Refuse to Serve: We Won't Work Against Innocent Palestinians. *Ynet*, December 9. https://www.ynetnews.com/articles/0,7340,L-4570256,00.html.

Lucchi, Nicola. 2011. Access to Network Services and Protection of Constitutional Rights: Recognizing the Essential Role of Internet Access for the Freedom of

Expression. *Cardozo Journal of International and Comparative Law* 19 (3): 645–678.

MacKinnon, R. 2008. Flatter World and Thicker Walls? Blogs, Censorship and Civic Discourse in China. *Public Choice* 134: 31. https://doi.org/10.1007/s11127-007-9199-0.

McDowell, Robert. 2012. The U.N. Threat to Internet Freedom. *Wall Street Journal* (21 February 2012). Available at https://goo.gl/xZYm4X. Last Retrieved on 12 Nov 2017.

McLuhan, Marshall. 1967. *The Medium Is the Massage: An Inventory of Effects.* New York: Random House.

McNeilly, Kathryn. 2015. Reclaiming the Radical in Universal Human Rights: Universality as Universalisation. *International Human Rights Law Review* 4 (2): 256–276. https://doi.org/10.1163/22131035-00402007.

———. 2017. *Human Rights and Radical Social Transformation: Futurity, Alterity, Power.* London: Routledge.

Nashif, Nadim. 2017. Surveillance of Palestinians and the Fight for Digital Rights. *Al-Shabaka Policy Brief*, October 23. https://al-shabaka.org/briefs/surveillance-palestinians-fight-digital-rights/.

Nielsen, Jakob. 2016. The Distribution of Users' Computer Skills: Worse Than You Think. *Nielsen Norman Group*, November 13. https://www.nngroup.com/articles/computer-skill-levels/.

Perugini, Nicola, and Neve Gordon. 2016. *The Human Right to Dominate.* Oxford: Oxford University Press.

Peters, Anne. 2016. *Beyond Human Rights – The Legal Status of the Individual in International Law.* Oxford: Oxford University Press.

Petersen, Gregers. 2014. Freifunk: When Technology and Politics Assemble into Subversion. In *Subversion, Conversion, Development: Cross-Cultural Knowledge Exchange and the Politics of Design*, ed. James Leach and Lee Wilson, 39–56. Cambridge, MA: MIT Press.

Rheingold, Howard. 1994. *The Virtual Community. Homesteading on the Electronic Frontier.* Cambridge, MA: MIT Press.

Said, Edward. 1999. *Out of Place: A Memoir.* London: Vintage Books.

Schaeffer Omer-Man, Michael. 2016. How Israel Is Trying to Enforce Gag Orders Beyond Its Borders. *+972mag*, August 9. https://972mag.com/how-israel-is-trying-to-enforce-gag-orders-beyond-its-borders/121266/.

Skepys, Brian. 2012. Is There a Human Right to the Internet? *Journal of Politics and Law* 5 (4): 15–29. https://doi.org/10.5539/jpl.v5n4p15.

Stepanova, Ekaterina. 2011. The Role of Information Technology Communications in the Arab Spring. *PONARS Eurasia Policy Memo* 159. http://pircenter.org/kosdata/page_doc/p2594_2.pdf.

Tawil-Souri, Helga. 2013. Networking Palestine, Creating and Limiting Media and Technology Flows: Television and Telecommunications Since 1993. In *The*

Oslo Accords 1993–2013: Twenty Years with What Results? ed. Petter Bauck and Mohammed Omer. Cairo: AUC Press.

Tawil-Souri, Helga, and Miriyam Aouragh. 2014. Intifada 3.0? Cyber Colonialism and Palestinian Resistance. *Arab Studies Journal* 22 (1): 102–133 http://connection.ebscohost.com/c/articles/96804537/intifada-3-0-cyber-colonialism-palestinian-resistance.

Turner, Mandy. 2015. Peacebuilding as Counterinsurgency in the Occupied Palestinian Territory. *Review of International Studies* 41 (1): 73–98. https://doi.org/10.1017/S0260210514000072.

UNHRC. 2016. *The Promotion, Protection and Enjoyment of Human Rights on the Internet*. https://goo.gl/xWFDjz. Accessed on 10 Mar 2018.

United Nations General Assembly. 1948. *The Universal Declaration of Human Rights (UDHR), Resolution 217 A (III)*. http://undocs.org/A/RES/217(III). Accessed on 10 Mar 2018.

Westra, Laura. 2011. *Human Rights: The Commons and the Collective*. Vancouver: UBC Press.

Wu, Tim. 2003. Network Neutrality, Broadband Discrimination. *Journal of Telecommunications and High Technology Law* 2 (1): 141–180. https://doi.org/10.2139/ssrn.388863.

CHAPTER 13

Conclusion: Changing Human Right Practices and the Battlefields of World Politics

Gabriel Blouin-Genest, Marie-Christine Doran, and Sylvie Paquerot

Looking back at the new human rights practices underlined in this volume, we are struck by the fact that some of our main arguments were already outlined in the Universal Declaration of Human Rights (UDHR 1948). In particular, the Articles 1 and 28 of the UDHR are particularly instructive of the transformative nature of human rights:

Article 1: "All human beings are born free and equal in dignity and rights."

Article 28: "Everyone is entitled to a social and international order in which the rights and freedoms set forth in this Declaration can be fully realized."

G. Blouin-Genest
Department of Political Science, Virginia Tech, Blacksburg, VA, USA
e-mail: gblouin@vt.edu

M.-C. Doran • S. Paquerot (✉)
School of Political Studies, University of Ottawa, Ottawa, ON, Canada
e-mail: Marie-Christine.Doran@uottawa.ca; spaquero@uottawa.ca

G. Blouin-Genest et al. (eds.), *Human Rights as Battlefields*,
Human Rights Interventions,
https://doi.org/10.1007/978-3-319-91770-2_13

Read together, these two articles show quite straightforwardly how human rights claims can be easily understood as political claims; claims for the transformation of the social order, at a specific moment and in a specific context, in which the "feeling" of dignity cannot be realized. The human rights practices illuminated by our different chapters bring at the forefront of the analysis the question of the order and context through which human rights are, or not, realized and implemented.

An "order in which" does not presuppose a fixed content or meaning, but rather imply rights as criteria of the legitimacy of an order in constant modification and change. Any order restricting or reducing the scope of rights should thus be modified in order to better implement the rights contained in the declaration, which constitutes the rights themselves *and* their full effect. Human rights are politically, contextually and culturally situated: they emerge as micro practices largely unrelated to the original inscription into international instruments.

The preceding chapters clearly illustrate this political process: in order to understand what human rights are, we should not primarily be concerned by their inscription in legal instruments or their recognition by this or that actor/country. What matters is what is made of them. If their legal inscription effectively tells us what will be practically implemented or the possibilities of recourse to enforce these rights, it does not explain the reasons, circumstances or contexts that fostered their emergence in public discourses and their uses by actors using them as tools for their social struggles. In other words, the legal inscription of human rights in legal instruments does not inform us in any way of lived "indignities", which in turn have generated the emergence of claims of dignity and recognition (Honneth 2000), and as such, of practices from below, from actors involved in day-to-day struggles about not necessarily specific human rights, but specific conditions linked with human rights. Human rights as battlefields represent these claims and struggles from below rather than the imposition of fixed meaning from above. These battlefields are the expressions of human rights struggles, rather than an end in itself or a specific role assigned to human rights in so-called liberal democracies.

Notwithstanding the liberal origin of human rights, and despite their legal inscription in the international system referring to a liberal and individualistic interpretation, contemporary re-appropriations of economic and social rights or civil and political rights by actors involved in their materialization frame them as political arguments, as the criterion of legitimacy of decisions and conditions of the "common" (Dardot and Laval

2014). In doing so, the very definition of the content and meaning of these rights becomes the object of contentious politics and is therefore both a tool for maintaining the existing order *and* to potentially resist this order.

Moreover, it is the very legitimacy of the political authority that is at stake since it is bound, by the Article 28 of the UDHR, to ensure an order such that human rights can actually be realized. The politics of human rights is ultimately a politics of the global order. As we have seen in several chapters, such as the ones by Doran, Bessant and Watts or Christiano, it is sometimes the state itself, or the political power, that monopolizes the realization of human rights at a given moment, with the objective to reduce the effective reach of human rights, especially political ones, which, precisely, make it possible to challenge the existing social order and the organization of power within society. In this sense, human rights as battlefields should be replaced in society's struggles for a broadening democratic space.

Political Subjects, Not Victims: Human Rights and Their Subjects

What are the subjects of human rights claims? How are they performed and characterized? Lamoureux (2013) suggests that the claims of human rights by excluded or vulnerable social groups are first and foremost a demand for inclusion "as is", to be recognized as being different. As such, these claims represent an effort to redefine the universal from below, from concrete specificities historically situated. In Ñusta Carranzo Ko's Chap. 8, for example, it is clear that the availability of contraception and contraceptive education is not truly universal and egalitarian but rather selective and enforced by coercion (forced sterilization) on poor aboriginal women, thus excluding them from their "humanity", and as such their ability and right to decide for themselves. Beyond compensation for the damage that these women have suffered, it is the recognition of their belonging to humanity, their inclusion in this universality—and democracy—that is reflected by their demands.

As shown also by several case studies presented in this volume, to frame a social or political claim in terms of human rights means not to consider the subject of that right as *victims*, who could eventually be compensated—this is the role of the courts—, but to challenge the conditions of the social order in which these rights are either denied or limited, to recognize the subject of these rights as political subjects and not only as victims. It is the universality of the human right subjects that is the challenge here. The discussion around the expression "*droits de l'homme*" in the French language (Chap. 3 by Bosvieux-Onyekwelu) eloquently illustrates how the universality of rights remains to be constructed and deployed in the face of the factual exclusions that persist in all of our societies. The distinction is particularly highlighted by the issues presented in Chap. 5 (Ozan Kamiloglu), focusing on the mobilization of the very political dimensions of human rights claims. The transformations of the order, of social relations and of the organization of power then represent the tools of contestation, the mechanisms through which this contestation is deployed.

The case studies of the second and third sections also make this clear: whether it is to question "habitus" (Bourdieu 1980) as in the case of the legal age of child marriage in Nigeria (Akinola), or more broadly women's rights; whether it is to claim a broader understanding of rights such as in the case of health (Blouin-Genest and Erb) or water (Paquerot), the rational of actors is not that of the victimization/compensation as sometimes suggested by the human right literature but that of the specifically political claim of transformation of the social order and power relations within it. Despite the fact that these demands are largely unsatisfied and unrealized, these processes of debate and translation do not change their deeply political nature.

Bringing Back the Conditions of Human Rights Practices

If, according to Article 28 of the UDHR, human rights are understood in terms of purpose and legitimate aspirations, national policies and international decisions should therefore be judged—and assessed—in light of this criterion and accepted only if they do not affect the implementation of the rights; whether it contributes to the goal or at the very least does not harm the potential realization of these rights. This kind of evaluation cannot be definitive because, on the one hand, the contexts in which these rights take effect change and evolve and, on the other hand, that transformations of the order will also lead to transformations in the conditions of the implementation of rights.

Changes in societies, either from a material, ideational and structural points of view, require different conditions for the concrete implementation of human rights. Taking seriously the right to life, for example, does not require the same interventions and the same rules in a society like the United States, where there are hundreds of mass killings annually, as in a country where peoples die from thirst or hunger. Similarly, the right to food does not mean the same thing in a subsistence agriculture context as in a society fed by agribusiness using carcinogen and hormonal disruptor pesticides. The right to adequate housing cannot cover the same requirements in a temperate environment as in a tropical environment. The social, environmental or technological contexts of human rights deeply affect their implementation and realization.

Chapter 12 (by Fabio Cristiano) on internet access illustrates the need for this constant reassessment in the light of the material transformations of societies, in this case from the point of view of the freedom of expression: "the framing of internet access as human rights pertains the basic recognition that access to the Internet and facilitates the enjoyment of political freedoms". The battle for the right to water (Chap. 4, by Sylvie Paquerot) shows how the transformation of the organization of economic relations has led to the demand for a new right, while the chapter on the right to health (Blouin-Genest and Erb) shows that the transformations of social relations generate the need to rediscuss the requirements of the right to health and the scope of this right, an issue that Surma Das (Chap. 9) explores in a similar fashion regarding maternal mortality.

It is also this rereading of the obligations underlining the implementation of each right that Thomas Pogge makes, in his analyses of extreme poverty (Pogge 2002, 2003, 2004, 2005), when he relates Article 25 of the UDHR to Article 28 and postulates that a violation on the part of those who impose the order to produce avoidable extreme poverty, considering that it is not a fatality but a consequence of the social relations resulting from this order:

> Are the rich countries violating human rights when they, in collaboration with Southern elites, impose a global institutional order under which, foreseeably and avoidably, hundreds of millions cannot attain "a standard of living adequate for the health and well-being of himself and of his family, including food, clothing, housing and medical care" (Universal Declaration of Human Rights §25)? The Declaration itself makes quite clear that they do when it proclaims that "everyone is entitled to a social and international

> order in which the rights and freedoms set forth in this Declaration can be fully realized" (§28). The existing international institutional order fails this test. (Pogge 2007, p. 36)

Populations and social groups who seize—and make claims about—human rights to demand a reinterpretation only further push reasoning already accepted by the human rights system a long time ago. For example, it is well-known that the UN Human Rights Committee has found it necessary to make general comments more than once about certain rights, including the right to life.[1] In Observation 6 (CCPR 1982), the Committee stresses, for example, that the right to life must be interpreted by considering positive obligations for States, especially with regard to infant mortality and life expectancy. Then, in 1984, the Committee felt it necessary to reconsider the interpretation of this article more specifically with regard to nuclear weapons (CCPR 1984). In the first case, this interpretation has consolidated the foundation of economic, social and cultural rights. In the second case, it is a specific dimension of the international context of the time that prompts the Committee to specify, from the point of view of nuclear weapons, what the order should be for the rights to be respected.

Human rights, as aspirations, require a discussion on the conditions for the effective implementation of these rights, and therefore of equal human dignity. As such, they must be constantly reiterated in the light of the social transformations that may affect their concrete realization. But they also serve to challenge the market society, "without common ends" in the words of Hayek, opening the space for ideological confrontations. In both cases, it is the meaning of democracy that is at stake.

Human Rights as the Battlefields of World Politics

Analyzing human rights in these terms makes it possible to show that their liberal origin, which is too often used to criticize them (see, e.g., Žižek 2005; Odysseos 2010 or Charvet and Kaczynska-Nay 2008), is, among other things, what makes them a powerful tool for social protest, as this liberal origin does not prevent actors from subverting their meaning, expanding as such their scope (as shown with multiple chapters in this volume). Indeed, it is for their own coherence that claims to use human rights can be seen as a request to the authorities to take into account these claims, even if it is to translate them, reduce them and even sometimes divert them from their original orientations.

It should be remembered that human rights, conceived as an end, refer to the Four Freedoms speech of President Roosevelt (6 January 1941), which were integrated into the preamble of the UDHR: "*Whereas* disregard and contempt for human rights have resulted in barbarous acts which have outraged the conscience of mankind, and the advent of a world in which human beings shall enjoy freedom of speech and belief and freedom from fear and want has been proclaimed the highest aspiration of the common people" (para. 2). Fighting fear and fighting wants acquires a legitimacy that is difficult for those in power, be they economic or political, to reject from the back of the hand. But the current neoliberal governance of the world is part of a perspective where the ends of action are neither discussed nor questionable: they are presented and framed as depoliticized. To define a problem or a situation in terms of human rights thus precisely constrains powers to reopen the question of the aims of action. In this sense, and contrary to some of the human rights literature that sees human rights as a risk of depoliticization (see, e.g., Žižek (2005)), it is precisely, this book argues, a re-politicization of questions/issues handled in a managerial way by the neoliberal governance human rights claims involved. Recognizing the political nature of human rights emerging "from below" is giving texture and volume to the political role played by every day's actions in the realization—and politicization—of human rights.

It is therefore a real political conflict that unfolds around human rights, a conflict that it is important in order to better understand the power relations that intervene and determine the outcomes of these conflicts. One can interpret these political conflicts as a confrontation of two opposed conceptions of the "good life", in the Aristotle meaning, and as Hayek pointed out in his time, since from a neoliberal perspective, a good society is a society without any common aim: "[a] Great Society has nothing to do with, and is in fact irreconcilable with 'solidarity' in the true sense of unitedness in the pursuit of known common goals" (Hayek 1976, p. 111). Hayek insists that "[t]he possibility of men living together in peace and to their mutual advantage without having to agree on common concrete aims, and bound only by abstract rules of conduct, was perhaps the greatest discovery mankind ever made" (Ibid., p. 136).

The fall of the Berlin Wall in 1989 has, in a way, clearly consigned the end of great narratives: the so-called victory of democracy and market is, according to some, the "end of history" (Fukuyama 1992). The idea of a social or political global project therefore becomes suspicious and the social forces fostering protests are forced to think and act within the frameworks of the system, of which they denounce the effects of domination, exclusion and marginalization. The "grammar" of human rights as we called it somewhere else (Blouin-Genest and Paquerot 2016), recognized at least in principle in most national constitutions as well as in international law, becomes in this context the legitimate vocabulary of contestation, both in terms of means and purposes, since it allows, on the one hand, the challenge of power and, on the other, the recognition of the legitimate meaning of action: an order such that human rights can find full effect. Opposition and resistance are therefore inscribed in the register of human rights and the terms of law, the result of "the capacity of social agents, outside the legal field, possibly via social movements, to mobilize the right to weigh on its redefinition or '(re) creation' in the sense of the cause they defend" (Commaille 2004, p. 14).

In that discussion, human rights from below clearly open the space to ideological confrontations: do we have common ends or not, and if so, are human rights a shared common end for humanity? As pointed out by Allard, "it is not so much a right that is at stake here as a world politics, whose law and judicial procedures are only an imperfect grammar" (Allard 2008, p. 82). Human rights as battlefields are the battlefields of world politics and its common, or not, ends.

Sovereignty of States or the People's Right to Self-Determination: What Democracy?

The contemporary context is characterized by an acceleration of economic globalization, desired and promoted by the political authorities represented by states. In doing so, they give up the primacy of the purposes and values of their people and often restrict fundamental freedoms for their choices not to be challenged. Yet, "international economic and trade law, in the context of today's globalized economy, is often seen as a general and organized offensive against the rights of people to self-determination and human rights, against the democratic gains and the international order as a whole, including the appropriation of common resources" (Ruiz Diaz 2004, pp. 3–4). Human rights as battlefields are also about the people's right to self-determination.

State sovereignty is therefore increasingly in contradiction with this fundamental right of people to self-determination (Flipo 2002, p. 409). As such human rights become the legitimate vocabulary to contest these orientations and refer to a conception of democracy which is not limited to delegating power to elites. The right to self-determination is precisely, the right to decide for oneself. Human rights play a key role here, as being the tool used—and claimed—for that self-determination. The contestation in the name of human rights shall therefore be analyzed from a political standpoint and not only from a legal one, since written positive law represents only the state of social and power relations at a given moment:

> [f]rom the moment when human rights are laid down as the ultimate reference, established law is doomed to questioning. There is always more question, as collective wills or, if one prefers, as social agents carrying new claims mobilize a force of opposition to that which tends to contain the effects of recognized rights. Where the law is in question, society, let us understand the established order, is in question. As effective as are the means available to a class to exploit for its benefit and to deny to others the guarantees of law, or those available to the power to subordinate the administration of justice or subject the laws to the imperatives of domination, these means remain exposed to legal opposition. (Lessard 2017, p. 35)

Human rights from below are therefore what ultimately nourish democracy. Let's be clear here, we don't mean by that *procedural* democracy, but democracy understood as a genuine process of emancipation, allowing the redistribution of power and the inclusion of all in the decisions concerning the actions and orientations of the community (what Dardot and Laval called the "common"), where individuals have a real capacity to choose and to act politically, "as equals in the definition of the common world, in short cease 'to be acted' to reach the capacity for action" (Lamoureux 2013, p. 60). This approach is distinct from the procedural vision of democracy in that it seeks the manifestation of a "power of doing together" rather than a "power over".

It must be remembered here that the people's right to self-determination is the subject of the first article of the two main international treaties on human rights (the International Covenant on Civil and Political Rights and the International Covenant on Economic, Social and Cultural Rights), devoting this collective right of human communities to decide for themselves, thus corroborating the very basic democratic principle. Indigenous people have well understood this, as they have articulated the struggles for their recognition around recognized human rights principles, no matter how liberal and Western they are. This struggle of indigenous people, like any other struggles for rights, has transformed, through a process of translation, the scope and meaning of the right to self-determination[2] itself, underlining how human rights, no matter what they are, are translated by actors involved in their practices at the micro level.

With the recognition of the right of indigenous people to self-determination, it is the recognition of the net distinction between the rights of people and the sovereignty of States that is consecrated and which has since been mobilized far beyond these struggles to legitimize the opposition to development projects imposed on people by political and economic powers around the world. In the context of these struggles for a real and deeper democracy, for a palpable self-determination, one sees unfolding many confrontations around the interpretation of the civil and political rights essential to the democratic broadening (Lefort 1981): freedoms of association, of conscience, of expression, of manifestation, and so on, questioned or shrunk at their simplest expression by power.

In this sense, the struggles for human rights from below seem well destined to renew the scope of the democratic principles, insofar as they are and will always remain a limit to power of a few over the rest. State sovereignty, in this context, has found its inherent limits: it is only justified to the extent that it translates the self-determination of the people—who are in a situation of legitimate political contestation when their rights are not fulfilled. In other words, what human rights struggles from below mean is that when the social and international order does not allow to fulfill all human rights, it is the order that must be changed, not human rights.

Paradoxically, we found this order to be challenged in practices of actors claiming these rights to contest the current norms, sometimes at the expenses of traditional or dominant understanding of human rights. Human rights as battlefields represent this paradox: they are tools used to challenge the dominant order, and are at the same time changed and modified by these claims. This is where the politics of human rights finds its most crucial importance: no matter what these rights are, their changing practices are the cornerstone of emancipation.

Notes

1. The Committee also found it necessary to make more than one comment in the case of Articles 3 (equality between men and women), 4 (derogation), 7 (prohibition of torture) and others.

2. We cannot delve deeper into the stakes of this struggle and this recognition, which would require the production of another work alone, but analyzes in this sense are numerous (Charpentier 1985; Christakis and Daudet 1999; Kohen 2007; Lavorel 2012).

References

Allard, Julie. 2008. La "cosmopolitisation" de la justice: entre mondialisation et cosmopolitisme. *Dissensus.*

Blouin-Genest, Gabriel, and Sylvie Paquerot. 2016. Environmental Human Rights as a Battlefield: A Grammar of Political Confrontation. *Journal of Human Rights and the Environment* 7 (1): 132–154.

Bourdieu, Pierre. 1980. *Le Sens pratique.* Paris: Les Éditions de Minuit, coll. "Le sens commun".

CCPR. 1982. *General Comments No 6*, 04/30/1982.

———. 1984. *General Comments No 14*, 11/09/1984.

Charpentier, Jean. 1985. Le droit des peuples à disposer d'eux-mêmes et le droit international positif. *Revue quebecoise de droit internationale* 2: 195.

Charvet, John, and Elisa Kaczynska-Nay. 2008. *The Liberal Project and Human Rights: The Theory and Practice of a New World Order.* Cambridge: Cambridge University Press.

Christakis, Théodore, and Yves Daudet. 1999. *Le droit à l'autodétermination en dehors des situations de décolonisation.* Paris: La documentation française.

Commaille, Jacques. 2004. La place du droit dans l'œuvre de Pierre Bourdieu. *Droit et Société*: 56–57.

Dardot, Pierre, and Christian Laval. 2014. *Commun: essai sur la révolution au XXIe siècle.* Paris: La Découverte.

Flipo, Fabrice. 2002. *En quoi la crise environnementale contribue-telle à renouveler la question de la justice? Le cas du changement climatique.* PhD Dissertation, Université de Technologie de Compiègne. Available at https://tel.archives-ouvertes.fr/tel-00957797

Fukuyama, Francis. 1992. *The End of History and the Last Man.* New York: Free Press. 418 p. isbn:ISBN 0-02-910975-2.

Hayek. 1976. *The Mirage of Social Justice.* London: Routledge and Kegan Paul.

Honneth, Axel. 2000. La lutte pour la reconnaissance. Cerf.

Kohen, Marcelo G. 2007. *Sur quelques vicissitudes du droit des peuples à disposer d'eux-mêmes.* Bruylant.

Lamoureux, Diane. 2013. *Le trésor perdu de la politique: espace public et engagement citoyen.* Écosociété.

Lavorel, Sabine. 2012. Le renouvellement du Droit des Peuples à l'autodétermination face aux changements environnementaux. In *The Renewal of the Right of Peoples to Self-Determination Faced with Environmental Changes*, 553–575.

Lefort, Claude. 1981. Droits de l'homme et politique. In *L'invention démocratique*, 45–86.

Lessard, Geneviève. 2017. *La Cour interaméricaine des droits de l'homme: un levier utile de démocratisation dans les Amériques? Le cas colombien*. Doctoral Dissertation, University of Ottawa, School of Political Studies.

Odysseos, Louiza. 2010. Human Rights, Liberal Ontogenesis and Freedom: Producing a Subject for Neoliberalism? *Millennium* 38 (3): 747–772.

Pogge, Thomas W. 2002. *World Poverty and Human Rights: Cosmopolitan Responsibilities and Reforms*. Vol. 65. Cambridge: Polity.

———. 2003. Ethical and Human Rights Dimensions of Poverty: Toward a New Paradigm in the Fight Against Poverty. *Philosophy Seminar*, All Souls College, Oxford, March, UNESCO Poverty Project..

———. 2004. The First UN Millennium Development Goal: A Cause for Celebration? *Journal of Human Development* 5 (3): 377–397.

———. 2005. Severe Poverty as a Violation of Negative Duties. *Ethics & International Affairs* 19 (1): 55–83.

———. 2007. Severe Poverty as a Human Rights Violation. In *Freedom from Poverty as a Human Right: Who Owes What to the Very Poor*. Oxford: Oxford University Press.

Ruiz Diaz, Hugo. 2004. *Réflexions sur les mutations du droit international (I); Le droit international et la mondialisation*. Comité pour l'annulation de la dette du tiers-monde (2 décembre). Available at http://www.cadtm.org/Le-droit-international-et-la.

Zizek, S. 2005. Against Human Rights. *New Left Review* 34: 117.

Index[1]

[1] Note: Page numbers followed by 'n' refer to notes.

G. Blouin-Genest et al. (eds.), *Human Rights as Battlefields*,
Human Rights Interventions,
https://doi.org/10.1007/978-3-319-91770-2

The manufacturer's authorised representative in the EU is Springer Nature Customer Service Centre GmbH, Europaplatz 3, 69115 Heidelberg, Germany. If you have any concerns regarding our products, please contact ProductSafety@springernature.com

Printed and bound by CPI Group (UK) Ltd, Croydon, CR0 4YY
07/10/2026
02229187-0001